## REVOLUTIONARY CONTINUITY

*Marxist Leadership in the U.S.*

# Revolutionary Continuity

*The Early Years 1848 – 1917*

**FARRELL DOBBS**

**PATHFINDER**

NEW YORK     LONDON     MONTREAL     SYDNEY

ISBN 0-87348-841-5 paper (formerly 0-913460-84-2)
ISBN 0-913460-85-0 cloth
Library of Congress Catalog Card Number 80-84850
Manufactured in the United States of America

First edition, 1980
Second printing, 2001

Pathfinder
410 West Street, New York, NY 10014, U.S.A.
Fax: (212) 727-0150
E-mail: pathfinderpress@compuserve.com

PATHFINDER DISTRIBUTORS AROUND THE WORLD:

Australia (and Asia and the Pacific):
    Pathfinder, 176 Redfern St., 1st floor, Redfern, NSW 2016
    Postal address: P.O. Box K879, Haymarket, NSW 1240
Canada:
    Pathfinder, 2761 Dundas St. West, Toronto, ON, M6P 1Y4
Iceland:
    Pathfinder, Klapparstíg 26, 2d floor, 101 Reykjavík
    Postal address: P. Box 0233, IS 121 Reykjavík
New Zealand:
    Pathfinder, P.O. Box 3025, Auckland
Sweden:
    Pathfinder, Vikingagatan 10, S-113 42, Stockholm
United Kingdom (and Europe, Africa except South Africa, and Middle East):
    Pathfinder, 47 The Cut, London, SE1 8LL
United States (and Caribbean, Latin America, and South Africa):
    Pathfinder, 410 West Street, New York, NY 10014

# Contents

# *Introduction*

Each worker who joins the revolutionary movement reaches that decision through a unique sequence of personal experiences. Yet there are certain broad phases of intellectual development that most who take this step share in common. In this country the newborn arrive upon a social scene permeated with capitalist ideology. By adulthood they have been conditioned to think in terms of shaping a future for themselves within the framework of the existing social order. Then, after a while, frustrations develop because of inequities built into the capitalist system. Recognition dawns that adjustments are needed in social relations and efforts follow to reform the present order of things. Attempts of that kind run head-on into capitalist resistance, however, as repeated clashes occur over economic, social, and political issues.

In the course of those conflicts some of the more rebellious become revolutionists and join a revolutionary socialist party. This brings unparalleled opportunities to achieve great leaps in social thought and political consciousness as they begin to understand why capitalism is irremediably bankrupt and precisely how the workers' struggle must be waged to replace it with a new, higher social order.

This opens the way for a meaningful reexamination of history, not with past events falsely presented or deliberately ignored, as is frequently the case in textbooks of the official educational system, but through honest, forthright accounts of what actually happened. In this way they can learn valuable lessons from the setbacks as well as the advances, from the mistakes as well as the achievements, of their revolutionary predecessors.

Such, for instance, were the phases through which my own social thinking evolved. Graduation from a Minneapolis high school in 1925 marked the end of my formal education. I had no chance to go on to college, but that didn't bother me at the time. It seemed good to have done with books, to be in a position to earn some money of my own which could be used as I saw fit.

At that point a new kind of education began for me in the school of hard knocks. No matter what job I tried the situation remained basically the same. Every employer demanded maximum labor for long hours and paid stingy wages. The result was a chronic gap between my growing needs and lagging income. Then, in 1927, I married Marvel Scholl, assumed family responsibilities, and found it harder than ever to make ends meet.

Those experiences reawakened my intellectual curiosity. I wondered how this social system operated, what efforts others had made to improve things for workers like myself, and how I might help bring about some of the needed changes. The way history was taught in high school had turned me off. So I started reading biographies, especially the lives of people whose careers were generally looked upon as successes. Before long those studies led to a revived interest in history and I began probing wider subjects. All this was done without any definite plan, however. I simply went to public libraries and read whatever books I chanced upon that looked like they might be useful.

By that time I was working for the Western Electric Company as an installer of telephone central office equipment. My wages had originally been very low. Gradually, though, my hourly pay was hiked and considerable overtime at premium rates significantly boosted my earnings. The outlook began to appear quite bright. Then I was promoted to job foreman, which brought me a higher salary in terms of regular hours. But there was a catch involved. I now had to put in overtime without extra pay and my overall weekly earnings dropped. I had wound up assuming greater job responsibilities for less money.

Somewhat later—in 1931—I was assigned to the company's division office in Omaha, Nebraska, given the title "planning engineer," and set to work estimating the labor cost of equipment installations. This, too, was presented as a promotion, but no raise in pay went with it. When I brought up the subject of money, my superiors advised me to be patient. The company was training me for the higher echelons of supervision, they said, which meant a start up the ladder toward a really big salary.

At first the prospects held out to me seemed promising; that is, until I discovered what was expected of top supervisors. The division superintendent had me sit in as a learner at high-level conferences held in his office. What I heard soon made it clear that in deciding important matters the sole factor was protection of company profits. The workers' needs were always treated as secondary and decisions affecting them were made with callous indifference to the impact upon their lives. This inhuman attitude was most shockingly revealed to me at a conference that selected a list of employees to be laid off because of the severe economic crisis.

Among those who got the ax was a worker I knew well from past association on the job. He had served the company loyally for a long time, but that had no bearing whatever in the top supervisors' view. They looked upon him only as a man who was getting old. He should be laid off, they decided, so the company could keep younger, more productive workers and at the same time avoid having to pension him later. This was the kind of thinking, I realized with revulsion, they were trying to teach me. My acceptance of it would have meant helping to impose upon others injustices of the very kind I had bridled against as a worker. To me that was unthinkable.

When I told Marvel about my dissatisfaction with the job, she responded sympathetically. We decided to turn away from Western

Electric and chart a new course for ourselves.

One aspect of my thinking about what to do next stemmed from a reading experience. While browsing in the Omaha public library I had come across H. G. Wells's *Outline of History.* Its ambitious scope appeared to promise valuable insights into existing social relations. A first reading produced no enlightenment of that kind, however, so I plowed through the ponderous tome a second time to make sure nothing had been overlooked. Again it proved to be a dry run, and this frustrating experience made me think that my desire for knowledge could be fulfilled only with college training.

Marvel and I decided to use my termination pay to start a small business in Minneapolis, Minnesota, our home town. In that way we expected to finance college educations for both of us. Personally, I intended to study political science and law with the aim of becoming a judge and using that position to dispense some justice.

Our idea about setting up a business reflected the degree to which we—like workers generally—had swallowed ruling-class propaganda that everyone has a chance to become "your own boss." We accepted the myth that it took only the accumulation of a little cash to establish our own "free enterprise" and then make good. The termination allowance of several hundred dollars I received upon leaving Western Electric seemed adequate for that purpose, so we used it to take over management of a neighborhood agency serviced by a dry-cleaning firm. There was no doubt in our minds that we could now get ahead financially, provide for our children's needs, and have enough left over to obtain the desired college education.

We naively embarked on that course in 1932, during the depths of the depression then paralyzing economic life. Before long, though, we discovered that the whole scheme was a pipe dream. Our adventure into the dog-eat-dog business world soon bankrupted us; and I wound up in late 1933 working long hours in a Minneapolis coal yard for starvation pay, able to provide Marvel and our (by then three) children no more than a hand-to-mouth existence.

Caught in those straits, I responded favorably when asked to participate in a campaign to unionize the coal workers. There was no way left in sight to find an individual solution to my problems, and the idea of united labor action seemed worth a try. After the union became strong enough, demands were made upon the fuel companies for improved wages and job conditions. They refused even to negotiate with us, so we went on strike. Our militant picketing halted coal deliveries and significant concessions were won from the employers.

During the heat of battle young workers like myself, who were new to the labor movement, became aware of our inherent power when acting collectively as members of a class. Some of us also perceived that a problem existed within the union's official leadership. Picketing had been guided by volunteer organizers within the ranks, who functioned competently as a team. Its effectiveness in forcing concessions from the bosses had been partially blunted, however, by the union business agent's mishandling of negotiations. Then, after the strike, this inept official began to denounce the most capable of the volunteer organizers as communists. That aroused not my hostility but my curiosity.

If those able fighters were communists, I reasoned, it should be possible to learn some of the things they knew by joining their party. So I asked and found that they belonged to the Communist League of America, the forerunner of the Socialist Workers Party, the organizational form then taken by the revolutionary Marxist movement. I entered its ranks in March 1934 and have remained there to this day.

Within the Communist League educational guidance of the kind I had been seeking finally became available. It began with study of Karl Marx's pamphlet *Wage-Labor and Capital* and Frederick Engels's *Socialism: Utopian and Scientific.* Removing the covers from those writings so they could be carried inconspicuously in my pocket on the job, I read them during long streetcar rides to and from work. For the first time my studies began to lead me to a scientific understanding of capitalism's inner mechanisms and of the socialist perspectives that necessarily flow from them and point the way toward the solution of the workers' problems. From then on, although busily engaged in union activity, I seized every chance to broaden my political knowledge. I read Leon Trotsky's *History of the Russian Revolution,* for instance, during a bout with the flu, and his *Third International After Lenin* while nursing a scalded foot.

In the spring of 1934 seasonal layoffs began in the fuel industry. Those who had been especially militant during the coal strike were first to get the ax, and I was among them. A number of us then put in full time as volunteer organizers, mobilizing the forces needed to extend the union's power throughout motor transport in the city. Two general strikes of trucking workers followed, both characterized by the employers' violent attempts to smash our picket lines. The strike leaders won support from working farmers, paid close attention to drawing in the unemployed, and saw women, inspired by the struggle, come forward and play a new, self-confident role. During those intensive struggles my political education was further enhanced by direct confirmation in life of the concepts in Marxist literature.

Before joining the labor movement I had been taken in by capitalist propaganda that the workers and employers have at least some basic interests in common; that workers, as well as employers, enjoy inviolable democratic rights within the prevailing system; that the government takes an impartial attitude toward industrial disputes; and that its "forces of law and order" safeguard the well-being of all.

The experience of the 1934 trucking strikes exposed every such pretense as a fake and a fraud. The workers, motivated by urgent need, were asking only to receive a fairer share of the fruits of their labor. They got a hostile response from the greedy employers, who put profit-making above everything else. When the workers exercised their democratic right to withhold their labor, the capitalist government tried to force a settlement on employer-dictated terms. Repressive actions taken against the strikers ranged from trickery by government mediators to murderous police assaults on picket lines and an attempt to restore trucking operations by military force.

In the course of the fierce struggles precipitated by the employers I learned another fundamental lesson. It had to do with an internal union problem. Unlike the strikers, who had everything at stake in the fight, the labor officials were generally interested in building lucrative personal careers based on collaboration with the ruling class. They disliked strikes and when one occurred their aim was to settle it quickly on the insufficient terms the bosses would offer. On top of that, they were given to acting in collusion with the capitalist government. As events showed, those proclivities created great dangers for the workers, dangers which were further magnified by the labor bureaucrats' viciousness against opposition from the ranks to their policies.

Young, inexperienced militants like myself didn't know how to handle such a problem. But an effective answer was provided by seasoned trade unionists within the Communist League, some of whom were direct participants in the battle then going on.

Under their guidance the fight against the bosses was at all times kept the focus of the workers' attention. Democratic election of a broad strike committee genuinely representative of the ranks was pushed through, and this committee was vested with the necessary authority by the embattled workers. With that kind of leadership, enough combat momentum was generated to override bureaucratic interference. It even became possible to jockey some union officials into a position where they felt impelled to make useful contributions to the struggle. All in all, the tactics used made a lasting impression on me, because they enabled us to beat the enemy class.

In addition to acquiring an understanding of class struggle realities at the industrial level, I went through a cram course in working-class politics during the strikes. An exceptional situation then existing in Minnesota made the experience a rich one. Unlike the rest of the country, there were three major parties in the state: Republican, Democratic, and Farmer-Labor. The Farmer-Labor Party was based primarily upon the trade unions, and it was organizationally independent of the two capitalist parties. Those positive features of the FLP merited encouragement. But there was also a negative side to its development.

Programmatically, the Farmer-Labor movement limited itself to proposals for only those social and economic improvements that were compatible with the present system. In addition, the top leaders were opposed to mass confrontations with the ruling class to achieve even these stated aims. They sought, instead, to confine rank-and-file activity to support of Farmer-Labor candidates at the polls, arguing that mass needs could best be met by reforms put through at the governmental level. When elected to public office, however, those candidates tended to put "official duty"—as defined by the capitalists—above their campaign promises. That trait was graphically demonstrated when the Farmer-Laborite governor of the state emulated the Republican mayor of Minneapolis in taking repressive action against the strikers. (My four-volume history of the teamster movement—*Teamster Rebellion, Teamster Power, Teamster Politics,* and *Teamster Bureaucracy*—available from Pathfinder Press, records these events in detail.)

These experiences with Farmer-Labor politicians taught me a further lesson. Independent labor political action requires more than an organizational break with the capitalist two-party system. If a mass labor party's program remains limited to seeking reforms compatible with capitalism, the workers will find themselves trapped in procedural norms designed to serve the interests of the ruling class; opportunists within the party, who put their personal ambitions above mass needs, will act as de facto agents of capitalism; and what was meant to be an emancipating social movement will degenerate into a narrow instrument that helps perpetuate the very injustices it initially set out to correct. Thus the hopes and aspirations of the working people become frustrated.

Those observations added a new dimension to my growing appreciation of the vital role played by the revolutionary vanguard party. Only such a party, it had become plain to see, could introduce into the mass movement the class consciousness needed to develop an effective program for independent labor political action. Only such a party could explain to the workers why a lasting solution to their basic problems requires a definitive break with the whole capitalist system; why the labor movement should orient toward assuming governmental power in its own name, so as to bring about a fundamental changeover to a new social order; and how to understand the strategic line of march and develop the necessary tactics to achieve those far-reaching objectives.

Along with knowledge about trade union methods and independent labor political action, education within the Trotskyist movement was extending my horizons beyond the local scene. Events in Minneapolis, I began to understand, were in a broad sense the concrete local manifestation of national trends; and those, in turn, were interrelated with and a reflection of international developments. Basic to this whole pattern, moreover, was an unremitting clash of class forces on a global scale. Toilers elsewhere were battling in one way or another to defend their class interests, just as the trucking employees were doing locally. We had a stake in all those struggles, my mentors explained, and our class allies should be backed to the fullest extent possible. When workers or the oppressed won a fight anywhere it helped the movement as a whole to progress. Conversely, if the bosses defeated any progressive movement, that meant a setback for the working class generally. That made it imperative, they stressed, to develop labor solidarity with the oppressed and exploited on a national and international scale. The goal was to weaken a common enemy—the brutal rule of imperialist capital.

There was still another way in which the educational guidance I received was broadening my outlook. It involved study of past developments in the trade union and political movements of labor and its allies throughout the world. The results were gratifying. Clues were provided concerning effective steps that could be taken in contemporary struggles. Study of earlier events offered safeguards against needlessly repeating errors. I got a more rounded feel for the class struggle as a historic process, a better grasp of social dynamics.

*     *     *

A cynic has said that we learn from history that people learn nothing from history. This may well be the case if one's insights into the historical process depend exclusively upon knowledge derived from academic and bourgeois sources, which ignore or downplay the central role of the class struggle as its motive force and a workers' government as its inevitable end product.

This study of the struggle for revolutionary Marxist continuity in the United States has been written from the viewpoint of the historic line of march of the working class. The narration of events is designed to bring forth the significance of the successive efforts of the working masses, and above all of the leading cadres, to attain a clearer class consciousness, a better understanding of their place and role under capitalism, and stronger forms of economic and political organization to oppose and combat the exploitation and domination of the capitalist rulers.

Because of the retarded ideological state of the United States working class compared to its counterparts in many other countries, its inability so far to break loose from the Democratic and Republican political machines and establish a mass independent labor party, and the small size of the revolutionary socialist forces within it, it may seem that very little or no progress has been made toward these goals. That would be a superficial estimate. So sterile and pessimistic a view is not warranted.

The various and repeated attempts of the working class and its most advanced leaders to promote and reinforce its independent industrial and political organization have left their mark. This achievement is most evident of course in the trade union field. When the ranks are aroused and set into motion, the U.S. union movement is one of the most powerful, well-organized, and combative against the corporations and their government in the world. What it still lacks to realize its potential is the proper kind of leadership.

This book records and critically reviews the ways in which the successive generations of proletarian revolutionists have participated in the movements of the working class and its allies and sought to steer them along the correct path. As I have explained, their leadership was not always fruitful or well thought-out. They had their share of defaults and disappointments.

Nonetheless, they maintained through the decades the continuity of revolutionary proletarian thought and kept the spirit of conscious anticapitalist resistance alive. Marxists today not only owe them homage for their deeds, their courage in the face of adversity, their perseverance in defending the welfare of the exploited and oppressed. We have a duty beyond this acknowledgment. That is to learn where they went wrong as well as what they did right so that their errors are not repeated.

That is the only way in which the heritage of the efforts of millions, often paid for in blood, can be put to good account and not squandered and nullified. For the Marxist program is simply the generalization of the strategic lessons learned by succeeding generations over the course of the class struggle as the toilers strive to replace the dictatorship of capital with their own.

Just as I have searched for accounts of past developments in the labor and socialist movements throughout my quest for political education, the current generation of fighters will need every bit of information that can be provided on the subject. For that reason I have undertaken this contribution to the history of revolutionary Marxism in the United States, beginning in this first volume with a sketch of the revolutionary continuity from which it stems. I hope today's worker militants will gain a measure of the enlightenment they seek from the experiences incorporated and lessons emphasized in these pages.

These volumes will trace three major threads through the history of the workers' movement in this country and its revolutionary continuity: (1) the fight for the economic organization of the working class into trade unions, and for organization along industrial rather than craft lines; (2) the fight for political and social consciousness and action by the workers' movement; and (3) the fight for the independent political organization of the working class, a labor party, to advance its interests and those of its allies against the interests of the ruling capitalist minority. Tying these threads together are the efforts by the Marxist wing of the workers' movement to gather the cadres of a proletarian revolutionary party needed to lead the fight to end capitalist rule, establish a workers' and farmers' government, and open the road to a socialist order.

These books will trace this record of working-class program, strategy, and tactics in the United States from three different vantage points. The first, which encompasses the entirety of this volume, is written from a historical standpoint, relying on prior narratives and the written record of participants.

Beginning in 1934, the vantage point will shift to that of a direct participant in the economic, social, and political battles of the working class. Whereas my four-volume teamsters series treated these years primarily from the standpoint of a revolutionist in the unions, this history will review these events from the perspective of constructing a proletarian vanguard party.

The vantage point will shift again, beginning with events in 1940, to that of a central leader of the Socialist Workers Party. This final part of the series will then trace the forementioned threads up to the 1960s, concentrating on the SWP's efforts to preserve, develop, and apply Marxism in the U.S. class struggle and to construct the nucleus of a revolutionary party of industrial workers in the United States.

I have had in view above all the oncoming generation of workers—Black, brown, and white, female and male—who are destined through their struggles to write the next chapters in the history of the emancipation of the toilers. Reliable knowledge of the past will help arm them to find the road to victory.

# 1

# European Ancestry

Forebears of today's revolutionary workers' movement date back to European cadres who issued the *Communist Manifesto* in 1848. That profound document, written by Karl Marx and Frederick Engels, opened a new era in the fight for social progress. A scientific and proletarian alternative to the various petty-bourgeois socialist programs and outlooks was advanced for the first time. Its revolutionary concepts can be paraphrased along the following broad lines:

Since human society advanced beyond primitive communal possession of the land and the products of human labor, struggles between the exploited and exploiting classes over the disposition of the surplus product have been the motive force of history. Oppressed and oppressors have been arrayed in constant opposition to each other at every stage of social evolution. They have carried on uninterrupted conflicts—now hidden, now open—that lead toward the revolutionary reconstitution of society at large; that is, to new social orders displacing outlived ones.

At a fateful turning point in that historic process the rising capitalist class developed as the key progressive element within feudal society. The capitalists (referred to in the Manifesto by the French term *bourgeoisie*) were characterized by their capacity to increase the productivity of labor by developing increasingly efficient methods of employing wage-labor in production. But the possibilities of the capitalist mode of production could be realized only by replacing feudal and other precapitalist social relations. So revolutionary struggles against the feudal aristocracy began, out of which capitalism emerged as the dominant social order.

As the bourgeoisie gained ascendancy in one country and continent after another it proceeded to reorganize social conditions according to its needs. Urban populations were greatly increased relative to rural ones, means of production were centralized, and property was concentrated in fewer hands.

At the same time another process necessary for the expansion and survival of capitalism became intensified. It involved constant revolutionizing of the instruments of production, thereby ceaselessly conflicting with the relations of production and thus with all social relations. This continual disruption of their social conditions brought incessant uncertainty into the lives of the masses.

The productive forces thus created under capitalism have already begun to come into fundamental conflict with the property relations necessary for the existence and rule of the bourgeoisie. That conflict is manifested in periodic economic crises, marked by the capitalist anomaly of overproduction in the midst of need. During these crises society suddenly finds itself put back into a momentary state of barbarism; it appears as if a famine or a devastating war had cut off the means of subsistence. Why? Because there is too much means of subsistence, too much production under a system regulated by capitalist greed for private profit. As this grotesque anomaly shows, the productive forces have become fettered by the maintenance of bourgeois property relations.

When economic crises develop, the bourgeoisie curtails production, thereby creating unemployment. It uses the crises to impose greater speedup on the workers, to stretch out the workday, and to lower the workers' expectations. It also seeks to revive commerce by the conquest of new markets and by more thorough exploitation of the old ones. That is to say, the way is paved for more extensive and more destructive crises later on.

In its quest for constantly expanding markets the bourgeoisie has striven and managed to build up world trade and foreign investment. Raw material is taken from the remotest zones. Industrial products are exported to every quarter of the globe and capital goes everywhere. As a result national seclusion and economic self-sufficiency gives way to the universal interdependence of nations; superexploited countries are made economically dependent upon the industrially advanced ones. Along those lines capitalism has set out to create a world after its own image, and in the process national isolation and narrow-mindedness become more and more impossible.

Both to advance its interests abroad and to assure its primacy at home, the bourgeoisie has restructured the government as an instrument for the management of its affairs as a class. Constitutions and codes of laws have been set up to assure economic exploitation of the laboring majority by the capitalist minority. Armed forces and other state instruments have been established as well, for the enforcement of ruling-class policy and maintenance of bourgeois rule.

There is a catch, however, in this scheme of things. The essential condition for the existence and for the sway of the bourgeois class is the formation and augmentation of capital; the condition for the increase of industrial capital is more and more intensive exploitation of wage-labor. Workers are paid less for their labor-power than the value they produce. The surplus value in the excess of products they turn out beyond their minimal needs of existence and reproduction is appropriated by the bourgeoisie in order to accumulate more capital. In proportion as capital is thus put to use, in the same proportion is the proletariat, the modern working class, developed and extended—a class of laborers who live only so long as they find work and who find work only so long as their labor increases capital. Hence, the development of society as a whole becomes more and more dominated by the conflict between the great classes directly facing each other, the bourgeoisie and the proletariat.

Proletarians, who must sell their labor-power for wages, are commodities like all other articles of commerce. As such, each worker is exposed to all the vicissitudes of competition with other workers, and to all the fluctuations of the market. These factors affect both chances for employment and the pay received for their toil. On the job they are subjected by the employers to the longest possible working hours and to speedup on production lines under hazardous working conditions. Upon receiving their pay the workers are set upon by other profit-gougers, such as landlords, merchants, and loan sharks.

Not only do many workers lose their jobs during economic crises; those who remain employed are subject to downward fluctuations in wages during such periods. On top of that, unceasing technological change makes job stability ever more precarious. Instead of gaining a more secure livelihood with the progress of industry, the workers tend to be thrust below the conditions necessary for their maintenance as a class. As a result pauperism develops, especially among the most oppressed layers of the proletariat.

Antagonisms bred by such injustices lead to clashes between workers and employers. These more and more take the character of collisions between the contending classes as the workers form trade unions to fight for improved wages, hours, and conditions. Now and then they are victorious in those struggles, but only for a time because the employers keep whittling away at them. The real fruit of their battles lies not in the immediate results, but in the expansion and reinforcement of the labor movement. Workers in different localities establish contact with one another; the numerous local struggles, all of the same character, become centralized into one national struggle between the contending classes. At the same time the proletariat increases in numbers with the development of industry; it becomes concentrated in greater masses; its strength grows; and it feels that strength more as a class.

Every class struggle is a political struggle. Therefore, organization of the workers as a class must include the formation of their own independent political party, a party that will represent a self-conscious movement of the immense majority, acting in the interests of the immense majority. In fulfilling that role the mass proletarian party must enter into struggle to protect and promote the welfare of the masses on all social levels. If the workers are to emancipate themselves from capitalist exploitation and oppression, they must at the same time free the whole of society from all exploitation and every form of oppression. To achieve that objective the working class must lead a fight for the conquest of political power, in order to overturn bourgeois rule and abolish the capitalist system.

Concerning the role of the middle classes—administrators, farmers, merchants, artisans, professional people, etc., also called the petty bourgeoisie—a contradictory situation exists. Many of them are thrust into opposition to the bourgeoisie, but since their objective is to safeguard their petty-bourgeois status within the existing capitalist order, their role is not inherently revolutionary. For some it can be conservative, even reactionary, because they vainly try to roll back history to an earlier epoch dominated by independent petty commodity production.

If sections of the middle classes do become revolutionary-minded, it is in view of their impending transfer into the proletariat due to erosion of their current class position under capitalism. They thus defend not their present, but their future interests; they desert their current standpoint to place themselves at that of the proletariat.

Thus, of all the classes that stand face to face with the bourgeoisie, the proletariat alone is the consistently revolutionary class. Proletarians are without productive property. Unlike the capitalists, they gain nothing through exploitation and oppression of others; to emancipate themselves they must abolish individual property in the means of production, thus eliminating the ultimate cause of exploitation and oppression. Their historical line of march leads to the overturn of bourgeois rule, laying the foundations for the sway of the proletariat that will abolish capitalism and open the way toward socialism.

Although competition among workers under the wage-labor system tends to divide them, the advance of industry reduces the possibility of individual solutions and increases tendencies to social thinking on their part by drawing them into close association on the job, where they have common problems. They are thereby impelled toward organization as a class and consequently toward formation of their own political party. Despite ups and downs, the objective thrust in that direction becomes stronger, the revolutionary potential of the proletariat more pronounced. For those reasons what the bourgeoisie produces, above all, are "its own gravediggers." Its fall and the victory of the proletariat are equally inevitable.

Coming to this conclusion after analyzing capitalist society along the above lines, the Manifesto charted a basic course for the communists of that time, which remains the central guide for today's revolutionary socialists. Communists, it declares, have no interests separate and apart from those of the proletariat as a whole. They do not set up any sectarian principles of their own, by which to shape and mold the proletarian movement.

The theoretical conclusions of the communists are in no way based on principles invented by any reformer; they merely express and project, in general terms, actual relations springing from the existing class struggle. In this way communists understand the line of march, conditions, and ultimate results of the workers' movement, leading to the conquest of political power by the proletariat.

Communists identify completely with the working class at all stages of its political development and act simply as its most conscious and organized contingent. They fight for the attainment of the immediate aims, for the satisfaction of the everyday needs of the working class, but in the movement of the present they also represent and act as guardians of the future of that movement. They never cease, for a single instant, to instill into labor's ranks the clearest possible recognition of the irreconcilable antagonism between the bourgeoisie and the proletariat. They support every revolutionary movement, everywhere, against the existing social and political order.

The subjugation of workers under capitalism, the Manifesto stresses, decreases national differences. Under the rule of the exploiters workers have no country to call their own. Their struggles are national only in the sense that they must first acquire political supremacy within each country; and in those national struggles communists point out and bring to the fore the common interests of the world proletariat, independently of all nationality. Socialism is above all an international movement. During the various stages through which the struggle of the working class against the bourgeoisie must pass, communists always and everywhere represent the interests of the movement as a whole. From this it follows that the communists are in practice the most advanced and resolute section of each country's working class, the section which pushes forward all the others.

The oppression of women, which began with class society, will end as class society and all its vestiges are eradicated. The Manifesto voiced proletarian indignation at the disgusting hypocrisy of bourgeois attitudes toward women whose degradation is rooted in the very system of private property the ruling class upholds. A far-reaching, radical perspective of women's liberation and the elimination of the family as an economic institution serving the needs of the exploiting classes are proclaimed as part of the workers' self-emancipation.

Once the workers take power, the Manifesto asserts, a basis will have been laid for democratic control of society by majority decision. Total reorganization of the economic and social structure can then begin. Among the first steps will be the abolition of private property based on the antagonism of capital and wage-labor. It is not the personal belongings of individuals, nor the small holdings of such toilers as working farmers, that will be abolished, but large-scale bourgeois property in the means of production: banks, industries, big landholdings, etc., which are used by capital to subjugate labor.

All instruments of production can then be centralized in the hands of the state—that is, in the hands of the proletariat organized as the ruling class—to increase the productive forces and the available wealth. In time that planned economy will lead to the disappearance of class distinctions, to the regulation of production by a vast association of the whole nation and federation of nations. Since political state power is by definition the organized power of one class for repression of another; since the proletariat will have crushed bourgeois efforts to block the social transformation; since it will have swept away capitalism and all it stands for—the conditions will have been laid for abolition of its own supremacy as a class. In place of the old bourgeois society, with its classes and class antagonisms, there will be a voluntary association of producers in which the free development of each becomes the condition for the free development of all.

Having set forth that liberating perspective for humanity as the goal, the *Communist Manifesto* ends with the battle cry: "The proletarians have nothing to lose but their chains. They have a world to win. Workers of all countries, unite!"

By 1848, when the Manifesto appeared, the European proletariat was becoming a major class force. Its growth had resulted from an industrial revolution that began in England during the eighteenth century and spread to other economically advanced countries. The technical change involved a leap from manufacture dependent upon hand labor to the factory system of machine production.

It was built especially on the crushing, brutal superexploitation of women and children, who constituted the majority of the work force in such vitally important industries as textile and apparel manufacturing. This was a conscious policy carried out in such a way as to destroy the power of the male-dominated skilled trades, divide the working class, and reap vast superprofits.

Under the preceding system capital had been used for collective employment of workers who had craft skills and often their own simple instruments of production—tools, hand looms, etc. Then came the invention of the steam engine and related devices, which led to a sweeping reorganization of productive relations. In industry after industry capitalist-owned machinery replaced the handicrafts in manufacturing processes. Control over the means of production became centralized in the hands of the bourgeoisie. The workers' simple instruments of production were rendered worthless and they lost whatever independence such possessions had afforded them.

Previously certain craft privileges had remained extant despite the introduction of some division of labor into the earlier manufacturing system. With the development of machinery, however, such privileges rapidly disappeared. Various steps in manufacturing processes were now divided among the workers to such an extent that no single worker any longer made an entire product with his or her own hands. Each produced merely a part of the given article, doing so through simplified forms of labor in which the movements were repeated mechanically. In short, skilled mechanics were reduced to common laborers serving as appendages of machines in commodity production. To a constantly increasing extent use of skilled labor became confined to tool and die making, machine repair, etc., and to work outside the manufacturing sphere.

A class of proletarians thus arose who owned nothing and had to sell their labor-power to a boss to exist. It was a class, moreover, which gained steadily in numbers and acquired greater inherent strength as machine production expanded.

It did not follow, though, that the proletariat automatically became conscious of its status as a class, or that it immediately perceived the irreconcilable antagonism between its interests and those of the capitalists. Such awareness had to develop through diverse and protracted experience and could be attained by the masses only a step at a time. Since Britain continued in the forefront of the industrial revolution for many years, the sharpening of labor struggles there may be used to illustrate essential factors involved in the evolution of class consciousness and the rise of proletarian movements throughout Europe.

At the outset the British factory workers merely sensed the need for collective resistance to the worst aspects of capitalist exploitation. As against bourgeois efforts to generate individual rivalries among them, they sought to engage in united defensive actions. At first this took the form in the Luddite movement of destroying the machines in the factories. Then mass demonstrations and strikes, usually of a spontaneous nature, occurred with increasing frequency. In the course of those struggles the workers, to some extent, initiated organizational combinations, but these did not last very long.

Efforts to create proletarian organizations ran head-on into a bourgeois conspiracy to prevent the workers from combining as a class. The employers' tactics included enactment of laws prohibiting such combinations, or unions. Worker-militants sought to get around the obstacle by forming secret societies, which intervened as best they could in spontaneous outbursts of struggle. Their efforts were aided by mass unrest caused by the alternation in employment between industrial upswings and crises of overproduction. As those cycles unfolded, social contrasts became more and more glaring. The capitalists grew increasingly prosperous, while destitution and misery became the lot of many in the working class. So great was the mass discontent thus generated, that pressure mounted steadily for the right to freedom of action and organization in defense of labor's interests.

During the first quarter of the nineteenth century the British proletariat attained definite shape as a class. In the same period its struggles won modification of laws prohibiting the formation of workers' organizations, and the achievement was used to good purpose. Trade unions were built in the various branches of industry. Within the separate industries local units moved toward formation of national federations. Efforts were also initiated to establish a general combination embracing all trade unions in the country.

Strikes conducted in an organized way became the principal method of struggle. Although the strikers often experienced defeat, there were also victories of a limited nature. Those battles within industry gave the workers needed combat experience. The victories served to strengthen the trade unions, and thus labor's combat potential grew.

Yet another advance began in the aftermath of an economic crisis in 1836–37. A political struggle against ruling-class policies was launched by forces within the British labor movement. It centered on demands for legislation expanding the workers' democratic rights. Although those demands—including universal male suffrage—did not go beyond efforts to win reforms within the capitalist system, this new development, known as the Chartist movement, had significant implications for a country already majority proletarian. This time the workers were not simply engaging in economic conflict with one or another individual capitalist at the industrial level; they were raising broad demands as a class on the political arena, which were directed against the bourgeois government.

Elsewhere in Europe there were variations, country by country, as to the precise manner in which independent organization of the proletariat was taking place. The interrelationship between the economic and political conflicts involved also differed somewhat as to form and sequence. But essentially the British developments reflected the limited degree to which class consciousness and struggle momentum had developed among the proletarian masses of Europe by 1848.

That was the objective setting in which Marx and Engels led a campaign to build a revolutionary formation capable of carrying out the far-reaching aims set forth in the *Communist Manifesto.* Work toward the desired end was conducted in two main spheres: within the existing mass movement, and among vanguard workers becoming advanced in class consciousness. To the extent that participation by revolutionists helped to raise levels of consciousness generated through spontaneous mass struggles, prospects for strengthening the vanguard were enhanced. Growth of the conscious vanguard served, in turn, to further intensify class-struggle perspectives and trends on a mass scale. Along those lines gains made in one sphere led to new advances in the other on an interacting basis.

Through this process it became possible to fuse vanguard con-

Left, Karl Marx. Right, Frederick Engels.

sciousness with mass power to a higher and higher degree, and thus help the workers go beyond partial, episodic struggles by one or another section of the class. They could be influenced toward development of coordinated class action—both economic and political—on the national arena; class solidarity could similarly be generated on an international plane. As determined by the dynamics of events, the workers could in time be mobilized and guided into a fight for state power and the transformation of society.

Numerically, the Marxist tendency was quite weak at the start. Such cadres as were available proceeded to form groups based on the program of the *Communist Manifesto,* doing so in the few countries where the tendency existed. One aspect of the activity of these groups, which took the name Communist League, involved propaganda and educational work designed to facilitate recruitment of radicalizing workers. Toward the same end scientific socialists in some instances entered other groups containing leftward-moving forces who might be won over to the revolutionary socialist line.

Parallel with those steps the Marxists sought to exercise influence within the mass movement. They made common cause with the proletariat in its economic struggles and in its fight for democratic rights. On a day-to-day basis they supported the general line of action possible in given situations, going through experiences with the workers from which lessons could be drawn. Illusions about collaborative relations between capital and labor could in that way be dispelled. Mistaken views could be criticized in an objective manner so as to help open-minded militants think in terms of the workers as a class facing the bosses as a class. Tactics based on explicit class-struggle concepts could then be introduced into economic conflicts. Explanation of the workers' need to defend their class interests in generalized form could be presented in a manner designed to lead them toward independent labor political action.

On the whole, this combination of united action and probing discussion served to give revolutionary views increasing weight among the workers. Sympathizers were developed, who collaborated more and more closely with the Marxists, and in the process some became revolutionists themselves. The correctness of the new program and perspective was confirmed in action in the crucible of the revolutions of 1848.

Within less than two decades these methods prepared the ground for creation of the first international organization embracing substantial numbers of politically advanced workers from several countries. Sufficient forces who agreed on how to proceed were available; and problems involving theoretical confusion on the part of some could best be worked out after bringing those forces together in a common organization. This approach concerning matters of theory and program fit in with the need to replace the existing conglomeration of socialist and semisocialist sects with a revolutionary political organization of the working class, one capable of leading the class toward fulfillment of its historic mission.

In striving to attain that objective Marx and Engels demonstrated the interrelationship between fusions and splits in building a political movement. Organizational fusions serve to establish close working relations with leftward-moving tendencies so as to help them acquire full revolutionary consciousness; in the process, rival political formations are reduced in number. Membership growth realized in that manner remains purposeful, however, only so long as the expanded movement adheres to a correct political course. If its theory becomes defective or its program proves wrong, numerical strength loses significance; because a movement so afflicted will fail to meet the test of class battle. When any of the basic theoretical or programmatic conquests are challenged, they must be defended at all hazards; and those who persist in deviating from the required line must be excluded from the organization. At that point, splits take precedence in assuring the building of a strong movement.

The international fusion process among different national sections of the proletariat took a qualitative step forward with the launching in 1864 of the International Workingmen's Association, better known in history as the First International. British and French vanguard workers took the organizational initiative in the step, which was formalized at a gathering in London. Marx wrote the program adopted by the new movement. It contained the following key points: emancipation of the working class had to be accomplished by the working class itself; this signified a struggle to end inequity through the abolition of class rule; the task was a social one, and was not limited to either local or national perspectives, but embraced all countries. The working class needed not only its own domestic social policy but its own internationalist foreign policy.

The International organized rallies and demonstrations in solidarity with the Polish struggle for national independence, as well as freedom of Ireland from British rule. It championed the war to defeat the Confederacy in the United States, projecting the need to transform it into a revolutionary war to emancipate the slaves and crush the slaveholding system and planter class.

Marx deliberately restricted the initial program of the International to points that allowed immediate and concerted action by the workers. In that way direct impetus could be given to class-struggle activities and to expanded organization of the proletariat. As progress was made toward those ends, a basis would be laid for the introduction later on of more rounded programmatic concepts and necessary differentiations from utopian, sectarian, opportunist, and anarchist currents.

Representatives from various countries were elected to an executive body called the General Council. It set up headquarters for the International in London. From the outset Marx and Engels— through their own teamwork and in their relations with others— provided an example of the manner in which that body should function. Objective collaboration, they taught by word and deed, was imperative between worker-militants and revolutionists from other classes who identified themselves totally with the proletariat through their commitment to the party. Those guiding the organization needed to act as a collective leadership that carried out its duties through the necessary divisions of labor. This had to be done, moreover, with a clear understanding of the new movement's character at that specific juncture and of the direction in which it was heading.

Formation of the First International did not reflect the coming together of established national parties. It was essentially a vanguard step intended to guide the workers in each country toward a showdown with the bourgeoisie; to concretely demonstrate in practice the vital need for an international outlook in the class struggle; and through those combined experiences to unite politically advanced elements around the Marxist program and develop a general staff of the world revolution.

The International's efforts toward work among the masses soon began to stimulate trade union organization generally. International campaigns to back major strikes in one or another country helped to raise the workers' sights beyond national horizons. Support of demands for progressive labor legislation provided a way to introduce more advanced political ideas into the trade unions, especially the need to form independent parties of the working class. On balance, however, mass action during the next few years after 1864 remained more or less confined to intensified trade union struggle.

The most notable exception occurred in Germany, where two workers' parties appeared during the 1860s. One, the General Association of German Workers, was organized by Ferdinand Lassalle; its effectiveness was impaired, unfortunately, by Lassalle's sectarian attitude toward trade union organization and by his tendency to engage in unprincipled political maneuvers with the German monarchic government. The other organization, the Social Democratic Workers Party of Germany, was launched by followers of Marx; they opposed Lassalle's maneuverist tendencies on the political arena and paid attention to building German trade unions.

During the same period some of the more advanced workers' formations in a few other countries affiliated with the International. The trend was encouraged through a flexible organizational policy that allowed separate groups within a given country to have equal status as sections of the world movement. Then, as permitted by time and changing circumstances, the separate groups were drawn toward fusion and united affiliation as a single section.

This flexible policy was equally useful in attracting and dissolving the socialist and semisocialist sects. All working-class socialists were invited to join the International, retaining their separate organizational identities if they so desired. In that way a means was provided for gradually integrating the minor sects into the movement as a whole. To a certain extent such a transition was accomplished through debates in connection with world congresses held during the 1860s and early 1870s. Differences were thrashed out and resolved between the Marxists and some of the sects, thereby achieving a greater degree of political homogeneity within the movement on the basis of common fundamental outlooks.

An exception to the regroupment trend developed in the case of the anarchists, led by Mikhail Bakunin, according to whom the main evil in society was not the capitalist system but the state as such, which they considered an entity standing above social classes. Capital was created by the state, they contended, and individuals possessing capital did so only by the grace of the state. Therefore, the state had to be abolished forthwith, after which the significance of capital would fade into obscurity. Full equality of the social classes would then prevail. There would be no overriding authority of any kind whatsoever, nor would there be any such thing as majority rule. Each social community would function on an autonomous basis, and each individual within the community would have complete freedom of action.

In striving for social change there could be no resort to political action, the anarchists held, for politics in any form simply helped to keep the state alive. Instead, propaganda and agitation should be conducted against the state, as such, to convince the masses of the need to abolish it on the morrow after the revolution. At the same time the International should be constructed so as to represent the anarchist ideal of future society, thereby serving as the initial means of social guidance once the state had been done away with.

Apart from a few workers who served as a facade, the Bakuninist cadres were petty bourgeois. The latter thought in terms of carrying on a personal war with the ruling class, acting as self-appointed representatives of the proletariat, and appealing to the lumpen layers of the society instead of the proletariat. Their tactics centered on one or another piece of ultraleft adventurism, along with terrorist acts called "propaganda of the deed." In that way, they expected to galvanize the masses into support of their struggle to rid society of the state.

The Marxists agreed that the state should ultimately be abolished. But talk of doing so without a previous social revolution, they explained, was utter nonsense. Under capitalism the state was constructed as a creature of the capitalists, not vice versa, as the anarchists contended. In carrying through a revolutionary social change the workers would need to wrest state power from the bourgeoisie and wield it for their own purposes. Their objective would not be to achieve "equality of the classes" but to move toward the abolition of class formations. The first task would be the crushing of bourgeois resistance to the overthrow of capitalism. Steps could then be taken to move toward a socialist order. As the process advanced, class distinctions within society would gradually disappear; there would no longer be any need for the use of state power by one class to repress another; and the state, having no further role to play, would wither away.

Anarchist notions that a minority of adventurers could substitute themselves for the working class were also refuted by the Marxists. Where a complete transformation of society is involved, they stressed, the masses must be in the thick of the action and they must grasp what is at stake. That imposes several requirements upon revolutionists: persistent dissemination of socialist propaganda, including the fact that the workers can win liberation only through their own efforts; support of trade union struggles; aid in developing mass political movements of the workers on a class basis; patient building of the revolutionary vanguard proletarian party; utilization of every opening to advance the class struggle stage by stage, as made possible through changing social reality.

The Marxists rejected with equal firmness anarchist plans to shape the International as an anticipation of their ideal for society at large. That would have meant suppression of the democratic principle of majority rule in favor of freedom for minorities to do as they pleased at any and all times. Instead of the organization developing as an effective political vanguard of the working class, adherence to the anarchists' formula would have made it a shambles.

Anarchist views—concerning theory, program, strategy, tactics, and organizational norms—represented an antithesis of Marxism. No common basis existed for the two tendencies to arrive at a homogenous political outlook. They could only engage in ceaseless rivalry for influence among the masses.

The Bakuninist movement had not taken shape until about three years after the First International was launched. It began with formation of a group called the Alliance for Socialist Democracy. That setup operated partly in the open and partly in secret, its actions being subject to centralized personal control by Bakunin. By the end of 1868 the Alliance had acquired significant numerical strength, and Bakunin, who had joined the International on his own, pressed from that vantage point for acceptance of the Alliance's application for admission as a body into the world organization. Since an anarchist scheme was obviously afoot to pack the 1869 congress, the General Council rejected the application.

An intensive struggle followed between the Marxists and the Bakuninists over the issues of program and leadership, as the anarchists persisted in their efforts to capture the International. Before the confrontation reached a climax, however, the world movement had to face still further difficulties issuing from the outcome of a revolutionary upheaval that erupted in France.

In 1870 Emperor Napoleon III of France launched a war of conquest against Germany. After a few weeks the main section of the French army was forced to surrender to the Prussians. The defeat precipitated a political crisis at home in which Napoleon III was deposed and a republic proclaimed. With German troops rapidly penetrating France, the Paris deputies to the former national legislative body—acting with the support of the aroused masses—formed the

Government of National Defense. All able-bodied males in the city were enrolled in the National Guard; and since workers constituted the great majority of the Guard, it meant the proletariat as a class was now armed.

Fearing the Parisian workers more than the German army, the bourgeoisie's so-called Government of National Defense soon plotted to disarm them. It could get no direct help toward that end from the invading forces that had laid siege to the city, because the bloody assault required would have aroused strong opposition within the German working class. So an armistice was arranged in January 1871 as an interim measure. The terms provided that the National Guard would keep its weapons and the Prussian troops would stay outside the city.

Suspecting that treachery was afoot, the workers reorganized the Guard and entrusted supreme authority to its central committee, which was democratically elected by the ranks. No attempt was made, though, to overturn the national government, whose loyalty was in question. The proletariat manifestly wished to avoid civil war. The bourgeois schemers, however, had no such inhibitions.

Louis Thiers, who had become head of the national government, demanded that the Paris Guard surrender its weapons. When the demand was ignored, he set out to force compliance through a combination of trickery, provocations, and military pressure. Finally, on March 18, 1871, the remnants of the defeated French army tried to seize the Guard's artillery in a surprise raid. The attempt failed, but it was nonetheless one provocation too many. In self-defense the central committee of the Guard proceeded to organize the Paris Commune as the city administration, and the Thiers regime thereupon fled in a panic to Versailles. Through those developments, a state of civil war came to exist between the Paris proletariat and the French bourgeoisie.

The formation of the Commune was an attempt for the first time to establish a workers' government. Its highest body consisted of democratically elected representatives of the masses. As safeguards against the rise of a bureaucracy, holders of public office were subject to immediate recall and their salaries were limited to the wage scale of skilled workers. Those elected were almost entirely workers or recognized representatives of workers.

The First International supported the Paris uprising unconditionally, even though it had no control over its decision making. Commune policy was shaped by leaders who in their majority were not socialists; and it could not be otherwise, for they had been selected out of a spontaneous mass movement. And the majority current among those who were socialists were non-Marxists, followers of the petty-bourgeois Pierre Proudhon and revolutionary-insurrectionist Auguste Blanqui. Despite flaws in carrying the struggle forward, which resulted from lack of rounded education as revolutionists, the course they set was eminently progressive. It went in the direction of upsetting the economic foundations and political superstructure of capitalist rule, thereby paving the way toward complete emancipation of labor and all the oppressed. Before they could carry the experiment very far, however, the steps toward fundamental reorganization of French society were cut short.

Apparently the Commune leaders still hoped to avoid the civil war that Thiers had already started. In any case they failed to march immediately on Versailles, where the then helpless national government had installed itself, and put an end to the bourgeois conspiracy against the working class. This reluctance proved to be a fatal mistake.

Theirs seized the opportunity thus afforded him to regroup his forces. The German government helped him by releasing French soldiers captured earlier. Once the counterrevolutionary Versailles army had been beefed up by the returned prisoners, it was hurled against Paris with indirect aid from the Prussian military. Bitter fighting ensued as the Parisians put up heroic resistance, women revolutionaries fighting shoulder to shoulder with the men. The attackers had too great a military advantage, however, and the Commune succumbed on May 28, 1871.

Terrible reprisals were then taken by the Thiers regime. Communards were executed in wholesale lots, women and men alike.

Arrests and imprisonment took place on a mass scale among those who escaped the slaughter. These savage reprisals continued in various ways until the bourgeois lust for revenge against the rebellious proletariat had spent itself.

After the Paris Commune was overthrown, Marx and Engels presented a scientific evaluation of the workers' struggle. This involved both the drawing of tactical lessons from it and a concrete enrichment of Marxist theory in the light of the 1870–71 events. Earlier, when drafting the *Communist Manifesto,* they had dealt with the question of the state in general terms. Attention had been centered on the need for the proletariat to use the organized apparatus and repressive forces of the state to proceed with the reorganization of society and to crush bourgeois resistance to the change. Concrete steps toward those ends were not specified, however, since historical experience had not yet pointed to the material solution of the problem.

A few years later—while analyzing the bourgeois revolutions and reactionary counterrevolutions of 1848–51 in France and Germany—they took note of the fact that the proletariat was moving toward the breaking of bourgeois control over the governmental apparatus. In view of what had happened, especially in the 1848 revolution in France, Marx pointed to the necessity of the proletarian revolution not attempting to use but smashing the bureaucratic-military state machine created by the capitalist class and constructing their own in its place. He also projected the concept of the dictatorship of the proletariat, using the term originated by Blanqui. Engels shared those conclusions—which Marx had drawn in his book *The Eighteenth Brumaire of Louis Bonaparte*—and when they were once again verified, in much richer detail, in 1871, he joined with Marx in presenting them as explicit lessons taught by the tragedy in Paris.

The workers, they explained, cannot simply lay hold of the ready-made machinery of state and wield it for their own purposes. It is imperative that the capitalists' standing army be abolished and replaced by the nation in arms. Similarly, the police must be abol-

Above, the proclamation of the Paris Commune in 1871.
Below, a membership card in the First International.

ished and necessary policing functions taken over by the working class. At the same time the existing governmental bureaucracy— legislative, judicial, or administrative—must be thoroughly dismantled. Every instrumentality used for capitalist repression of the masses has to be done away with. Only in that manner can a firm basis be laid for creation of a workers' state.

The Paris Commune, they explained, demonstrated that to carry out those measures a dictatorship of the proletariat is needed. The proletariat is the only class that is consistently revolutionary. It alone is capable of uniting all the exploited and oppressed in a struggle to displace the capitalists, to overcome their inevitable resistance to social change, and to reorganize society on a socialist basis. During that process the proletariat will constitute the ruling class. Its aims will be the opposite, however, of those nurtured by the old ruling class, which—no matter what form of government it used at a given time—consistently maintained a repressive dictatorship of the bourgeoisie. In contrast, the dictatorship of the proletariat will be genuinely representative of the masses, whose needs will be its sole concern. It will constitute the most democratic government that has ever existed in extending the rights and ensuring the welfare of the working people.

What is more, it will be a government with a historically limited life span. After capitalism has been eradicated and a classless society established, the social transition will have been completed. The state, which had continued to function in its final form as the dictatorship of the proletariat, will, at the same time, finish its process of withering away.

While the Marxists thus sought to deepen revolutionary consciousness within the proletariat on the basis of events in France, and succeeded on a world scale for the first time in establishing Marxism as the scientific socialist current in the workers' movement, the frightened bourgeoisie throughout Europe launched a witch-hunt against organized labor. That attack, together with the demoralizing effect of the Commune's fate, caused a general decline in the workers' combat momentum. As a result, the International was deprived of realistic possibilities for practical action in relation to the mass movement.

At the same time, it faced exacerbated internal difficulties caused mainly by the anarchists, who responded to the post-Commune wave of reaction by intensifying their ultraleft sectarian activities. Simultaneously, they stepped up their efforts to capture organizationally the International, hoping to exploit its moral authority that had been earned within the working class. That made it imperative to carry through a definitive break with them so as to keep the world movement's theory and program on a correct axis. The definitive split took place at the Hague congress in 1872. Bakunin and other anarchists who had penetrated the organization were expelled. A public declaration was then issued disclaiming any responsibility for their activities.

Shortly thereafter the General Council moved its seat from London to New York. There were several reasons for the step. Little could be done in Europe because of the slump in labor activity and due to the especially fierce persecution of Marxists by the bourgeoisie. There was also the problem of continued organizational maneuvers by the anarchists, which could best be counteracted by moving the leadership apparatus to the other side of the Atlantic. In addition, it was hoped, useful political work might be conducted within the United States. Before long, though, experience showed that the manifold problems confronting the International heavily outweighed any possibilities for constructive activity, and it was dissolved in 1876.

Although its life span was comparatively short, the First International had accomplished a great deal. Both trade union and political organization of the workers had been accelerated. Class solidarity on an international scale had not only been generated in terms of proletarian consciousness; a way to give it concrete organizational form had been demonstrated. Marxist theory, program, strategy, and tactics—concerning all aspects of the class struggle—had come to be embraced by a growing revolutionary vanguard. Substantial clarification about the dangers of petty-bourgeois radicalism, sectarianism, anarchism, and labor opportunism had been obtained. It followed that the enforced dissolution of the International signified not an end but an interlude in international organization. A new world movement was bound to arise; a revived formation standing on the accomplishments of the old one; a bigger, potentially stronger organization built on expanded growth of the labor movement as a whole and based explicitly on a Marxist program.[*]

Objective trends were already preparing a resurgence of the class struggle. A general economic upswing was under way in Europe. It tended for a time—along with the downfall of the Paris Commune—to produce conservatism among the workers. But that was only the initial aspect of the changing situation. Before long the accelerated growth of industry gave fresh impetus to the labor movement. Trade union organizations developed on a more extensive scale and limited gains were made in the building of socialist parties in one and another country.

A change in trends took place in yet another sense. It took years for the French workers to recover from the bloodletting of 1871, and in those circumstances the political center of gravity in the European class struggle shifted from France to Germany. Industrial expansion had lagged in the latter country up to the middle of the nineteenth century. Now, though, it was gathering increased momentum and the struggle potential of the German working class rose accordingly.

With these favorable winds beginning to blow, the German Marxists lent themselves to a regroupment of revolutionary cadres. The effort centered on an approach to the General Association of German Workers, now headed by followers of Lassalle who took over after his death in 1864. A fusion came about between the Marxist and Lassallean forces, which was consummated at a unity congress

---

[*] Engels dealt with the dissolution of the First International and the political basis of its possible successor in an 1887 letter to Friedrich Adolph Sorge. See appendix, page 219.

held at Gotha in 1875. The expanded formation was designated the Social Democratic Party of Germany.

Marx, whose views were solicited by his followers during the unification process, saw grave dangers in the program adopted by the new party. He carefully delineated its deviations in theory by writing *Critique of the Gotha Programme*. It merits careful study. Further criticisms relating to opportunist traits manifested with the party leadership were made in letters written by Marx and Engels during October 1877 and September 1879. It was a grave mistake, they warned, to make compromises on such basic matters out of a desire to speed party growth. This was being done not only in the case of the Lassalleans. Instead of seeking a thorough grasp of scientific socialism, diverse halfway elements—with varied theoretical outlooks—were bringing remnants of bourgeois and petty-bourgeois prejudices into the party with them. Catering to those prejudices would only produce confusion within the movement. The halfhearted elements had to be pressed toward wholehearted adoption of the proletarian point of view; otherwise they would be an adulterating factor in a workers' party.

Around the time that Engels wrote the 1879 letter to August Bebel and others in the German party, a new development served to stiffen the Social Democratic Party. The Anti-Socialist Law was enacted in Germany. It illegalized socialist propaganda and put the party under close police surveillance. The party didn't respond by mistakenly going underground. Instead, its leaders sought legal avenues through which to fight back. They found the key one to be parliamentary activity, from which the repressive law had not excluded the organization.

With help from Marx and Engels, the German comrades proceeded to demonstrate how revolutionaries can use the vote as a weapon. They transformed the franchise, which is a means of deception used by the bourgeoisie, into at the same time an instrument for advancement of the proletarian cause. Legal propaganda and agitation during election campaigns provided a way for them to get in touch with the masses. Ruling-class candidates had to deal before all the people with issues raised by the socialists. Socialists elected to the Reichstag (German equivalent of the U.S. Congress) had a platform from which to speak freely to the workers on all subjects. Not only were they able to get around the gag law in that way, but election returns gave a partial indication of their relative strength among the masses. A certain sense of proportion was thereby provided, which served as a safeguard against both unnecessary caution and untimely boldness in carrying on other party activities.

As the fight against bourgeois repression went forward along the above lines, the Social Democratic vote in general elections reached new highs; the party won respect among the workers; its ranks became firmer, better attuned to battle; and their activities produced increasing support within the broad labor movement.

Before the campaign against the Anti-Socialist Law ended with its repeal, a loss was suffered that came as a heavy blow to the entire world proletariat. On March 14, 1883, Marx died. With his strong hand no longer at the helm, Engels stepped forward to take the lead in maintaining the continuity of scientific socialism within the revolutionary movement. It was a difficult task, one that would later seem to have become almost a lost cause before powerful reinforcement was received from an entirely new quarter—the Russian Bolsheviks.

In the immediate situation labor was achieving significant advances throughout Europe. Trade unions were experiencing steady growth. Socialist and labor parties were gaining strength in a number of countries. Progress had become such that it was both realistic and advisable to develop cooperation among the various national movements by means of a newly constituted world body. Organization of the Labor and Socialist International—the Second International—was brought about through a congress held at Paris in 1889.

This time it was not a matter of a skeletal formation promoting the building of trade unions and workers' parties within those countries where it had influence, as had been the case with the First International. Already-existing working-class parties and trade unions of considerable substance were coming together on the international plane. They were impelled toward that step by common need for collaboration through a broad exchange of views, for the development of joint world perspectives, and for the organization of mutual assistance in the class struggle. In short, the Second International represented a movement with great potential for coordinated class actions on a mass scale in industrially advanced countries.

To realize this potential, an initial course had to be charted in line with existing objective conditions. Despite intermittent slumps, the economic expansion was maintaining its overall momentum, which meant that the rate of employment remained relatively high. In those circumstances the workers generally were not inclined to go beyond efforts to wrest economic and social concessions from the boss class within the framework of the existing system. They did stand ready, however, to fight for demands of that limited nature, and as its first step the International had to help them do so.

Sectarians within the movement opposed that course. They contended that winning economic and social reforms simply reconciled the workers to capitalism. It was necessary, they held, to rapidly precipitate a revolutionary confrontation between labor and capital. Efforts to promote ultraleft adventurism of a similar nature were also made by the anarchists, who persisted in the line they had put forward during the days of the First International.

As against those views, the Marxists fought for a clear revolutionary course of action on the part of the Second International. It was necessary, they explained, for revolutionists to go through the workers' experiences with them, fighting for their needs step by step. Only in that way could the toiling masses develop political consciousness to the point where, at an objectively determined conjuncture, they would be ready for a showdown battle to overturn the capitalist system. Those arguments prevailed within the movement and its activities remained relatively free of ultraleft coloration.

A different type of problem developed in the case of opportunists, who were ready to adulterate revolutionary principles as a means of winning immediate if unstable support. One category arose within the officialdom of the trade unions. It drew its main support from the labor aristocracy of skilled, better-paid workers. During the extended period of capitalist prosperity those workers tended to degenerate politically, putting their falsely perceived self-interest presented by the bureaucrats, ahead of class solidarity, at the expense of the large masses of proletarians. Using the labor aristocracy as a base, the union bureaucrats palmed off the more favorable situation of the skilled workers as representative of conditions for the class as a whole. They became increasingly reluctant to make any vigorous fight in defense of labor's broad needs and interests. Instead, the bureaucrats cravenly sold their principles to the bourgeoisie at the price of small concessions to the union ranks. At the same time, of course, they were careful to assure handsome incomes for themselves.

Another wing of the opportunist tendency crystallized at the parliamentary level. To a large extent it consisted of petty-bourgeois functionaries adhering to the Second International, who collaborated with the trade union bureaucrats inside and outside parliament. In combination the two categories represented an alien petty-bourgeois tendency that introduced programmatic confusion and political disorientation into the labor movement.

These misleaders took as their point of departure the situation imposed upon the International by the objective conditions existing at the time of its birth and growth. The necessity of going through a temporary phase of struggle whose tactics were aimed at obtaining limited immediate economic and social gains was elevated by them into a strategic perspective. Instead of concentrating on preparation of the masses for revolutionary action later on, they advanced perspectives of lasting class peace and of the achievement of socialism through a gradual process of reform. This line led to their becoming coopted politically into the service of the capitalist class.

As a cover for their revision of Marxism, the opportunists resorted to political trickery. Marx had set forth a revolutionary course leading transitionally from struggles around immediate social and democratic demands to the overthrow of capitalism. Although involving a complex of demands, his was a unified revolutionary strategy. The opportunists now purported to divide that conception into two separate and distinct parts, which they in practice made mutually exclusive. One aspect centered on day-to-day application of a minimum program; the other on a maximum program for revolutionary change in the vague and remote future. The so-called minimum program, which was the real one, remained entirely subordinate to the maintenance of capitalism and was applied on a strictly reformist basis. Mention of the maximum program was relegated pretty much to abstract literary treatment and to fake oratorical homage on ceremonial occasions.

Engels led the revolutionary Marxists in attacking this revisionist line. While revolutionists support the workers' struggles for immediate gains, they emphasized, no concessions to reformism were necessary or defensible. There was a world of difference between fighting for worthwhile reforms and adopting a reformist strategy and outlook. The primary objectives are to deepen class consciousness; to expose the irreconcilable antagonisms between the proletariat and the bourgeoisie; to use each confrontation as a means of intensifying the class struggle as a whole; and to weaken the authority and maneuverability of the enemy. That principled course was now being abandoned by the opportunists. In turning the fight for reforms into a strategy, they stripped the revolutionary content from the workers' struggles around immediate demands. To compound the error they were crossing class lines in politics, even going so far as to participate in bourgeois governments. These were impermissible actions representing class collaboration of the worst kind. Such a course was bound to be self-defeating for the workers, who could conquer only along the path of a consistent and uncompromising class struggle strategy.

Citing the *Communist Manifesto*, the revolutionary Marxists outlined the realistic course for proletarian revolutionists. In the various stages of development through which the workers' struggles must pass, revolutionists both participate in the movement of the present and attend to the future of that movement. They not only take part in all phases of the developing class struggle; in doing so they consciously use each phase as a means to speed the proletariat's march toward the conquest of power.

The revisionists ducked a showdown over issues of basic policy by pointing to their maximum program as evidence of continued adherence to Marxist objectives. Criticism of their minimum program was treated as simply a dispute over tactics, and they went right ahead with the application of their false strategy.

Then, on August 5, 1895, Engels died. That removed the day-to-day influence of his well-earned authority within the movement, which had served to slow down the opportunists. Before long they grew bold enough to bring their revision of Marxism out into the open. Eduard Bernstein, a German Social Democrat, did the main theoretical job.

Marx had been proven wrong, Bernstein contended, on several counts. Despite Marx's predictions to the contrary, all signs indicated that capitalist economic crises would become rarer and less significant. As the productive forces continued to develop, mass living standards would steadily rise. A more balanced distribution of national income would result. Gradual, uninterrupted progress along those lines would blunt and diminish class contradictions. Step by step, the workers could win increased political liberties. Political democracy could in time be filled with new social content. Instead of the state being an organ for the repression of one class by another, as Marx had insisted would always be the case, the state could be gradually changed into an instrument for the conciliation of classes. Through political freedom, democracy, and universal suffrage granted by the bourgeoisie the incentive for further class struggles would be destroyed. By means of gradual reforms the present capitalist society would evolve toward socialism.

In 1899, a wing of the French social democrats took this position to its logical conclusion; Alexandre Millerand accepted a post in the same bourgeois government in which General Gallifet, the butcher of the Paris Commune, was minister of war. Initially, even the reformist Bernstein wing of the International condemned "Millerandism." But in little more than a decade, it had become standard practice for labor opportunists to act "responsibly" in government posts on the basis of capitalist ground rules—especially when this was needed to help defuse the threat of proletarian revolution.

Despite resistance from the revolutionary forces, this reactionary direction of the right wing became—in practice—the guideline for shaping the Second International's strategy. As the movement continued to expand under the prevailing conditions, the parliamentary reformists and trade union bureaucrats grew increasingly cocky. Numerically, the organization did acquire impressive dimensions. Yet that salutary accomplishment was fatally undermined by the revisionist policy and practices. The true situation, which continued to remain obscured for a time, was revealed in a terrible way only fourteen years after the turn of the century.

Before taking up that subject, the situation in the United States should be reviewed. Social contradictions had caused intensification of the class struggle in this country as well, but because of the operation of pronounced national peculiarities, the tempo had lagged behind the pace of European trends.

# 2

# *Indigenous Origins*

Prior to 1865 a combination of factors retarded industrial growth in the United States. One of the young nation's difficulties stemmed from the period when the original states were colonies, used by England as a source of raw materials and as a market for its finished products. This exploitation put a big crimp in the development of colonial manufacture. It remained confined generally to artisans who made and sold their own products and to the appearance of an occasional small master having enough capital to employ a small number of skilled workers.

Then, after the revolutionary war of 1775–81 brought national independence, things changed. The native bourgeoisie increased capital investments in industry, as did foreign investors. Manufacture based on employment of workers with craft skills began to grow and a start was made in establishing the factory system of machine production.

During the recurrent capitalist crises of overproduction that followed, the bigger investors used the hard times to squeeze out smaller ones. Increased concentrations of capital were amassed in fewer hands. By the 1840s these large-scale investments were accelerating the growth of the factory system. But fuller realization of capitalism's potential for industrial expansion in this country remained obstructed, this time by economic and political contradictions that had existed from the beginning within the United States itself.

The southern part of the nation was then ruled by a planter aristocracy that had shaped an agricultural economy based on slave labor. For their own reasons the plantation owners had supported the rebellion against English oppression. But their interests were no less opposed to being overshadowed by industrial capital, with its necessarily free wage-labor, so they resisted industrial encroachments into the southern region. In national politics the slaveholders, counterposing their own class aims to those of the northern bourgeoisie, strove to preserve and advance the slave economy through use of the federal government, which they dominated. As a result the manufacturers were unable to implement national policies required for unfettered extension of machine production. This obstacle to the more rapid evolution of wage-labor caused a lag in the social and political development of the industrial working class.

At the time of the revolutionary war only a nucleus of wage earners existed. Independent commodity production was the prevailing mode of production. During the subsequent industrial upsurge, wage-labor began to expand, but it consisted to a large extent of skilled workers in various crafts. Although machine production had increased by the 1840s, unskilled factory labor remained a small percentage of both the active population and the working class. Hence the working class remained immature. It had yet to become decisively proletarianized through full-scale mechanization of industry; it contained a big sector with a narrow craft outlook; and due to exceptional circumstances then existing its composition was unstable.

This instability resulted from a significant turnover in the labor force. Employers paid the least they could get away with for the longest possible hours of toil. That made things difficult at all times for the wage earners, and, when laid off during economic depressions, their situation rapidly became critical. Government agencies provided no relief whatever for the unemployed and their families.

Left entirely on their own, they got by as best they could.

Those hardships caused workers to seek a new way of life and there was an opportunity at hand. Free land, taken from the Indians, was available for settlement along the frontier, which was steadily pushed westward. Numerous workers seized this chance to become small farmers, hoping in that way to improve their situation. Repeated turnovers resulted within the labor force in the eastern industrial centers, and these turnovers impeded unionization, the development of class-struggle momentum, and the rise of class consciousness.

In some instances migration to the West reduced the supply of highly skilled labor enough so that skilled workers could use their favorable position on the labor market to establish better wage standards. Some who found themselves in that advantageous situation undertook to save enough money to set themselves up in business as self-employed artisans, hoping to go on from there to become small masters at least.

Both of these trends served to slow down the rise of a hereditary proletariat and to generate alien class sentiments within the labor movement. The petty-bourgeois mentality developed by those who aspired to become small entrepreneurs or professionals came into play, as did that of others who were beginning to anticipate their interests as farmers. The ideas thus propagated among wage earners had the effect of blurring class differentiations and promoting a class-collaborationist outlook. Since the central conflicts perceived were between slave owners and free labor, and between independent producers and large banking and merchant interests, the irreconcilable antagonisms between labor and capital were obscured. This gave quite an advantage to the rising bourgeoisie.[*]

Class consciousness on the workers' part was further impaired

---

[*] The questions of the impact of availability of land, homesteading, and the western migration on the development of a hereditary American proletariat were dealt with extensively in Engels's letters to U.S. socialists, and in his articles. See appendix, pages 227–29, 230–39, 246–47.

by illusions that victory in the revolutionary war and the first ten amendments to the Constitution, had established the principle of majority rule in the United States; that supreme authority rested with the people at large; that full democratic rights and civil liberties were guaranteed to all males—except the slaves.

The actualities were quite different. Inequalities and injustices were not confined to the slave system. In the industrial North only one right was fully guaranteed: the right to acquire private property in the means of production and circulation and to carry on "free enterprise" through exploitation of wage-labor. Those having the capital needed for this purpose constituted only a tiny part of the population. Yet their stranglehold on the industrial structure enabled them to establish political control and exercise governmental authority. What amounted to the dictatorship of a minority dedicated to protect and expand capitalist property relations was thus created. A great deal of care was taken to mask its class nature with the trappings of formal democracy in order to deceive the masses, who believed in their revolutionary heritage.

All in all, many obstacles confronted the workers in fighting to defend their class interests. But one overriding factor—the impact of capitalist exploitation upon their daily lives—pushed them toward self-organization. Often preceded by spontaneous struggles, trade union locals sprang up here and there. These craft formations of skilled workers acted separately, each concentrating on its own immediate efforts to win higher wages, shorter hours, and better job conditions. At the outset there was little or no connection between various craft setups.

Experience gained through these isolated struggles led to recognition of the need for organizational coordination. Central labor bodies consisting of all local unions within a given city began to take shape. Some of the skilled crafts launched national formations embracing specific craft units located in various cities. Efforts then followed to create a national federation of all the unions in all the crafts.

Parallel with this trend a broad campaign was opened in the mid-

1820s to institute a ten-hour work day. Since the employers imposed exceedingly long hours of labor, there was great incentive for this struggle; and it was conducted militantly. The specific goal was attained in certain instances and at least some cut in hours was generally won.

As labor's aggressiveness increased, it was met by an employer counterattack. Due to the political climate that existed after the war for independence, the bourgeoisie hesitated to push through laws banning worker combinations as had been done in England. Instead, the courts were used as a ruling-class instrument. Compliant judges decreed that struggles organized by the workers constituted a conspiracy and leading militants were convicted on that charge. These victimizations did harm to the union movement, but the attack failed to halt the labor upsurge.

The workers were dealt paralyzing blows, however, when a severe economic depression began in 1837. Widespread layoffs created massive unemployment with crippling effects upon the trade unions. Seizing the opportunity thus presented, the bosses cut wages and lengthened the hours of those still holding jobs. They also launched a direct union-busting offensive. During the difficult period that followed, the recently formed general federation of labor crumbled, as did the national organizations of the skilled crafts and the city central bodies; even a good many local unions went under.

When the depression ended and the workers again developed struggle momentum in the 1840s, there was a good deal of lost ground to be regained. Efforts began accordingly to reconstruct and extend the trade union formations on the local and national levels; also to revive the campaign for a ten-hour day, which had suffered reverses during the economic crisis. Those steps were accompanied by a new dimension to organized labor's activity involving sporadic attempts to unionize factory workers.

Developments in the trade union sphere had been accompanied by the rise of numerous local labor parties in industrial areas. In the main they were made up of skilled workers. These formations put up candidates in city elections and in some cases on a statewide basis. The platforms on which they campaigned for public office put forth demands along the following general lines: legal recognition of labor's right to organize; enactment of ten-hour legislation; greater taxation of the rich and easing of the workers' tax burden; creation of a public educational system; elimination of restrictions on universal free-male suffrage; and democratization of the process of government.

But attention was diverted from the necessary interconnection of political action with trade union struggles, as some of those demands were taken up by middle-class elements. With this blurring of class lines in politics, notions arose that labor could solve its problems by helping to build a two-class political formation. This opened the way for petty-bourgeois ideology to dominate the movement. Political action thus became divorced from the initial trade union base and the workers' parties as such passed out of existence. They were superseded by catch-all political setups advocating one or another panacea for the ills of capitalism.

At that juncture a new ideological tendency arose within the labor movement, resulting from an influx of political immigrants after the defeat in Europe of the 1848 bourgeois-democratic revolutions. Among these immigrants were German cadres who were adherents of the concepts which had recently been set forth in the *Communist Manifesto*. They began to propagate those ideas here, and the origins of modern revolutionary socialism in the United States trace back to the pioneer role of these immigrants in striving to create such a movement.

(In the late 1840s, the potato famine in Ireland and the harsh conditions it imposed on the masses of that country, drove thousands of Irish workers and poor farmers into the United States. While these immigrants were not a major factor in the development of the socialist movement at this time, they entered the ranks of American labor as militants in the trade unions.)

In 1852 Joseph Weydemeyer organized the Proletarian League, based on German-American socialists in New York, and began the systematic distribution of Marx's writings in German. Under his leadership the league sought to deepen labor's grasp of class politics. Struggles conducted by the trade unions over immediate issues on the job, these Marxists explained, should be accompanied by independent political action. Generalized demands reflecting the needs of the entire working class could in that way be incorporated into a broad program, and the many local struggles could be raised to a higher plane in the form of political confrontations between the workers and the capitalists nationally. In taking this course labor would of necessity back all victims of capitalist exploitation and oppression, seeking to win them as political allies. But the movement could not be allowed to fall into the hands of petty-bourgeois peddlers of social nostrums. Leadership of anticapitalist political action had at all times to be assumed by the workers and for that purpose they, as a class, had to build their own mass party.

Another problem given attention was the sectarianism prevalent among German-American workers, whose numbers had gradually swelled over the preceding years. Instead of developing political communication with the English-speaking workers, they usually issued publications and conducted meetings in the German tongue. Comparable narrowness prevailed among them in trade union matters. They tended to concentrate on building their own ingrown formations of skilled hands who had learned a trade in the old country.

This sectarianism on the part of German-American workers retarded mobilization of the class as a whole. It accentuated the tendency among skilled workers to concentrate on narrow craft unionism, which could not serve the needs of unskilled factory labor or other layers of the oppressed. It thus gave an edge to middle-class reformers seeking to line up workers politically in support of their pet schemes.*

Correction of those shortcomings, the Marxists stressed, was

---

* Engels wrote several letters to American socialists on the problems of sectarianism among the German-American socialists and of language divisions among the proletariat. See appendix, pages 221–23, 224–26, 244–45.

urgent. All sections of the labor movement should join in promoting the unionization of unskilled workers along with the skilled. Collective attention should also be paid to the development of more advanced class-struggle concepts within labor's ranks, with special emphasis on the need for combined trade union and political actions on a mass scale. To serve that end, petty-bourgeois ideology had to be refuted, so the workers could be guided toward assumption of the necessary leadership role in political struggle against the capitalists.

As a first step in that direction, the Proletarian League initiated a broad labor formation of an ad hoc nature. Its aim was to draw the craft unions into direct collaboration with provisional organizations of unskilled workers. As a tentative mechanism for rapid mobilization of the unskilled—and the unorganized generally—geographical units were established on a city-wide scale. With these units serving as a staging area, those workers were then to be assimilated into a redesigned trade union structure embracing both skilled crafts and factory employees. The idea caught on to some extent, but no lasting advance resulted. There was still too little proletarianization of labor, still too much relative weight carried by the self-centered craft unions, for the attempt to succeed.

After a time Weydemeyer moved to the Chicago-Milwaukee area, where he again took up political work. Friedrich Sorge, another German immigrant, assumed leadership of the eastern socialist movement. In 1857 Sorge reorganized the former cadres of the Proletarian League as the Communist Club of New York.

The new group continued socialist propaganda in the labor movement along the lines initiated earlier by Weydemeyer. But anticipating the coming showdown, its activities—like those of other Marxists scattered around the country—began to focus more and more on the abolitionist fight against enslavement of Blacks. Then, in 1861, the antagonisms between the capitalist and planter classes erupted into civil war. Recognizing the progressive character of the bourgeois "free-labor" struggle against the slave system, followers of Marx responded to President Abraham Lincoln's call to arms.

Thereafter the socialists centered their activity on participating as Union Army soldiers in the military side of the war, which caused their work in the labor movement to dwindle for an extended period.

Crushing the slavocracy in 1865 brought the capitalist class definitive control over the nation. A general recasting of governmental policies and social institutions followed, so as to bring them into full conformity with bourgeois needs. That cleared the way for qualitative leaps in machine production, railroad construction, etc., already accelerated by the Civil War. Huge concentrations of capital were amassed to finance large-scale enterprises. Big corporations came into existence. Giant trusts were formed by industrial and banking combines in moves to establish monopolies. This trend soon produced a bumper crop of multimillionaires who fattened on harsh exploitation of wage-labor and wanton depredation of national resources. These plutocrats became the real power behind the bourgeois-democratic governmental facade, and they dealt brutally with all who resisted their ruthless methods of coining superprofits.

Expansion of the factory system also led to transformation of the working class. Unskilled laborers serving as appendages of machines became an increasingly larger section of the class and the weight of the skilled workers declined proportionately. As these contrasting trends revealed, wage-labor was becoming substantially proletarianized. This signified that—in terms of objective developments—the country was entering a new phase. Capitalism, which had just triumphed over the planter aristocracy and which was making fewer and fewer compromises with the independent producers, was already beginning to create "its own gravediggers."

This period also saw the definitive end to a progressive role for any wing of the bourgeoisie or its political parties.

By 1877, radical reconstruction had gone down to bloody defeat, and not only Afro-Americans but the entire working class had suffered the worst setback in its history. The defeat was engineered by the dominant sectors of the industrial ruling class, who were incapable of carrying through a radical land reform in the old Confederacy and rightly feared the rise of a united working class in which Black and white artisans and industrial workers would come together as a powerful oppositional force, allied with free working farmers.

The rural poor and working class were forcibly divided along color lines. The value of labor power was driven down and class solidarity crippled. Jim Crow, the system of extensive segregation, was legalized. Racism was spread at an accelerated pace throughout the entire United States. The ideological basis for imperialist expansion was laid. All the conditions were created for the forging of the new Afro-American oppressed nationality.

At the same time, the Marxists had been weakened in the aftermath of the Civil War. Isolation from the civilian work force, casualties in the war, and the death after the war of Joseph Weydemeyer—Marx and Engels's principal collaborator in the U.S.—virtually decimated the organized Marxist current in the United States.

A considerable part of the growing proletariat consisted of immigrants from European countries and to some extent from Asia. A few million had arrived here before the Civil War, but that proved to be only a start. During the postwar decades the capitalist government stimulated immigration in order to swell the labor force available to the industrial moguls until the influx became a veritable flood. Being of different nationalities, the newcomers had difficult problems of communication. Language barriers existed between the various groups and most of them were alien to the English tongue. Isolated within new surroundings, they became prey to the most severe forms of capitalist exploitation, which in some cases including tricking them into playing the role of strikebreakers. This presented serious problems to the labor movement. Contact with foreign-born workers had to be developed through many different languages; comparable adjustments were required in methods of organizing them; and all this had to be done in a way that created full labor solidarity against the boss class.

The accelerated immigration from abroad far exceeded the rate at which workers from the eastern region of the United States were moving westward to take up farming. A mushrooming of the labor forces concentrated in industrial centers resulted, and the trend gained further momentum as the area of western land available for settlement diminished. Artisans and small masters constituted a smaller and smaller percentage of production relative to the dominant factory system. Economic conditions were locking a hereditary, a permanent working class into the cities, one which was steadily growing in social weight.

In those circumstances more and more workers began to think of themselves as part of a distinct class. Goaded by hardships suffered at the hands of capitalist exploiters, they groped for a way to act together in defense of their common interests as a class. Bitter struggles developed in which the employers resorted to acts of extreme violence in efforts to repress organized labor. Those experiences made the existence of class antagonisms quite plain to see, but the steps required to advance the workers' cause were not so readily apparent. Because of the rapidity with which social and economic changes were occurring; because of social confusion resulting from the swift changes; because of the relative immaturity of the working class—it would take time, experience, and the aid of a revolutionary vanguard to develop an effective class-struggle strategy.

Stimulated by changing objective conditions, the socialist cadres around the country undertook to gear themselves for intensified party-building activity. Following the Civil War small groups were reactivated or newly organized in New York, Chicago, Milwaukee, St. Louis, and San Francisco. Although these groups operated separately on a local scale, a means had already been provided through formation of the First International in 1864 to draw them into coordinated functioning. Both Sorge and Weydemeyer accordingly pressed for immediate affiliation of the various local formations to the world movement. As an interim step in the process, which began in 1867, each group was designated a section of the International and cooperation between the sections was promoted by its General Council, seated in London.

The socialist movement here was still almost entirely German-American in composition. There were two main political tendencies among its cadres. One consisted of adherents of Marxism. The other tendency espoused the line that had been developed in Germany by Ferdinand Lassalle before his death in 1864.

The Lassalleans thought socialism could be achieved by outflanking the capitalists. To do so, they advocated that the workers form producers' cooperatives as a means of freeing themselves from the wage-labor system. Top priority should be given to electoral action based upon full use of universal male suffrage to increase their political strength, and force through government financing of such projects. Trade union activity had to be subordinated to "socialist" objectives of that kind.

At the same time that they exaggerated the emancipating role of the ballot, it should be noted that the Lassalleans generally opposed extension of the vote to women and urged the labor movement to organize to prevent women from entering the labor market.

These utopian and regressive concepts diverted the workers from a class-struggle course in industry and also disoriented them politically. History had already shown that ruling minorities, such as the capitalists, would not peacefully accept a majority decision to strip them of their privileges. Every stage of social development had taken massive revolutionary action to enforce measures of that nature. Under the existing electoral procedures, moreover, male suffrage—to the degree that it existed—lacked the fully democratic character presupposed by the Lassalleans. Universal male suffrage, a conquest of the workers' movement, remained an instrument of bourgeois rule. All elections were to bourgeois institutions. Thus, instead of allowing a true expression of majority will, it was rigged to entrap dissidents into indirect support of the evils they sought to abolish. On top of that, a movement seeking to reform capitalism out of existence was bound to become honeycombed with petty-bourgeois elements, which meant that workers drawn into it would become mired in the swamp of reformist politics.

As against the Lassallean outlook, the Marxists stressed the need for socialist activity in the trade unions. It was in that sphere, they emphasized, that the workers were organizing themselves and engaging in battles with the capitalists. Revolutionists should be in the unions to fight side by side with the workers in the industrial conflicts that developed and to help them draw correct lessons from their experiences. In that way organized labor could be steered toward adoption of a class-struggle line. Labor could be led to champion the needs of the oppressed. Sentiment could be generated for the initiation of independent working-class political action based on the trade unions. And in the course of those efforts, native-born workers could be recruited into the revolutionary vanguard party needed to lead the struggle for basic social change.

Means were at hand to test the conflicting views in the crucible of class struggle. The developing worker upsurge had led to formation in 1866 of the National Labor Union, a broad trade union federation. Its affiliates included national organizations and city assemblies of craft unions, all of which consisted mainly of skilled workers. William H. Sylvis, head of the iron molders' union, was the principal leader in creating the federation and shaping its perspectives.

The central aim of the National Labor Union was full mobilization of the toilers for militant struggle against capitalist exploitation. As an initial move in that direction, the founding convention in Baltimore called for organization of unskilled workers so as to achieve unified action by the class as a whole. Toward the same end, a nonexclusionist policy was followed, with all tendencies in the movement accorded the right to freely express their views. Politically, Sylvis advocated from the outset the building of a union-based labor party, and after a couple of years delay that task was finally accepted as official policy.

As a broad issue around which to promote unified action, a campaign was launched for enactment of eight-hour day laws throughout the country. This move coincided with a similar proposal made by the 1866 congress of the First International, which called for a reduction in hours of labor as a prerequisite to meaningful improvement in working conditions. A practical basis was thereby laid for collaboration between the two organizations, and at the National Labor Union's 1867 convention Sylvis played a leading part in pressing for affiliation to the International. Although the convention declined to take that formal step, it left the door open for continued fraternal cooperation with the world socialist movement of that time.

Soon afterward the sections of the International in this country, which were just being established, sent cadres into the National Labor Union to help carry out the progressive aims it had adopted. The Marxists began to develop constructive relations with Sylvis for that purpose, only to have the process cut short when he died in 1867. None of the union officials who survived him proved capable of filling the leadership void created by his death; nor could the Marxists do so, for they lacked the necessary influence within the movement. This helped lay the federation membership open to the machinations of reformist tendencies.

Earlier Sylvis had participated in a campaign to establish producers' cooperatives and to seek a means of financing them by pressing the government for reforms in the nation's monetary system. That fact now served as a peg for the Lassalleans to push their own line inside the National Labor Union. They discouraged carrying forward class-struggle activity within industry. To escape from capitalist exploitation, they advised that labor organize politically to win state aid for the development of producers' cooperatives. Those views were shared by some officials within the federation, who helped launch a movement that became known as the National Labor Reform Party. Its platform contained a call for monetary reform, as well as specific legislative acts in the interests of labor, such as an eight-hour day law.

The initial rank-and-file response to this step demonstrated that many workers were ready to act politically as an independent class force. They campaigned vigorously through their unions for the candidates of the new party in the 1869 elections. Impressive support was registered at the polls, and in a few instances these nominees were elected to public office.

It soon became apparent, however, that the party was not to be based upon and controlled by the workers' unions. The leadership put major emphasis on a quest for petty-bourgeois allies, whose ideology was arbitrarily imposed upon the movement. Currency reform, which attracted rural and urban middle-class support, was given precedence over issues of immediate concern to organized labor. This change of policy alienated the workers, and the party lost the bulk of its voter support in subsequent elections. Desertions then followed among the petty-bourgeois elements, who went back into the capitalist political parties. Before long the whole structure came apart, and the National Labor Reform Party was not the only casualty of this mistaken attempt to act through a two-class party. The National Labor Union was dragged into oblivion with it.*

As the trade union federation began to crumble, the Marxists shifted the central focus of their activity during the early 1870s to support of strikes conducted by various unions. A heartening upturn in socialist recruitment followed. In membership composition the cadres expanded somewhat beyond the German-Americans to include foreign-born workers mainly of Bohemian, Irish, and Scandinavian origin; also in this category were French militants who had come here after the Paris Commune was crushed in 1871. But relatively few native-born workers were drawn into the socialist ranks at that juncture.

The gains achieved served to attract middle-class reformers of diverse shades into the sections of the International in this country. In each case they sought to use the movement as a vehicle through which to propagate their own peculiar shibboleth, and without exception they were opposed to an orientation toward activity in the trade unions. Their conduct within the organization became so dis-

---

* In 1871, Marx wrote to Friederich Bolte about the need for independent working-class political action. See appendix, pages 215–18.

ruptive that the General Council helped to expel them. A stipulation was then made by the existing affiliates nationally that at least three-fourths of the membership in any new sections formed had to consist of workers. It was further stipulated that all sections had to support labor struggles in industry and help promote trade union growth.

Around the same time Friedrich Sorge was designated secretary of the General Council and the International's headquarters was moved from London to New York. This development, stemming from the difficulties the movement faced in Europe, had a salutary effect here. New means were provided to establish a somewhat more centralized leadership on the eve of a conjunctural turn in objective developments.

Beginning in 1873 the capitalist economy fell into the worst crisis experienced up to then in the United States. Millions lost their jobs and unemployment remained high for several years. Taking advantage of the social turmoil and demoralization created by depression conditions, the boss class proceeded to inflict reverses upon organized labor. Wages were cut, hours of work lengthened, and the trade unions, lacking a federation to coordinate defensive actions, were dealt one setback after another.

In that critical situation the Marxists initiated the mobilization of resistance to the capitalist onslaught. They began by formulating demands for relief measures on behalf of the jobless and rallying forces to fight for those demands. Mass demonstrations were organized jointly with trade unions ready to act. When police assaulted the demonstrators a hue and cry was raised throughout the labor movement. Gradually the ranks regained their fighting spirit and the way was opened for a revival of trade unionism as events pushed workers still holding jobs into new struggles. At the same time the socialist movement acquired new adherents through those activities and it gained in influence within the mass organizations.

But the Lassalleans, who remained impervious to the lessons of the National Labor Union's downfall, were not impressed by such accomplishments. They pointed to the adversities thrust upon organized labor during the economic depression as confirmation of their view that nothing significant could be achieved through struggles in industry. Therefore, they insisted, the socialist movement should turn away from trade union activity. Efforts to draw the masses into electoral action should be given top priority. The socialists had to take the lead in sparking such a development, putting aside work for a labor party linked to industrial struggles and based on the unions.

Determined to get on with the implementation of that line, they broke with the International and formed their own organizational setup. Support was received in the venture from a number of socialist militants who had simply become impatient with the slow pace of political work in the trade unions.

In 1874 this rump formation ran a few candidates for public office. The anticipated response from the working class did not materialize, however, and the election returns were a big disappointment. This experience caused some of the militants involved, who were not hard-core Lassalleans, to reconsider their views. No longer certain that the Marxists were wrong in their outlook, these forces began to favor reunification of the socialist movement.

The following year a fusion took place between the Marxist and Lassallean cadres in Germany. As noted in the foregoing chapter, Marx and Engels criticized the programmatic concessions made by their followers at the Gotha congress in 1875 where the fusion was brought about. But many of the German-American socialists tended to put aside that dangerous aspect of the development. Their interest centered on the positive fact that the Marxist and Lassallean tendencies had gotten together in their old homeland, and sentiment grew for the attainment of political accommodations through which unity could be restored on this side of the Atlantic.

Then, just as the First International was being dissolved, the various socialist groups in this country sent delegations to a joint convention held in Philadelphia. There a decision was reached to unite all the cadres within a single organization called the Workingmen's

Party of the United States. The program adopted by the gathering represented an attempt to reconcile conflicting political views and so was abstract. On specific questions of policy, the Marxist approach to trade union work was endorsed, and, in deference to the Lassalleans, local election campaigns were held permissible where the party had sufficient influence among the masses. Platforms advanced in such campaigns were to be restricted to local issues handled in keeping with the program agreed upon at the convention.

In substance the Workingmen's Party was a loose federation of disparate tendencies. It lacked homogeneity in vital matters of theory, program, and strategy. Consequently no solid basis existed for objective consideration of disagreements over party-building tactics in a manner that would safeguard the organization's internal equilibrium. Disputes that arose over what appeared superficially to be tactical questions led to irreconcilable factional squabbles because they were rooted in unresolved political differences.

It didn't take long for Lassallean maneuvers to lay bare the new party's internal contradictions. Shortly after the unity convention the Lassalleans initiated local election campaigns that put forward their program. The Marxists objected to this violation of official policy, stood aloof from the electioneering, and fixed their attention on the trade unions. Factional contention ensued with both sides helping to engender—in terms of the immediate situation—the separation of union building from political work on the electoral plane as mutually exclusive forms of activity. The party was unable to develop a principled line for combining labor struggles in industry with independent working-class political action. This default soon led to further programmatic disorientation.

By the spring of 1877 the cumulative hardships stemming from prolonged economic depression had generated widespread discontent among the exploited masses. So great was the social unrest, in fact, that the first substantial upsurge of class struggle precipitated a general confrontation between labor and capital.

The conflict opened when new wage cuts were imposed by railroad companies. This was one blow too many for the workers involved, who launched spontaneous walkouts on one railway line after another. A few among them belonged to weak craft unions. But in the main they were unorganized and without ready-made means of conducting a strike. Under those circumstances organizational improvisations, including formation of an ad hoc leadership, had to be devised in the heat of battle.

As the walkout gained momentum some of the Lassalleans momentarily put aside their opposition to trade union activity and joined with the Marxists in calling for all-out support of the railroad workers. Cadres of the Workingmen's Party extended help to the strikers in solving their organizational problems. In a couple of cities this led to formal inclusion of socialists, who were not necessarily railroad workers, in strike committees. A substantial contribution was thereby made to what rapidly developed into an effective shutdown of virtually the entire railway system.

Capitalist efforts to crush the walkout became increasingly brutal as it grew in scope. This counterattack took place behind a smokescreen of antilabor propaganda laid down by newspaper editors, church dignitaries, and other "civic leaders." It began with the hiring of strikebreakers at premium pay to run trains. The private railway police assigned to protect the scabs were beefed up and steps were initiated to form antilabor vigilante gangs.

At the same time, all levels of government went into action against the workers. City police and state militias were used to break up picket lines. Strikers were clubbed and jailed. Both official and extralegal armed bodies fired upon workers' gatherings, killing some and wounding many.

Those vicious assaults provoked a widening of the struggle. Large numbers of workers came to the direct aid of the embattled railroad strikers and the walkout was extended to other industries. The high point of the movement was reached in St. Louis, Missouri, where labor solidarity became manifested through a general strike in which socialists functioned as key leaders.

By then the national government had entered the conflict on the side of the bosses. Federal troops used extensively as the main repressive force tipped the scales against labor. The railroad strikers were finally driven back to their jobs in defeat.

Despite the setback received in the immediate struggle, the labor movement had gained new potential. Many workers had become more aware of their common interests as a class. They had also become more perceptive of the solidarity among the employers as a class in opposing them, as well as the antilabor character of the capitalist government. These advances in consciousness gave rise, in the aftermath of the strike defeat, to the initiation of working-class political action. Labor parties arose spontaneously in many cities to run candidates for government office in the 1877 elections.

For those parties to act effectively, the workers' demands as a class had to be generalized in political form. Safeguards were required to maintain rank-and-file control over electoral policy. Care had to be taken, as well, to assure that—in seeking political allies—labor continued to function at all times as an independent class force.

To achieve such objectives the workers needed help from the revolutionary vanguard. But the Workingmen's Party had lost the leadership capacity shown during the brief span when the ranks were somewhat more united than usual in support of the railroad strike. Entirely different courses of action were put forward by the rival formations within the organization, and both failed to meet their obligations to the working class.

As the leaders of the Marxist tendency appraised the new situation, an objective basis did not yet exist for creation of a mass labor party. There was neither a high enough degree of class consciousness among the workers for them to act as a truly independent political force, they contended, nor the trade union strength required to maintain control over a broad electoral formation. Hence, the socialists were confined to two immediate tasks. One of these was through propaganda and education to help the workers acquire political class consciousness from their experiences in industrial conflicts. The other task was to promote the revival of trade union activity in the aftermath of the strike defeat and to press for creation of a labor federation through which the various unions could act in concert. It would be a mistake, they held, for the party to bypass those functions in order to center attention on election campaigns. The socialist movement lacked the broad influence needed to carry weight as an independent political factor on the electoral arena, and activity of that kind would serve to divert its cadres from trade union work.

In adopting such an outlook, the leaders of the Marxist tendency left aside the question of what to do about the labor parties that were developing spontaneously. This omission had an adverse effect upon new members recruited into the Workingmen's Party during the railroad strike, who thought the revolutionary party should have given major attention to activity on the electoral plane.

Under those circumstances, the Lassalleans were able to win extensive support for their line. The capitalists' use of state power to defeat the railroad workers proved, they argued, that trade union struggles were ineffective. It was therefore imperative to use the vote in a fight for control of the government, since this was the precondition for meaningful advancement of labor's cause. Many party members accepted that view. Campaigns were launched in city and state elections, and the balloting registered an increase in the socialist vote.

A convention of the Workingmen's Party followed in December 1877. By that time the Lassalleans had won a clear majority, which they used to recast the organization. Its name was changed to the Socialist Labor Party of North America (SLP). The official program was modified in a manner that gave precedence to electoral activity carried out in accordance with their views. Several party campaigns were then conducted during the next two years. During 1878 many workers continued to look for whatever means could be found to express their dissatisfaction with the status quo, and the SLP achieved further successes in the elections. It also enjoyed a substantial growth in membership.

By 1879, however, conditions were beginning to change. A new industrial upturn was gaining momentum; trade union activity was on the rise; and the workers were losing interest in political campaigns. Serious reverses followed for the party. Much of its previous electoral support was lost and a number of the new members recruited somewhat earlier dropped out of its ranks.

At that point the Lassalleans began to maneuver toward an alliance with a political movement dominated by petty-bourgeois elements. This outfit had originated during the depression as the Greenback Party, a name derived from demands for monetary reform that included federal issuance of currency known as "greenbacks." This movement was based initially on farmers and sections of the urban middle class. Later on some of the labor parties that had arisen as independent formations in 1877 merged with the Greenbackers. A revised platform was adopted embracing both the currency reform question and several labor demands. For a limited period this political combination, rechristened the Greenback-Labor Party, attracted a good deal of electoral support.

In connection with the 1880 national elections the Lassalleans forced through a decision in the SLP to support the Greenback-Labor presidential ticket. One group in the party, which up to then had favored concentration on independent SLP electoral activity, refused to carry out that line. It was led by Albert R. Parsons and August Spies, who were soon to be martyred in a capitalist frameup. The Parsons-Spies group urged the nomination of SLP candidates, and when that proposal was rejected, the group acted on its own to run a party ticket in the Chicago elections.

During the presidential campaign the Greenbacker candidates subordinated labor's demands to the currency reform issue. This alienated most of the workers who had continued to manifest some interest in electoral activity, and the Greenback-Labor Party made a poor showing at the polls. After that—as had happened earlier in the case of the National Labor Reform Party—the petty-bourgeois elements in the movement returned to outright capitalist politics.

The ignominious outcome of the Lassallean maneuver caused an exodus of frustrated workers from the Socialist Labor Party. These militants, disheartened by the defeat of the railroad strike, had gone along with the notion that labor's problems could be solved through use of the electoral mechanisms. Efforts toward that end had led, however, to the Greenback-Labor fiasco, and a number now abandoned the SLP to give anarchism a try. This shift in political direction on their part coincided with the arrival of anarchist immigrants who came here after the enactment in 1878 of the Anti-Socialist Law in Germany.

Prominent among those immigrants was Johann Most, who soon assumed leadership of the anarchist movement in the eastern part of the United States. Under his influence, the line developed in that region for the struggle against capitalism centered on advocacy of terrorist attacks carried out by individuals acting on their own initiative.

A different concept was put forward in the West, where Parsons and Spies were the leading figures among former socialists who had gone over to the anarchists. Their group opposed the substitution of individual acts of terror for collective struggle by the workers. Anticipating the anarcho-syndicalist course later to be fully developed, it advocated continued use of the trade unions—not to fight for immediate gains at the industrial level, but as a means of mobilizing the masses for direct action leading to the overthrow of capitalism.

In 1883—the year that Marx died—the two anarchist formations held a joint convention. All present were opposed to election campaigns and against fighting in any manner for reforms within the capitalist framework. They were likewise agreed on use of direct action to meet repressive force with revolutionary force. Concerning the manner in which the latter aim was to be carried out, the Parsons-Spies group took advantage of its preponderant weight at the gathering to establish a policy of promoting mass action, as against Most's advocacy of individual terrorist acts.

Meanwhile, the Marxist tendency had sought to help strengthen organized labor within industry. Collaboration had been established with leaders of the eight-hour day movement to accelerate the trade union upsurge that began around 1879. Objectives set by the Marxists included both the expansion of existing craft formations in the skilled trades and a campaign to unionize unskilled workers. In addition, they made a concerted attempt to promote the building of a labor federation. Significant gains were recorded only among the craft organizations. Neither the plans concerning the unskilled nor the perspective of a broad federation came to fruition. But some progress was made in convincing union militants of the need to strive toward those ends, and that facilitated emergence of a left wing in the Order of the Knights of Labor (K of L), which was rapidly gaining prominence in the mass movement.

The K of L had been founded back in 1869 by a group of garment cutters. It was conceived as a secret organization to safeguard the membership from victimization by employers. Workers in other skilled trades soon entered the movement and each craft was allowed to form its own separate unit. Broad assemblies were then fashioned to provide a means of joint cooperation between the various crafts. During the next few years the membership functioned through this diffuse structure, acting as part of the general labor movement. It was not until the mid-1870s that an independent body was formed on a national scale.

Major changes in the basic character of the K of L were initiated at its 1878 convention. Membership growth experienced during the class battles sparked by the railroad workers had created strong pressures for abandonment of craft union concepts. A shift in perspectives resulted. Steps were undertaken to organize all workers—unskilled as well as skilled—uniting them into a single powerful body. Notions of maintaining secret functions were dropped before long, and a decision was made to act entirely in the open. Those actions led to stepped-up recruitment through which the organization became the dominant factor in the ensuing labor struggles.

Workers drawn into this promising movement were unable to fully exert their collective strength, however, because of leadership defaults. Terence V. Powderly, who assumed the central post of Grand Master Workman in 1879, adopted a reformist, class-collaborationist outlook. His program focused on advocacy of cooperative enterprises and monetary reforms, together with electoral actions designed to achieve those aims. In regard to the workers' economic struggles, he called for arbitration of industrial disputes in place of "futile" strikes. Powderly urged the organization to stay clear of labor radicalism, and at the same time he facilitated entry into its ranks of alien class elements—including employers if they wanted to join.

This line alienated many unions existing apart from the K of L. Instead of linking up with the Knights in a common movement, they formed a separate national body called the Federation of Organized Trades and Labor Unions. The new federation, launched in 1881, advocated concentration on action in support of the workers' immediate demands, including resort to strikes. It opposed compulsory arbitration and other class-collaborationist aspects of Powderly's outlook.

Samuel Gompers, leader of the cigar makers' union, played a major role in creating the federation. In that early stage of his career he collaborated with the Marxists on some issues, especially in stressing the need to build strong unions as the first step toward drawing the workers into united action. Even at that point, though, a disagreement arose that—as will be seen later—portended a deepening clash over basic union policies. Gompers sought to shape the federation as an essentially craft structure based on skilled labor. But a majority of the delegates to the founding convention, among whom were several Marxists, overruled him. A decision was made to undertake the organization of unskilled workers in basic industry, along with skilled hands in the various trades.

Workers adhering to the Marxist tendency set out to build left wings inside both the Federation of Organized Trades and Labor Unions and the Knights of Labor. In the latter movement their efforts were facilitated by spontaneous outbreaks of rank-and-file militancy that often culminated in hard-fought strikes, despite the Powderly regime's distaste for actions of the kind. At the same time, however, realization of the gains thus made possible

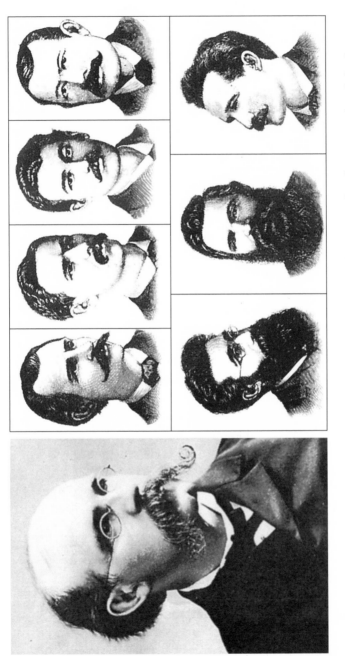

Left, Terence V. Powderly, Grand Master Workman of the Knights of Labor. Right, the Haymarket defendants, (clockwise from top left) Albert R. Parsons, Adolph Fischer, Louis Lingg, George Engel, August Spies, Samuel Fielden, Michael Schwab.

was badly hampered by contradictions within the Socialist Labor Party.

The Lassalleans, whose concepts were in several respects akin to Powderly's, ganged up with him inside the K of L. They backed his downplaying of union struggles for immediate demands and his advocacy of multi-class political alliances in the electoral arena. Further impetus was thereby given to the infusion of petty-bourgeois elements into the K of L leadership, and the antagonisms within the organization between official policies and membership needs became more pronounced.

It was not the Lassalleans alone, though, who retarded the progress of the Socialist Labor Party. A bent toward formalistic thinking prevailed among leaders of the Marxist tendency, especially on the question of independent labor political action. They concentrated on organization and education of workers at the trade union level. Their propaganda centered on projection of a militant course in industrial conflicts and on efforts to win immediate acceptance of socialist ideas. They appeared to assume that this would lead to mass recruitment into the revolutionary vanguard party and open the door to a direct struggle for a workers' government. No provision was made in their programmatic outlook for transitional stages in building a mass revolutionary movement. Spontaneous labor party trends were considered premature, not worthy of serious attention, and that made it all the easier for reformists to misguide the workers politically.

Engels put his finger on this aspect of the SLP's difficulties in a letter of November 29, 1886, to Sorge. "The Germans have not understood how to use their theory as a lever which could set the American masses in motion," he wrote; "they do not understand the theory themselves for the most part and treat it in a doctrinaire and dogmatic way as something that has to be learned by heart, which will then satisfy all requirements forthwith. To them it is a credo and not a guide to action. What is more, they learn no English on principle. Hence the American masses had to seek out their own path and they seem to have found it for the time being in the K of L, whose confused principles and ludicrous organization seem to correspond to their own confusion. But from all I hear, the K of L are a real power, especially in New England and the West, and are becoming more so every day owing to the brutal opposition of the capitalists. I think it is necessary to work inside them, to form within this still quite plastic mass a core of people who understand the movement and its aims and will therefore take over the leadership, at least of a section, when the inevitably impending breakup of the present 'order' [of the Knights of Labor] takes place."*

Engels was referring to events between 1884 and 1886 in his remark about "brutal opposition of the capitalists." Around 1884 another economic recession set in. It led quickly to an upsurge of mass support for the demand to establish an eight-hour day as a means of providing jobs for the unemployed. A decision was made by the Federation of Organized Trades and Labor Unions to set May 1, 1886, as the deadline for putting the eight-hour provision into effect. During the campaign that followed in support of this decision, new members were recruited in great numbers by the existing trade unions and increased militancy was imparted to the labor movement.

When the Powderly regime in the Knights of Labor tried to ignore the eight-hour movement, it was thwarted by rank-and-file enthusiasm for the cause. Not only that. K of L members, seeking to use their own organization as an instrument for struggle, conducted militant strikes during 1885. In every instance the workers picketed effectively, but little was accomplished because of the class-collaborationist leadership's ineptness in dealing with employers. Nevertheless, these actions prepared the way for the K of L to reach its zenith the following year as a national movement embracing all

---

* Marx and Engels, *Letters to Americans 1848–1895* (New York: International Publishers, 1953), pp. 162–63. Engels wrote several letters to American socialists on the problems of dogmatism and sectarianism. See appendix, pages 221–23, 224–26, 240.

categories of the work force. New combat momentum was generated in other trade union sectors as well, and organized labor moved toward a major clash with the ruling power.

On May 1, 1886, the deadline set for inauguration of the eight-hour day, a gigantic strike wave developed. From coast to coast workers downed their tools, established picket lines, and held mass demonstrations. Then, in Chicago, Illinois—where outstanding labor solidarity was manifested—the capitalists launched a savage counteroffensive.

By that time the anarchists led by Parsons and Spies had emerged as the most influential radical tendency within the Chicago labor movement. At first they had been rather indifferent to the eight-hour demand, dismissing it as a reformist compromise with the capitalist system. But when it became apparent that the demand had drawn large masses into united action, they made common cause with the workers in the eight-hour fight as a means of promoting a general confrontation between labor and capital. Acting through trade unions under their sway, the anarchists helped to strengthen the effectiveness of the strike.

As the struggle unfolded, the Chicago police harassed the strikers day after day, trying to provoke an incident that could be used as a pretext for a full-scale attack on the trade unions. A labor rally to protest the police provocations was held at Haymarket Square on May 4. It was a peaceful assembly that was about to adjourn when a large body of cops descended upon it, demanding that those present disperse immediately. At that point a bomb exploded among the police, killing one instantly and wounding others. The forces of "law and order" then fired upon the assembled workers, inflicting many casualties.

This tragedy provided the capitalists with an alibi for a general assault on the eight-hour movement. Through a combination of witch-hunting and police repression labor's ranks were divided, the strike undermined, and the workers forced to return to their jobs. Even under those adverse conditions, however, some reductions in hours were achieved because the formidable strength displayed by the trade unions had thrown a scare into many employers.

As part of its antilabor campaign the ruling class demanded vengeance against those held responsible for the Haymarket bombing, and the blame was fixed upon the anarchists, who had issued propaganda urging the workers to arm themselves in self-defense. Eight of them were brought to trial before a rigged jury that—acting out of prejudice against the defendants' ideas—convicted them without the prosecution having presented any proof of guilt. After losing appeals made to higher courts, four victims of the frame-up were hanged: Albert R. Parsons, August Spies, George Engel, and Adolph Fischer. Another of those scheduled to be hanged, Louis Lingg, escaped that fate only by committing suicide. Michael Schwab and Samuel Fielden, both of whom had initially been doomed to execution, later had their sentences commuted to life imprisonment. Oscar Neebe received a fifteen-year prison term.

In a political sense, the Haymarket episode put an end to the anarchists' leading role within the trade unions. Their movement was reduced to little more than a small band of intellectuals, who were located in the eastern part of the country and who exercised no appreciable influence among the masses.

The situation was different, though, concerning the individual anarchists charged with murder. They were honored throughout the mass movement as courageous fighters who had been singled out by the capitalists in an attack that was really aimed at the entire working class. When the jury found the eight defendants guilty, organized labor nationally launched a pardon campaign on their behalf. Following the executions a vast body of Chicago trade unionists attended the funeral of those whose lives had been taken by the capitalist government. The pardon campaign was continued thereafter until finally, a few years later, Governor John P. Altgeld of Illinois reviewed the trial proceedings and declared all the defendants innocent. Altgeld then freed the frame-up victims serving prison terms and granted pardons posthumously to those who had been hanged.

By the time this legal vindication of the martyred trade unionists was achieved the labor movement had already recovered from
the 1886 setback, and its revolutionary vanguard had entered into a
new stage of development.

# 3

# Gains and Setbacks

During the 1884–86 labor upsurge large numbers of both native-born and foreign-born workers joined trade unions. This widening discontent with existing social conditions led to an expansion of the workers' united struggles as a class, which manifested itself in a series of strikes over economic demands. Then, early in 1886, the conflict assumed political characteristics with a massive strike wave in support of the eight-hour day. While trade unions directed this demand against one or another particular employer in economic struggles, it had broader significance. The workers as a class were pressing a political issue against the capitalists as a class, explicitly so in calling for laws to limit the hours of labor.

The indicated next step for trade unionists was building their own political organization, and they moved instinctively in that direction. By the fall of 1886 labor parties, with platforms that varied from city to city, had again sprung up in several industrial centers and were running candidates for public office. This time, it should be noted, the Marxist tendency in the Socialist Labor Party took a more positive attitude toward the rising movement for political independence.

A major campaign was organized in New York City, where the Knights of Labor, the Federation of Organized Trades and Labor Unions, and the Socialist Labor Party acted jointly to launch a mass party in labor's name. A majority chose Henry George to head the new party's slate as its nominee for mayor. He was the leader of a petty-bourgeois sect that advanced a taxation scheme as a cure-all for the evils inflicted by capitalism. It centered on the notion that all social ills were rooted in the private ownership of land. George advocated a gradual increase in the land tax until it was equal to the full rent of the land, thereby expropriating all land rent for public use. All other taxes were then to be abolished, a concept which led to popular designation of the George sect as "single taxers."

But this strategy left the existing social relations of production untouched. Without the expropriation of the decisive forms of productive property, the industrial and financial bourgeoisie would remain free to exploit the toiling masses, who produce the surplus value that is the source of all rents, interest, and profit. And they would continue to use their ownership of capital to maintain political sway over the nation. Hence, the whole proposal was reformist to the core.

Nevertheless, the "single tax" panacea of Henry George, the main candidate, was included in the New York party's platform. The socialists—who rejected the "single tax" fallacies—backed the campaign organized around the George ticket, because what was decisive was organized labor's stepping forward into the political arena as an independent class force.

Labor party campaigns launched in other cities were supported by the Socialist Labor Party for the same reason. The various platforms for these independent mass political actions focused on issues of immediate concern to the workers in each locality. Little or no attention was given to the "single tax" idea, which remained limited essentially to New York.

The labor slates, taken as a whole, made an impressive showing in the November 1886 elections. Henry George, for example, got almost a third of the total vote cast in New York. Elsewhere, candidates put forward by the organized workers were in a few instances elected, and the overall results of the balloting maintained interest in the developing independent political action. The workers' mood opened the door to uniting the several local labor parties as the first step in building a national political movement. Engels took up this perspective in the letter of November 29, 1886, to Sorge, cited previously, centering his remarks on the New York situation.

"The first great step of importance for every country newly entering into the movement is always the constitution of the workers as an independent political party," he counseled, "no matter how, so long as it is a distinct workers' party. And this step has been taken, much more rapidly than we had a right to expect, and that is the main thing. That the first program of this party is still confused and extremely deficient, that it has raised the banner of Henry George, these are unavoidable evils but also merely transitory ones. The masses must have time and opportunity to develop, and they can have the opportunity only when they have a movement of their own—no matter in what form so long as it is *their own* movement—in which they are driven further by their own mistakes and learn through their mistakes. . . . If there are people at hand there whose minds are theoretically clear, who can tell them [the workers] the consequences of their own mistakes beforehand and make clear to them that every movement which does not keep the destruction of the wage system constantly in view as the final goal is bound to go astray and fail—then much nonsense can be avoided and the process considerably shortened" (*Letters to Americans, 1848–1895*, pp. 163–64, emphasis in original).[*]

To follow this advice the socialist movement needed to act flexibly in collaborating with the existing labor parties, city by city, to help them shape a common program. If the party's initial program dealt with important aspects of labor's interests as a distinct social class; if it set forth aims upon which all concerned were agreed—it could

---

[*] Engels dealt with the George campaign and its significance for American workers in several letters and articles. See appendix, pages 221–23, 224–26, 230–39.

help advance toward a mass nationwide working-class party. At the start the Marxists within the labor party would have to tentatively and partially indicate the course required for the workers' emancipation from capitalist exploitation. Time and experience could then make it possible for the party to develop explicit anticapitalist political goals and strategy.

The Marxist cadres in the SLP tried to carry out the policies advocated by Engels, but new developments soon made this impossible. During the New York campaign the Henry George ticket had attracted considerable middle-class support. After the elections George used these forces to narrow the labor party's strategy to the "single tax" line at the expense of working-class demands, and to overcome socialist opposition he bureaucratically expelled SLP members. This enabled him to make agreement with his "single tax" scheme the test of loyalty to the party, thereby undermining what had been a promising political movement and converting it into a narrow cult.

In other cities as well middle-class campaigners in the labor parties played similar roles. After the elections they sought freedom to convert the parties into vehicles for their pet notions by demanding that radical influence be eliminated, by which they meant primarily the SLP. This created great confusion within these organizations and they, too, began to fall apart. Labor's misplaced reliance on petty-bourgeois leadership in the electoral sphere had once again halted the organization of an independent political class force.

Still another problem confronting the workers generally had been reflected in one aspect of the New York situation. The labor slate had been supported by local trade union bodies affiliated to the Knights of Labor. In taking the step they had forced a reluctant Powderly—who opposed the formation of labor parties and favored reliance on multi-class political blocs—to give lip service to independent working-class political action. Although merely an incident, this typified the internal contradictions resulting from the circumstances in which the K of L had developed.

Like the labor parties, the Knights of Labor originated in the spontaneous appearance in different localities of units that became only loosely associated. Later those formations were drawn into closer relationships through creation of a semicohesive national body. After that their horizons expanded, reaching beyond the original, narrow concepts of craft unionism to the perspective of uniting the workers—skilled and unskilled—into a single, all-inclusive movement. As the K of L membership grew rapidly during the following period it began to mirror the conflicting levels of consciousness existing within the working class. Its program remained unclear and contradictory, as did its course of action. What held the structure together was the membership's growing realization of the need for class solidarity, and the unremitting daily pressures under capitalist rule that made it imperative to persist in the search for ways and means to protect labor's interests.

Efforts to develop an effective program were repeatedly frustrated, however, by the class-collaborationist outlook of the national leaders. This created internal frictions, which steadily became more pronounced. The ranks sought to use their inherent strength as a united class force to confront the boss class, power against power. Wanting no part of a class-struggle course, the Powderly hierarchy relied on petty-bourgeois members who had been allowed to enter the movement for support against rebellious workers. This deepened the gulf between official policies and the workers' aspirations, opening the way for a struggle to establish rank-and-file control.

As matters turned out, though, no left-wing leadership appeared that was capable of mobilizing the workers to thrust aside the misleaders in the Knights of Labor. Instead, the Powderly administration—reinforced by its middle-class allies and by the Lassalleans—mounted an offensive against rank-and-file dissidents. The attack began in the fall of 1886. Although it was aimed at every trade unionist who opposed the official line, skilled workers were singled out as the direct target. They were accused of being preoccupied solely with their own narrow interests and of disregarding the broader needs of unskilled labor. Historically, the skilled trades had tended to be self-centered. But this time the charges leveled against them were purely demagogic on two main counts.

For one thing, the policies set by the top officials violated the basic interests of both the unskilled workers they purported to defend and the skilled hands whom they blamed for the union's internal problems. Those policies included obstructing use of the strike to fight for immediate demands; rejection of class-struggle perspectives in general; and unprincipled political concessions to petty-bourgeois "friends" made in the search for concessions to labor through reform of the capitalist system. It was the repercussions from that class-collaborationist line, not selfishness on the part of skilled workers, that caused mounting discontent in the ranks.

Secondly, the national leadership had arbitrarily reversed an earlier decision taken by the K of L. In creating an all-inclusive formation along industrial lines, a place had correctly been provided for skilled workers by establishing special units through which they could handle specific problems they faced. This facilitated the harmonious unification of skilled and unskilled labor within a common movement. Now, however, that practical basis for united action was summarily canceled. Units of skilled workers were transferred into catchall assemblies that included both unskilled workers and various middle-class types. In effect, the skilled trades were being disfranchised to gag criticism of the officialdom.

Parallel with that step, raids were conducted against craft units of the Federation of Organized Trades and Labor Unions. Members won to the Knights of Labor were relegated to the catchall assemblies, and Federation unions' bargaining rights with employers were challenged. These actions, too, ruptured labor solidarity and gave the boss class an edge against the workers.

A sharp clash ensued between the Powderly regime and skilled workers both inside and outside the K of L. Then, in December 1886, a national convention was held by unions representing the skilled trades. A decision was made there to regroup the forces opposed to Powderly's line as the American Federation of Labor (AFL), with Samuel Gompers as its president. The Federation of Organized Trades and Labor Unions was dissolved into the new national body, and units of skilled workers in the Knights of Labor began to switch their affiliation to the AFL.

When class-conscious militants voiced concern that the great predominance of skilled trades in the AFL might cause it to disregard the interests of unskilled workers, Gompers denied that such would be the case. But subsequent events proved him wrong. Due to its composition, the new federation had an inborn tendency toward adoption of narrow, craft-oriented perspectives. The unresolved contradictions inside the Knights of Labor had given rise to a retrogressive current within the trade union movement.

At the same time, the Socialist Labor Party was emerging as the major radical grouping in the country, owing to the swift decline of anarchism after the Haymarket episode and to socialist backing of the labor parties in the 1886 elections. Organizational improvements were taking place as well. More extensive English language communication with native-born workers facilitated their recruitment and assimilation into the party. The socialist movement was getting into a better position to shed its German-American complexion and expand its influence throughout the working class.

During 1887 the socialists fought to keep the independent labor parties alive. Their efforts failed, though, when the petty-bourgeois maneuverers split the movement, causing an ebb in the mass political upsurge. The SLP then ran candidates of its own in scattered election campaigns but received few votes from the workers. These disappointing experiences created frustration inside the party, and a dispute arose over perspectives.

Some within the Marxist tendency interpreted the sudden decline of the labor parties as proof that efforts to promote independent working-class political action were premature. The SLP, they contended, should concentrate all its attention on union-building activities in order to establish a firmer base for independent labor political action later on; and notions about conducting socialist election campaigns should be put aside because they would only interfere with carrying out the necessary trade union work. By this time, however, a considerable number of the Marxists had learned something from Engels's attempts to advise them. These cadres rejected sectarian abstention from spontaneous working-class political upsurges. They urged ongoing promotion of such developments within the unions, seeking to give them impetus through socialist election campaign propaganda.

The Lassalleans—by now reduced to a minority in the party—continued to downgrade trade union work. Their line called for major emphasis on electoral activity. They still counted on galvanizing other forces into motion, with whom they would form political blocs on a producers' cooperative-monetary reform program.

These differences over perspectives resulted in a sharp internal struggle. It came to a head in 1889 when the Lassalleans held a rump convention at which they split from the party, disguising their minority status with the spurious claim that their setup constituted the official SLP. But Lassallean influence was definitively on the wane, and they managed to maintain an organized tendency in the labor movement for only a few more years.

Before the end of 1889 the SLP majority also gathered in convention. The proceedings demonstrated that the losses from the split had been more than compensated for by gains in political clarity. During the internal dispute progress had been made toward correcting sectarianism within the Marxist tendency. This enabled the convention to chart a course that put the party in a better position to strengthen its trade union work and at the same time press for independent labor political action. Socialist election campaigns could now be used more effectively to advance this perspective in the unions, since the Lassalleans would not be present to use electoral activity to promote unprincipled political blocs with middle-class elements.

Still another advance was recorded in popularizing socialist propaganda when the convention adopted a document setting forth labor's rights in language that paraphrased the 1776 Declaration of Independence. As that step demonstrated, serious attention was being given to ways and means of extending socialist influence within the working class as a whole.

Meanwhile, a new situation had been developing in the trade unions. A year earlier Powderly had opened a campaign to expel those who opposed the official policies from the Knights of Labor. This violation of internal democracy intensified frictions between the membership and leadership of the organization, accelerating its decline in strength and influence. Increasing numbers of workers turned away from the K of L, seeking to solve their problems through affiliation with the American Federation of Labor. They found it encouraging that the AFL, during the early stages of its rise, was relatively democratic, that it upheld labor's right to strike, and that it stood ready to take such action where necessary.

Adjusting to this change, the Socialist Labor Party concentrated on work inside the AFL. Militant party cadres helped build the new organization and played a leading role in its battles with the employers, striving in the course of those activities to influence the federation's evolution in a progressive direction.

In one particular sphere the SLP made a special contribution. Spontaneous walkouts frequently occurred in industries that employed mainly foreign-born workers and forced them to labor under the worst conditions. Party branches among the foreign-born stepped into those situations. Using the language understood by the workers, they helped organize them into unions and carry forward the fight in defense of their needs. Through such accomplishments—along with concerted support of workers' struggles—the party won new members and broadened its influence within the trade unions.

While backing labor's cause at the industrial level, the Marxist cadres also sought to build up sentiment for independent working-class political action. This propaganda could not by itself stimulate a quick revival of the earlier labor party movement based on the trade unions. But these efforts did bring political gains in another respect. Candidates nominated for public office in socialist election campaigns began to receive increased working-class support and votes.

Socialist prestige was further heightened in a less direct manner.

By convention decision the AFL took the initiative in setting May 1, 1890, as the date for resumption of the united labor struggle for an eight-hour day. This step coincided with the founding congress of the Second International, held in 1889. Gompers informed the congress of the AFL's intentions and asked the International to support the eight-hour campaign. It agreed to do so, accepting the date set in the United States as the occasion for collective action.

On May 1, 1890, workers' organizations in this country took to the streets in mass demonstrations and some called strikes in support of the eight-hour movement. Similar actions were taken abroad, varying in form according to the prevailing conditions. All in all, labor mounted an unprecedented show of force on a world scale. That accomplishment had the effect of elevating May Day, which dated back in the United States to the 1886 struggle, into an international workers' holiday celebrated by the labor movement everywhere.

Actions led by the American Federation of Labor registered significant gains. Hours of work were cut and a number of unions were able to establish the eight-hour day on a relatively firm basis. The AFL grew as a consequence. Fresh layers of workers were organized and the way was opened for it to become the representative in industry of all toilers. New opportunities thus existed for the Socialist Labor Party, which had played a substantial role in the eight-hour fight, to build a strong left wing in the AFL based on a class-struggle program. But at that point an internal development was about to impel the party in a different direction.

Around 1890, Daniel De Leon, who had taught international law at Columbia University in New York, joined the Socialist Labor Party and soon became one of its leaders. From the start he fully identified himself with the working class and turned his back forever on the academic world. Unlike some intellectuals who presumed to act as leaders, he did not consider revolutionary activity an avocation to be practiced on a part-time basis.

A dedicated student of Marxist theory, De Leon made important contributions to the education of workers by concretizing and

Left, Eugene V. Debs. Right, Daniel De Leon.

popularizing class-struggle fundamentals. He related these basic ideas to labor's problems of the day, often using historical references to further illustrate the lessons involved. In doing so he produced many pamphlets that remain useful today.

His legacy was quite different, though, when it came to strategic and tactical concepts. In that sphere he seemed unaware of important lessons taught by history. Large numbers of workers embrace revolutionary views only insofar as day-to-day experiences drive home to them basic truths about the class struggle. They take limited strides forward and make partial retreats, often acting collectively at important points, on the way to making a qualitative leap in their consciousness. The challenge for convinced revolutionists is to recognize that pattern, support and take part in the struggle for immediate goals set by the workers, and in doing so help them make the transition onto higher planes of action and class consciousness.

Several advantages result from accomplishing this. Past gains made by the movement are easier to maintain. Individual militants can be won to the revolutionary party, which strengthens its capacity to act, and new progress can be made as permitted by changes in the objective relationship of class forces.

But this transitional approach to party building, originally taught by Marx and Engels, was rejected by De Leon, the new leader of the Socialist Labor Party. Instead, impatient with the masses, he set the party cadres on a forced march to speedily revolutionize the labor movement. His methods had the opposite result. The policies he enforced created widespread confusion. Ground won by the party previously was soon lost, and it continued to suffer one reverse after another.

De Leon showed little interest in trade union efforts to improve the workers' immediate situation; and instead of the strategic line of march that included an independent working-class party based on the trade unions, he concentrated on attempts to rapidly force organized labor onto an anticapitalist political course. The transitional step of organizing a labor party—the very process of which could transform the labor movement and open the door to mass anticapitalist political action and a mass revolutionary party—was beyond his understanding. In his view a labor party would inevitably fall prey to the class collaborationism extant among union officials; only the SLP could represent the workers' revolutionary interests, and it had to serve at once as the vehicle for mass labor political action, with or without the workers.

As a move in that direction the SLP intensified its electoral activity. In the 1892 elections it nominated a presidential ticket for the first time, and received nearly 15,000 votes in the six states where the ticket was on the ballot. Viewed as a socialist propaganda campaign to explain the necessary strategy for labor against the employing class, the election returns were gratifying. But since the party presented itself as the vehicle for mass political action, the results were negligible.

While making this shift in electoral policy, the De Leonists tried to maneuver direct SLP affiliation to the American Federation of Labor. Such a step, they hoped, would enable them to bring that organization under party control. In New York, where De Leon had a strong personal following, unions led by the party withdrew from the AFL Central Labor Union. The seceders established a setup they called the Central Labor Federation—with the local SLP unit as one of its affiliates—and requested an AFL charter as a separate central body. Gompers refused the request because a political party was included in the formation, and the next AFL convention upheld him. The refusal did not imply a ban on socialists belonging to AFL unions in their respective trades. But the federation, which desired to remain a trade union movement, correctly held that a political party could not properly become an affiliate.[*]

Nevertheless, De Leon attacked Gompers's action as unprincipled. He charged that the federation refused to accept the Socialist Labor Party as an affiliate because the union leadership was preoccupied

---

[*] Engels criticized De Leon's maneuver in an 1891 letter to Hermann Schlüter. See appendix, page 242.

with immediate economic issues at the expense of independent labor political action; and that meant the organization had been rendered ineffective as a workers' instrument of struggle. He then called upon socialists in the AFL to break with it and lead their unions into the Knights of Labor.

A significant number of SLP trade unionists ignored De Leon's directive. They understood that the AFL's rapid growth offered the possibility of changing it from an essentially craft union body into an industrial union federation embracing unskilled factory workers as well as the skilled trades. There were also prospects of leading this expanding movement to form an independent labor party. Work toward those ends could be carried on, moreover, in an atmosphere where socialists were accepted on the basis of their capabilities as trade unionists. So these SLP members remained in the AFL, striving to build a left wing that could take on mass dimensions.

By the time of the AFL's 1893 convention another economic crisis had set in. That enabled union delegates who were socialists to cite the dire effects of the industrial slump in motivating a resolution they introduced. It centered on advocacy of independent labor political action sponsored by the unions. Programmatically, the resolution included a call for nationalization of certain key industries as an initial step toward collective ownership of the means of production and distribution. The general line of the resolution was endorsed by a majority of the convention. It was then referred to the affiliated units for consideration in advance of the next annual gathering where final action was to be taken.

During the interim Gompers successfully maneuvered to gut the resolution of its main provisions. His actions caused such widespread indignation that the 1894 convention ousted him from the AFL presidency. This created an opportunity for the left wing to become a major force in the federation. But the SLP members guiding it got no help from the party leadership, and they were unable to cope with the counteroffensive mounted by the right wing. Gompers was reelected president the following year, and his regime dominated the AFL from then on.

De Leon, meanwhile, had mustered what forces he could in an attempt to take over the Knights of Labor. SLP-led unions in New York, which had left the AFL at his bidding, served as the main contingent. They soon gained control of the Knights' strongest assembly in that city and used it as a base for broader operations. De Leon himself was included in the New York delegation to the 1893 K of L convention, where he made the opening move in a bid for leadership. A jerry-built power bloc—formed with J. R. Sovereign, head of an affiliated farmers' movement, and with disgruntled K of L officers—removed Powderly from the presidency and elected Sovereign in his place. After that De Leon tried to have Sovereign appoint an SLP member editor of the Knights' official journal to get more of the leverage needed for the party to dominate the union organization.

But matters worked out differently. Sovereign failed to appoint a De Leonist editor of the union journal. His regime was then denounced by the SLP, and that led in 1895 to expulsion of the socialists from the K of L. As the crowning irony to De Leon's adventure, the expulsions hastened the demise of a once-powerful movement already dying when he attempted to capture it.

The SLP leader's next sectarian adventure was the attempt to build a new union movement that would be revolutionary from the start. It was intended to displace both the American Federation of Labor and the Knights of Labor. But forthright projection of that aim would have aroused strong opposition among SLP members still active in the AFL. So De Leon contrived to confront the party with an accomplished fact. The New York unions that had spearheaded the earlier entry into the K of L were pulled out of that organization and used to launch a new formation, the Socialist Trades and Labor Alliance (STLA). A scattering of De Leonist-influenced unions in other cities were also drawn into support of the move.

At the Socialist Labor Party's 1896 convention the STLA was depicted as a movement to organize the unorganized workers into industrial unions; to guide the ranks onto a class-struggle course; and to imbue the broad labor movement with revolutionary proletarian concepts. On that basis party endorsement of the new union formation was secured.

After that De Leon's ploy began to unfold more concretely, as did its disastrous consequences. The Socialist Trades and Labor Alliance developed into a highly centralized body functioning under rigid control of the party leadership. It paid scant heed to workers' struggles for immediate gains, holding that none of their problems could be solved or even alleviated through such activity. The top officials called for construction of revolutionary industrial unions that would unite with the Socialist Labor Party to abolish capitalism, in which all the existing social evils were rooted. Toward that end they urged class-conscious trade unionists to leave the other labor formations and join in building the STLA.

Special efforts were concentrated on pulling militants out of theAFL. This weakened the left wing in the federation and antagonized workers who resented the raids on their established unions, thus strengthening Gompers's hand. At the same time the Socialist Labor Party—which bore responsibility for STLA policy—rapidly lost standing within all wings of the organized labor movement.

While De Leon was leading the party further and further out of contact with the mass movement in the early 1890s, a series of industrial conflicts erupted. The main actions included strikes in the steel, coal, hard-rock mining, and railroad industries. These were large-scale struggles during which unorganized workers were drawn into battle on the union side. Without exception the corporations declared war on their dissatisfied employees. Every available strikebreaking device was used, from the hiring of scabs and thugs to repressive measures by state militias and federal troops. The strikers fought back bitterly, and armed clashes left dead and wounded on both sides. In the end, though, the strikes were broken. Many workers were victimized, and there was no revolutionary party to help them draw the lessons of their experiences so their next fight could be more effective.

By this time the accelerating class-struggle tempos had convinced the ruling class that catchall conspiracy indictments were outmoded as a means of curbing strikes. Workers so charged had to be tried and convicted before the courts could penalize them. That procedure took more time than the capitalists could spare when they wanted to break a strike here and now, and it also failed to invoke large-scale repression.

The employers solved their problem by resorting to court injunctions against industrial stoppages. They had judges issue orders outlawing strike activity. Police and soldiers could then be immediately used to club, shoot, and jail workers in the name of upholding law and order; heavy fines could be levied against unions to cripple them financially—in short, the ruling class could quickly take whatever "legal" repressive action it chose to break a given strike. What has since become known as "government by injunction" was made a normal capitalist practice.

This shift in tactics did not mean that conspiracy indictments were abandoned. They continued to be used when expedient for other capitalist purposes; for example, to strip the workers of competent leadership and to blunt radicalization of the labor movement.

The viciousness of the injunction weapon was demonstrated in an 1894 strike against the Pullman Company, the leading manufacturer and operator of railway sleeping cars. Eugene V. Debs, a railroad worker and union organizer, led the strikers. He had played the central role in founding the American Railway Union, which united all categories of rail labor on an industrial basis. This organizational medium now proved highly effective in mobilizing support for Pullman employees who walked off the job after their pay was cut. A widespread tie-up of the rail system was brought about by union crews who refused to operate trains having Pullman cars attached.

President Grover Cleveland soon intervened on the side of the railroad magnates. He first secured an injunction against the Pullman boycott. Federal troops were then sent to enforce the court order, and their brutal intervention brought death or injury to numerous workers. Parallel with those steps Debs and other strike leaders were arrested on conspiracy charges. When they obtained release on bail pending trial, the federal authorities immediately re-arrested them. This time they were charged with violation of the injunction, convicted of contempt of court, and sentenced to jail terms. By then the strike had been broken.

With the federal government joining in savage attacks of this kind on organized labor, the Gompersites decided to make a bid for a general compromise with the ruling class. As an inducement they abandoned any pretense of unionizing the unskilled and semiskilled workers in basic industry. AFL activity became restricted more and more to organizing the skilled trades—a relatively privileged minority of the working class constituting a labor aristocracy—with the aim of securing capitalist acceptance of narrow craft unions as "partners" in industry and politics.

Debs and the militants associated with him had a different reaction to "government by injunction." In their view the crushing of the American Railway Union was simply an episode, though a tragic one, in the class war. It changed nothing concerning the need for a broad labor struggle against capitalist oppression and exploitation. Accordingly their outlook focused on twin aims: formation of industrial unions through which the workers could present a strong united front against the corporations; and initiation of anticapitalist political action on a mass scale.

Earlier Debs had been influenced by the populist movement, especially by the People's Party launched in 1891 by a coalition of reform groups. Although consisting primarily of working farmers, it was mainly small merchants and professionals who put the dominant petty-bourgeois stamp on the party. Its central plank demanded free coinage of silver in the hope that if more money were put into circulation the high interest rates exacted by bankers on loans needed to finance farming and small business operations would be driven down. This was a vain hope. It was not the amount of currency in circulation that determined the interest rates, but rather the supply of money capital relative to the demand for bank loans. Hence, the problem of usurious interest rates faced by working farmers, small business proprietors, etc., could not be solved through free coinage of silver. The cross they bore was not a cross of gold; it was a cross of capital.

Most people were unaware of those facts, however, and mass support of the People's Party developed rapidly, especially among farmers. Then with the onset of an economic crisis in 1893, increasingly strong backing came from workers nursing hopes that an expanded money supply, the issuance of more dollars by the government, would reverse the slump in industrial production and restore jobs to the unemployed. Under these circumstances the populist candidates received a sharply higher vote in the 1894 elections. Large numbers of workers, as the election returns showed, were being drawn by populist illusions into acceptance of petty-bourgeois political leadership.

This major problem for the socialist movement was discussed by Engels in a letter of January 16, 1895, to Sorge. "America is the *youngest,* but also the *oldest* country in the world," he said. "Over there you have . . . in the mountains stagecoaches dating from the seventeenth century alongside the Pullman cars, and in the same way you keep all the intellectual old clothes discarded in Europe. Anything that is out of date over here can survive in America for one or two generations. Karl Heinzen [a bourgeois democrat], for instance, not to mention religious and spiritualist superstition. Thus the old Lassalleans survive among you, and men like [Lucien] Sanial [a leading French-American De Leonist], who would be superannuated in France today, can still play a role over there. That is due, on the one hand, to the fact that America is only now beginning to have time, beyond concern for material production and enrichment, for free intellectual labor and the preparatory education that this requires; and, on the other hand, to the duality of American development, which is still engaged in the *primary* task—clearing the tremendous virgin area—but is already compelled to enter the competition for first place in industrial production. Hence the ups and downs of the movement, depending upon whether the mind of the industrial worker or that of the pioneering farmer gains predominance in the average man's head" (*Letters to Americans, 1848–1895,* pp. 269–70, emphasis in original).

Engels's comment about Sanial touched indirectly on the Socialist Labor Party's growing inability to cope with objective conditions. This was evidenced in this instance by their one-sided attitude toward the populists. The De Leonists simply denounced them as reformists and advised labor to disregard the whole agrarian movement. Their line missed the main point. The industrial workers needed to identify with the progressive aims of the working farmers so as to draw them into an alliance fighting the common capitalist enemy; an alliance in which labor would be in a position to assume the guiding role in the fight against capital, thrusting aside the populist politicians who had misled the exploited and militant working farmers. But the SLP failed to recognize that need. Instead, it adopted a sectarian attitude toward the working farmers, leaving them entirely at the mercy of the petty-bourgeois and bourgeois misleaders.

The silver-mine owners, whose profits would greatly benefit from free coinage of their product, showed greater tactical flexibility. They allied themselves with the petty-bourgeois leaders of the populist movement, whose policy then shifted to the right. This came about when the Democratic Party added a free-silver plank to its platform for the 1896 elections and nominated for president William Jennings Bryan, a free-silver advocate. The People's Party then endorsed Bryan's candidacy. With that fatal step, the populists were drawn so deeply into capitalist political service that their party soon disintegrated.

Debs went along with the populists in backing the Democratic ticket, and he found that reliance on petty-bourgeois politicians led to entrapment in the capitalist two-party system. This experience convinced him that the workers must lead their allies in anticapitalist political action through labor's own political party. He also concluded that a social revolution was needed to solve labor's basic problems, a view he had come to embrace after studying Marxism while in jail for defying the injunction against the Pullman strike. Debs made these changes in outlook public in January 1897, when he proclaimed himself a socialist. As a gifted orator equipped with unshakable revolutionary convictions, he thereafter became the foremost popularizer of socialism among the toiling masses.

On the organizational side Debs began with efforts to unite various socialist and semisocialist groups that had arisen spontaneously during the radicalization of the 1890s. These were small but growing formations that the De Leonists had been incapable of attracting to the Socialist Labor Party. Several of them responded to Debs's overtures.

As a preliminary step toward socialist unification, the surviving cadres of the American Railway Union sponsored a political discussion open to all tendencies. This initiative led in 1897 to the founding of a new party, the Social Democracy of America. From the outset it advanced as a central political goal a utopian scheme to colonize workers from the industrial East in western states where they were to form producers' cooperatives. As the superiority of the cooperative system over capitalism was in that way to be made evident, the utopian strategists contended, the movement would spread nationally and bring a socialist society into being. Another tendency, based in Wisconsin, consisted mainly of ex-SLP members who had been alienated by De Leonism. They were led by Victor L. Berger, an Austrian-American teacher, who opposed the colonizers and advocated a transition from capitalism to socialism through gradual reform of the existing system. Debs, on the other hand, went along with the colonizers for a time; but he also helped out wherever possible in trade union struggles, a policy the utopians dismissed as futile. A contradictory and confused internal situation thus prevailed with the different party tendencies acting unilaterally on the basis of incompatible aims.

The resulting frictions provoked a sharp dispute at the Social Democracy's 1898 convention. The Bergerites pushed their line at the gathering, and Debs pressed for greater attention to both independent working-class political action and industrial struggles. When a majority of the delegates voted to continue centering party work on colonization, the Berger group withdrew from the Social

Democracy. Debs, together with labor militants led by him, followed suit. The cadres of these two currents then acted jointly to establish the Social Democratic Party of America later in 1898.

All utopian notions were thrust aside by the new organization. It began to act as part of the existing labor movement with the aim of furthering the class struggle politically. The leaders did not, however, contemplate building a broad labor party based on the trade unions. They assumed that the Social Democratic Party could serve as the workers' independent means of mass political action. Trade union activity was accompanied by extensive nomination of party candidates for public office, who campaigned on that premise. Before long some of those candidates won local election contests, and at the same time the party itself rapidly gained new members.

These achievements, together with the industrial struggles of the period, had an effect on the Socialist Labor Party. An internal party dispute broke out during 1899 in which De Leon's sectarian course came under attack. The opposition was led by Morris Hillquit, a New York lawyer, and Max Hayes of the Cleveland typographers' union. They called for a more flexible approach to the trade unions and to the prosocialist groups that had recently sprung up. De Leon vetoed that line. A bitter factional struggle ensued, with each side claiming to represent the party majority. An open split resulted when the opposition faction held its own convention in January 1900 at which a decision was made to seek unification with the Social Democratic Party.

The proposed amalgamation got a mixed reception within the Social Democratic Party. It was favored by the Debs wing and opposed by the Bergerites. This divided opinion gave rise to a heated internal controversy, but a complete break over the issue was avoided through an interim arrangement for a united-front presidential campaign in the November 1900 elections. Debs of the Social Democratic Party was nominated for president of the United States and Job Harriman, a San Francisco lawyer representing the Hillquit-Hayes faction of the SLP, for vice-president. A vigorous socialist campaign was then conducted with the result that the united front's presidential ticket polled almost 100,000 votes, a new high for the socialist movement.

Inspired by the gains recorded in the national elections, the collaborating groups issued a call for a joint convention of all socialist formations to establish a single, broad party. A favorable response was received generally, with the notable exception of the De Leonists. When the convention assembled in July 1901, those present represented a great majority of the existing socialist cadres. Of equal significance, about four of every five delegates were native-born. Socialism in this country had advanced beyond its earlier German-American makeup; it was becoming a truly indigenous movement.

The convention launched an all-inclusive organization named the Socialist Party of America (SP). Although a unified national party in form, the SP was actually a loose coalition of diverse regional and local groups. There was no unified strategy for leading the workers to power. Political concepts within the party ranged from some grasp of Marxism to a purely reformist outlook. A great majority of the founding members had, in fact, rather limited political consciousness, as did most of the leaders. Such were the cadres who had joined in a collective effort to wage an effective struggle for socialism; and instead of getting help from the De Leonists, they would have to cope with that tendency as an obstacle to creation of a viable Marxist vanguard.

By this time the Socialist Labor Party had almost entirely lost touch with the mass movement. Its fortunes had also declined in the electoral arena, where the Debs-Harriman ticket had outpolled the De Leonist candidates nearly three to one in the presidential elections of 1900. In addition, large membership losses had been sustained by the SLP, and the Hillquit-Hayes split wasn't the only cause. Numerous individuals had been expelled for taking issue with the party leadership on various matters. This dictatorial attitude enabled De Leon to keep the organization "purified" according to his concepts of Marxism, but it also had the effect of reducing the party to a corporal's guard.

A similar fate had befallen the Socialist Trades and Labor Alliance. Attempts to use it to create revolutionary unions on a shotgun basis had totally failed. By the turn of the century the STLA had lost the bulk of its affiliates. Such union bodies as remained within its fold were more artificial than real, consisting primarily of SLP members and sympathizers who now found themselves caught in a bind. They could take no meaningful action through the STLA, and they had no way to exert influence in the American Federation of Labor, where the main unionized forces were assembled.

In these circumstances it became all the easier for Gompers to take a more brazen step toward implementation of his class-collaborationist line. He did so in 1900 when the National Civic Federation was formed with the stated aim of maintaining peaceful labor-management relations. This organization consisted of employers, top AFL officials, and so-called public representatives who were merely capitalist puppets. As this makeup indicated, its real object was to prepare new blows against labor. The ruling class had decided to use the craft unions as a means of splitting the workers' movement. To serve that end employers would recognize narrow formations of skilled hands, provided they complied with certain restrictions. There were to be no attempts to unionize the masses of unskilled and semiskilled workers, and independent labor activity was not to be extended beyond industry into politics.

Within industry the craft unions were to be granted limited concessions as to wages and conditions, if they reciprocated by according the bosses a free hand to carry on operations in a profitable manner. Work stoppages were to be avoided. Union officials were to cooperate with management in repressing troublemakers so as to maintain harmony on the job. This employer-designed pattern for collective bargaining could not have been more thoroughly rigged against the workers. Yet it was accepted by the top AFL hacks and codified under the deceptive slogan, "A fair day's work for a fair day's pay."

Politically, the craft-union officials complied with the ruling-class demand that labor's role be strictly confined within the capitalist two-party system. Democrats or Republicans were supported for public office, depending on their ratings as "friends of labor"—that is, the capitalist politicians who were the least hostile to the trade unions. If an occasional governmental concession to labor was obtained through such "friends," a heavy price had to be paid for it. The workers were steered away from efforts to form their own mass party, an indispensable step in defending their interests as a class; and the capitalists remained free to use governmental power against the trade unions.

V.I. Lenin, leader of the Bolshevik Party in Russia, characterized this line in an article written toward the end of 1912. "The state of affairs in the American labor movement shows us, as it does in Britain," he noted, "the remarkably clear-cut division between purely trade unionist and socialist strivings, the split between *bourgeois labor policy* and socialist labor policy. For, strange as it may seem, in capitalist society even the working class can carry on a bourgeois policy, if it forgets about its emancipatory aims, puts up with wage-slavery and confines itself to seeking alliances now with one bourgeois party, now with another, for the sake of imaginary 'improvements' in its indentured condition. The principal historical cause of the particular prominence and (temporary) strength of bourgeois labor policy in Britain and America is the long-standing political liberty and the exceptionally favorable conditions, in comparison with other countries, for the deep-going and widespread development of capitalism. These conditions have tended to produce within the working class an aristocracy that has trailed after the bourgeoisie, *betraying* its own class" (*Lenin on the United States* [New York: International Publishers, 1970], pp. 56–57, emphasis in original).

To further their bourgeois labor policy, the top leaders of the AFL proceeded to completely differentiate themselves from radical concepts. Gompers set the tone. At the organization's 1903 convention he repudiated his past expressions of sympathy with socialist aims and harshly denounced the Marxist movement. This attack was in reality a declaration of war against every worker who opposed any part of the official AFL line. The challenge had to be met and—as matters then stood—militants in the union ranks could look only to the recently formed Socialist Party for leadership. In doing so, however, they were to face many obstacles because of the party's internal characteristics.

From its inception the SP functioned in a decentralized manner. Considerable autonomy was exercised by the various party units, leaving the national administration no way to effectively coordinate day-to-day activities. On specific questions of policy, moreover, decisions made by the National Executive Committee were subject to reversal through membership referendum. Such organizational standards were in themselves enough to cause internal confusion, and the situation was made even worse by the SP's all-inclusive heterogeneous political character. Many differences existed within its ranks over basic policy. These differences led to a rapid polarization of left and right wings, each using the loose procedural norms to act on its own in pursuit of contradictory objectives.

Still another tendency soon crystallized in which Morris Hillquit played a key role. It consisted of centrists who wavered between revolutionary and reformist positions. They leaned toward the left or veered to the right depending on the pressures at a given time. Their vacillation was so pronounced that even when impelled leftward for the moment during a mass upsurge the centrists substituted opportunist methods for a class-struggle course.

The right wing, headed by Victor L. Berger, constituted only a small part of the SP's founding cadres. But size alone did not determine these reformists' relative weight within the party. From the outset they were organized on a tight basis and guided by an aggressive leadership with clear aims. In addition, the Bergerites could act with confidence of getting significant support from the regime in charge of the Second International. Engels had died in 1895. Opportunists, who were transforming Marxism into its opposite, were gaining more weight in the International and were, in practice, more and more pushing a reformist line. This development gave right-wing socialists in the United States both important backing from abroad and help in expounding their own revisionist concepts.

Eduard Bernstein's theories (summarized in chapter one) had by then become well known in the Second International; and even though Bernsteinism was rejected by majority vote at every world congress, the right wing of the International—covered by the centrists—sought constantly to put his revisionist line into practice wherever possible. Here in the United States the Berger tendency publicized Bernstein's concepts, which envisaged the evolution of capitalist society toward socialism through gradual reforms. At the same time a program was developed for adaptation of Bernstein's outlook to the conditions existing in this country. Top priority was given to the initiation of reforms at the municipal level. Through successes registered city by city along such lines, it was expected, the nation's social system would ultimately acquire socialist characteristics.

In keeping with that perspective the concept of fighting to establish a workers' government nationally was superseded by efforts to win control of city administrations in local election contests. The question of expropriating capitalist industry was similarly put aside in favor of emphasis on developing municipal ownership of utilities. Among the various civic improvements advocated was better sewage disposal, and the stress placed on that point became a peg for party militants—who opposed the whole right-wing program—to sarcastically dub it "sewer socialism."

The left wing of the Socialist Party, in contrast to its better-organized counterpart on the right, was a loosely knit formation. It also suffered from lack of firm internal guidance. Eugene V. Debs, the most outstanding figure in the party, sided with the left politically. But he had no clear Marxist strategy to establish a workers' government. Thus he did not see the need for a politically homogeneous combat party and so did not accept full party leadership responsibility. No one else came forward to assume that role. On top of that, reformist degeneration within the Second International made it much more difficult to receive international guidance in shaping a revolutionary course. So the SP militants on the left, who had only limited knowledge of Marxism, found themselves pretty much on their own. They had to grope along as best they could in the face of a complex situation within the labor movement as a whole.

As against Berger's reformist line, the left wing had a class-struggle outlook. It rejected the notion of creeping toward socialism a city at a time, recognizing that steps to break the capitalists' stranglehold on the whole economic structure were fundamental to the desired social change. It also understood that the workers had to take political power nationally in order to carry through a revolutionary transformation of society. The left wing assumed, however, that nothing more was involved than gaining control of the existing governmental apparatus through the electoral process. It seemed unaware of the lessons learned by Marx in the revolutions of 1848–49 and reinforced after the defeat of the Paris Commune—that the workers cannot simply lay hold of the ready-made state machinery and wield it for their own purposes; that the entire ruling structure set up by the capitalists must be dismantled, beginning with the standing army and the cops, and a new kind of state organized to serve the workers' ends.

Neither the left nor the right grasped this crucial problem. Throughout the party it was assumed that nothing more than the installation of socialists in governmental positions was needed to carry out a social revolution. What to do about the probable reaction of the ruling class once the socialists were backed by a majority of the population was not even considered. Nothing was said about the need for a socialist-led workers' government to prepare the firmest defensive measures against efforts by the counterrevolutionary capitalist minority to subvert majority rule through force and violence.

All tendencies held a common view of the socialist strategy and tactics needed to oppose Gompers's policy of tying labor to capitalist politics. It was taken for granted that the Socialist Party would be able to serve as the medium for mass working-class political action. A strategy for working through transitional steps in the rise of class consciousness to that political level was reduced to a mechanical formula—party support of labor struggles in industry, combined with socialist educational activity in the union ranks. This approach was expected to result in ever-larger numbers of workers leaping directly from an elementary trade union outlook to membership in the SP and the adoption of socialist perspectives.

Thus all SP tendencies opposed the building of an independent labor party based on the trade unions, looking upon such a formation as an obstacle to speedy growth of the socialist movement. But instead of serving the intended purpose, this policy had the opposite effect. It obstructed the transitional steps necessary for the development of mass working-class political consciousness in the manner recommended earlier by Engels, and it helped Gompers keep the AFL membership bogged down in the capitalist two-party system.

During the first period of the SP's existence, the focus of activity was determined by the left wing, then the strongest tendency in the party. Using its dominant position to advantage, the left drew the centrists into a bloc and isolated the Bergerites. This made it possible for a big majority in the party to influence the broad labor movement along class-struggle lines. Advocacy of militant union policies, along with help to striking workers, generated sympathy for the socialist movement. Working-class support of its candidates for public office increased, and accelerating recruitment more than doubled the party's membership during its first three years.

The Western Federation of Miners—whose principal leader, William D. Haywood, joined the Socialist Party—was influenced in this way. Although originally affiliated to the AFL, this union of hard-rock miners had severed that relationship because of the craft-union concepts and the class-collaborationist policies imposed by the Gompers regime. It had then sponsored establishment of a broad, more militant labor federation in the West based on the industrial form of organization. Gompers, who denounced this action as "dual unionism," immediately began preparations for an AFL raid on the western organization's membership. The new federation answered his belligerence by extending its campaign into the East through an expanded body called the American Labor

Union, directly challenging the AFL in its main territory. A head-on clash developed, centered on the issue of industrial versus craft unionism.

When Haywood looked to the Socialist Party for backing in this fight he got a mixed reaction. With Debs setting the example for all militants, the party's left wing extended full support to the industrial unionists. But the Bergerites took an opposite stand. Their primary concern was to secure official AFL endorsement of socialist candidates in municipal elections. In return they were ready to accord unconditional authority to the Gompers hierarchy to determine union policy. This position was presented under the guise of "party neutrality" in internal union disputes, and the Hillquit tendency went along with it.

At the SP's 1904 convention the dispute came before the delegates in the discussion of a resolution on the trade union question. Since the resolution was vaguely worded, however, its adoption failed to fix a definite party line. Contradictory policies continued to be followed by the different tendencies. While the left carried on a struggle for the industrial form of organization, the right and center sided with the hard-core craft unionists.

The left wing did gain an advantage through the convention's nominees for the 1904 elections. Debs was named presidential candidate and Benjamin Hanford of the New York typographical union was named the vice-presidential nominee. Debs set a revolutionary tone in the national campaign along the lines of the left's basic outlook, thereby shoving into the background the reformist propaganda advanced by Bergerite and centrist candidates at the city level. Thousands upon thousands of workers, inspired by Debs, volunteered to be campaigners. An impressive showing resulted as the Debs-Hanford ticket received over 400,000 votes, about four times the number cast for the Debs-Harriman slate in 1900. The potential for the party to become an effective revolutionary instrument was clearly on the rise. What was needed was a growing left wing, acting with political sagacity as the vanguard of the working class.

# 4

# A Disoriented Movement

While running for president Debs continued to press the industrial union issue. His initiative evoked a widening response among workers, and in January 1905 an informal conference of socialist and trade union militants was held to consider a plan of action. Their aim was to immediately institute the industrial form of organization on a broad scale, accompanying this step with infusion of class-struggle concepts into the union movement. To achieve those ends they had to overcome interrelated obstacles: the Gompers regime's craft union, class-collaborationist policies in the American Federation of Labor; and the unprincipled backing extended to the craft union hierarchy by the Berger and Hillquit tendencies in the Socialist Party. How then, the conferees undertook to decide, could their cause be best advanced?

Viewed from today's more detached vantage point, it appears that an effective fight might have been conducted by taking the next steps within the AFL. In fact such a course seems called for in the conditions prevailing at the time. By 1905 rapidly increasing concentrations of capital were creating huge industrial complexes that employed large numbers of unskilled and semi-skilled workers, and the relative weight of skilled hands in the labor force was being reduced accordingly. From this it followed that trade unions based on the skilled crafts had been rendered obsolete as a predominant form of labor organization. A structural change had become imperative, for only by organizing along industrial lines could the factory workers conduct trade union struggles against the harsh exploitation to which the capitalists subjected them. This organizational bind—which stemmed from the craft union officialdom's indifference to the needs of the most oppressed workers, who constituted a majority of the proletariat—was generating mass pressures on the official leadership for a change in policy; and those pressures could have given an edge to the industrial union advocates in an internal AFL struggle.

As class lines became more sharply drawn within basic industry, an upsurge of trade union consciousness had developed among the workers. This trend gave socialist militants an opening to press for an AFL organizing drive throughout industry. By thus allying themselves with factory employees ready to enter the union movement they could have drawn broad masses into the fight for a change in its organizational form. That approach could have been doubly effective, moreover, because it would have been applied within the framework of running battles against the employers. And it would have strengthened the class position of both skilled and unskilled workers.

While going through common experiences with the workers in such activities, the revolutionary socialists could have helped them both to perceive the bankruptcy of official AFL policy and to grasp the need for adoption of a class-struggle course. In that way an increasingly strong left wing could have been built within the federation. This left wing could have led a fight for complete internal democracy, for rank-and-file control over all union affairs. A campaign of that nature could have resulted in the removal of class collaborationists from official union posts and their replacement by tested, militant leaders elected on a clearly defined program which met with membership approval.

Progress within the AFL along the above lines could have brought parallel growth of the left wing in the SP. The right-wingers and their collaborators among the centrists could have been discredited and isolated. A revolutionary party could have been created, a vanguard force able to provide the political leadership needed by the working class and its allies.

As the struggle over basic policy grew more acute the class collaborationists might have fomented a split in the AFL, for such is the common practice among their ilk when the aroused ranks push their backs against the wall. Two union formations, qualitatively different in character, would then have existed as rivals. One would have consisted mainly of the most exploited sections of the working class, thereby representing the major force both in size and in potential dynamism. The other formation would have been stripped down primarily to a section of the labor aristocracy, a minority of relatively privileged workers who assume conservative attitudes so long as their skills enable them to obtain special concessions from the employers. In such a development the reformists would no doubt have been able to dominate the latter setup for a time, but sooner or later its ranks would also have become attracted to the rise of a strong industrial union.

The skilled workers, too, were subjected to capitalist exploitation. Therefore, although better off than the unskilled factory hands, they still had need for class-struggle policies to defend and advance their interests. For that reason many of them could have become inspired to ally themselves with the industrial unionists in one way or another. Potential for such action had, in fact, been manifested during the best days of the Knights of Labor, which united skilled and unskilled workers in battle against the employers. What broke up that dynamic alliance was not backwardness on the part of the skilled workers. Labor unity was shattered by the class-collaborationist policies of the Powderly regime in the K of L.

In the aftermath of that regressive development the Gompersites had been able to establish control over the American Federation of Labor. But they, like Powderly, had adopted class-collaborationist policies that ran counter to the needs of all workers, skilled and unskilled alike. The trend of events had thus made it possible to strip the Gompersites—and along with them the social reformists—of any substantial base from which to obstruct swifter growth of revolutionary socialist influence in the labor movement.

An altogether different situation arose, however, in actual practice. The January 1905 conference decided to call for the launching of a national industrial union separate and apart from the AFL. Various independent unions already structured on an industrial basis were counted on to respond at once. With their help, it was assumed, AFL bodies favoring organization on an industry-wide scale could be induced to come over to the new movement. The combined forces thus assembled could then open a campaign to recruit unskilled and semiskilled workers neglected by the Gompersites, thereby outflanking the craft-oriented federation.

A national convention followed in June 1905 at which the Industrial Workers of the World (IWW) was founded. The Western Federation of Miners, which constituted the strongest force in the new movement, sent a delegation to the gathering. Other affiliates of the American Labor Union were also represented, as were the remnants of the Socialist Trades and Labor Alliance fostered by the De Leonists. In the case of the AFL, however, only a handful of local unions responded to the convention call. Included among the delegations in attendance were three of the most prominent labor and socialist leaders in the country: Debs, De Leon, and Haywood. As their readiness to act jointly at the trade union level signified, new hope was envisaged of strengthening the broad labor movement and deepening class consciousness within its ranks.

Organizationally, the IWW set out to build local industrial unions that were to be combined, industry by industry, into national formations. The latter formations were then to be linked up by means of an all-embracing structure of a generalized nature, a concept that became popularized through the slogan of "One Big Union."

On the setting of policy and the handling of internal union affairs, the convention took a stand opposite to the AFL officialdom's growing tendency to usurp the power of decision. It was stipulated that supreme authority rested with the IWW membership. A policy of political nonexclusion was also established. All workers were invited into the organization, regardless of their political views.

A majority in the ranks of the new movement were nonpolitical trade unionists with two specific aims in mind. They wanted strong organizations built on an industry-wide basis; and they intended to use those instruments for militant struggle against the employers, as contrasted with the class-collaborationist line of the AFL officialdom. In striving toward such ends most of them were ready to listen with an open mind to views expressed by radical workers in their midst. The latter included members of the Socialist Party's left wing, Socialist Labor Party elements led by De Leon, and anarcho-syndicalists. Of these separate tendencies, those identifying themselves as socialists wielded the greatest influence among IWW members at the outset. The anarcho-syndicalists did not, as yet, carry much weight in the union.

All the radical groupings were agreed on the fundamental character the IWW should assume. They acted in concert to institute the concept that it would function from the start as a revolutionary union. It was to serve as the medium through which to mobilize the workers in a struggle for power, the objective being to abolish capitalism and establish a socialist order.

But this perspective didn't square with the current reality. Class consciousness was still at an elementary level among the vast majority of workers. They had many grievances about the conditions under which they were forced to exist, but most workers were unaware that the antagonisms between themselves and the employing class were irreconcilable. Hence they were not consciously anticapitalist. They were ready as yet for nothing more than a struggle through the trade unions for economic and social reforms under the existing system. If in those circumstances the IWW was to make headway, it had to start from the current level of mass consciousness and involve the workers in trade union actions, so that through these experiences they could begin to generalize their thinking in class terms. Gradually, along those lines, an expanding vanguard could be developed that understood the need to abolish capitalism.

This process had to be a recurrent one, moreover, because the masses in basic industry were yet to be organized. To the extent that this task was accomplished, new layers of backward elements would be drawn into the movement, one after another. As a result the IWW would constantly embrace both members having limited class consciousness and others who were acquiring a revolutionary outlook.

Still another task was posed. The vanguard forces needed a special means of functioning in an organized manner; that is, they needed to come together in a revolutionary party. Through that instrument their own political education could be broadened and deepened. They could act collectively to promote intensified class struggles within industry, to help the union ranks draw political lessons from their experiences in battle, and thereby to prepare the way for a working-class advance toward the overthrow of capitalism. The irreplaceable role of such a party was not clearly defined, however, by anyone in the IWW leadership. None of them conceived of a party with a homogenous Marxist program necessitating a revolutionary centralist combat character. The subject was treated only obliquely under the loose heading of "political action," and differing opinions on the strategy of political action were expressed by the various radical tendencies in the union.

By this time De Leon was changing his mind about the Socialist Labor Party's role in the class struggle. Earlier he had tried to subordinate the trade unions to the SLP with the aim of the party striving for state power through electoral and parliamentary action. Then, as the IWW came into being, he began to reverse that outlook.

Socialist industrial unions were proclaimed the main instrument for the transformation of society. These, he now held, were to be class-conscious organizations of the working class whose functions would be to abolish capitalist productive relations and institute collective ownership and operation of the means of production and distribution. To do so the unions were to take direct possession of industry. They would then replace the capitalist political government with an industrial one organized by the workers on the basis of democratic representation from the various useful occupations.

The SLP's role was recast accordingly by De Leon. It was to educate the workers as to the nature of capitalist society, urge upon them the need to abolish the bourgeois state, and press for the creation of revolutionary trade unions as the vehicle through which to reconstruct the social system. Electoral campaigns were to be conducted by the party to win support of socialist perspectives at the ballot box. Once the necessary backing had been registered in this manner the basic social change was to be carried out; and if the capitalists tried to prevent fulfillment of the majority will expressed in the balloting, the trade unions were to halt production as a means of forcing ruling-class acceptance of the new system.

Somewhat comparable views were advocated by the main section of the Socialist Party's left wing. These were set forth primarily by Debs, who by now had come to think in terms of subordinating political activity to trade union action. He projected as the main task for socialists the building of revolutionary industrial unions through the IWW. From its inception the IWW's central objective was to be the overthrow of capitalism. The affiliated bodies were to be organized along lines reflecting the various categories of production and distribution within the national economy. In that way an essential structure was to be formed through which to create a cooperative commonwealth and build a socialist society. Then, when the unions were strong enough, industry was to be taken over by means of a general strike and a trade union state established.

Although giving precedence to trade union efforts along the foregoing lines, Debs continued to stress the need for independent working-class political action. Use of the SP as a propaganda medium for revolutionary unionism was only one aspect of what he had in mind. He attached much importance to continuation of party activity on the electoral terrain. Election of socialists to public office, he stressed, could weaken capitalist control of the state apparatus and make it harder for the ruling class to oppose revolutionary action through the trade unions.'

A minority view was presented within the SP left wing by William E. Trautmann, who was a representative of the party's Ohio section on the National Executive Committee and edited the brewery workers' union journal. Trautmann held that the new industrial union movement should adopt the principles of revolutionary syndicalism with the aim of setting up a workers' cooperative republic. His role as a syndicalist was overshadowed, though, by that of Vincent St. John, a militant with an outstanding record in the Western Federation of Miners. St. John soon became the chief organizer of an anarcho-syndicalist tendency in the IWW.

Classical anarcho-syndicalism, which tried to outflank Marxism from the left and in so doing revised some of its key tenets, had arisen somewhat earlier in France. The French section of the Second International had turned increasingly to reformist activity in the parliamentary sphere. This trend caused many socialist militants to leave its ranks and ally themselves with anarchist trade unionists who spurned parliamentary reformism. From there the former socialists went on to embrace anarchist rejection of all "politics" and opposition to continuation of the state in any way. Together with their new allies, they undertook to convert the trade unions into revolutionary instruments of the working class. The aim was to overthrow capitalism by direct action at the point of production, adapting the struggle to the methods and forms of the trade union movement. It was from this combining of anarchist concepts with emphasis on building revolutionary "syndicates," from the French word for trade unions, that the tendency derived its name.

French syndicalism, being essentially national in character, had no direct influence on the IWW during its formative period. By the time significant contact developed between the two movements syndicalism had evolved quite fully as an indigenous phenomenon in the United States.

It had been projected in rough form by Albert R. Parsons and August Spies as far back as the 1880s when they left the Socialist Labor Party to join the anarchists. In taking that step they had at the same time rejected the anarchist concept of substituting terrorist acts by individuals for collective action by the working class. There was need, Parsons and Spies had contended, to use the trade unions as a means of mobilizing the masses for direct action to overturn capitalism. They made an ill-fated attempt to apply that line during the 1886 battle for the eight-hour day that had culminated in their martyrdom.

Then, after the turn of the century, a more concrete syndicalist line was advanced by St. John and others. According to their outlook, all political activity was to be abandoned. Revolutionary unions were to be built with the object of abolishing capitalism by direct action on the economic field. Industrial strikes were to constitute the key mode of revolutionary struggle. This course of action was to reach a climax in a general strike to halt all industrial production, so as to paralyze the ruling class and clear the way for workers' control of the economy. After that the capitalist state was to be replaced by a republic of labor based on representation organized through the trade unions.

In assuming that a general strike would paralyze the ruling class, the syndicalists underestimated the repressive powers of the state. They failed to perceive that a workers' victory could be achieved only through revolutionary political struggle to wrest state power from the capitalists; that the new state then had to be organized as an instrument for defense of the revolutionary conquests. These errors caused them to lose sight of the interconnection between industrial struggles and independent labor political action. As a result they sought to steer the workers away from their most vital political task in the fight to overthrow capitalist rule—the building of a revolutionary vanguard party.

Although the left socialists and syndicalists had important differences, they held certain basic ideas in common. All were agreed that revolutionary unions should be the main vehicle for anticapitalist struggle; that the general strike should constitute the prime weapon; and that the reorganization of society should be carried out by the trade unions. This harmony in outlook also extended more or less to the question of the state power, except in Debs's case. De Leon shared the syndicalist illusion that massive economic action by the workers would automatically bring down the capitalist state. Debs, on the other hand, emphasized the need for a political fight to nullify the state's repressive powers.

The main difference between these radical tendencies centered on the issue of political action. Struggles at the trade union level should completely displace political activity, the syndicalists contended, and labor should organize no political party whatever. As against that concept, both socialist tendencies advocated the building of a revolutionary party. Its role should be to conduct electoral and parliamentary activity, they argued, parallel to trade union work. At the same time, though, the socialists gave the syndicalists an edge by conceding that party building should be subordinated to the creation of a revolutionary union movement. That concession led to a compromise in the policy statement adopted at the IWW's founding convention, an accommodation that merely confused the issue and settled nothing.

In approving the preamble to the IWW constitution a majority of the delegates agreed on the following declaration: "Between these two classes [workers and employers] a struggle must go on until all the toilers come together on the political, as well as the industrial field, and take and hold that which they produce by their labor through an economic organization of the working class, without affiliation with any political party."

The crucial passage in this declaration—"come together on the political, as well as the industrial field"—had the surface appearance of endorsing political action as perceived by the socialists. During the discussion preceding the vote, however, the syndicalists presented a contrary view. Participation in politics, they claimed, had nothing to do with political parties. The IWW's political action would take place through revolutionary strikes to gain political ends; hence the specific provision that it would proceed "without affiliation with any political party." As this interpretation of the preamble indicated, the syndicalists aimed to line up the IWW against any form of political organization of the workers; and in pushing that line thereafter, they were to profit from the betrayal of the right wing and the political bankruptcy of the centrist leaders in the Socialist Party.

During its first year the new movement concentrated on attempts to win the affiliation of AFL bodies, accompanying the effort with a propaganda campaign for industrial unionism. Gompers reacted with charges that the IWW was conducting a "dual union" raid on the AFL. His line, which fogged the issue of industrial versus craft organization, was backed by the SP right wing and most of the Hillquit tendency. Except for a few centrists, only the left wing mobilized party support for the industrial union cause. Debs led the effort through a tour of the industrial East; and many left-wing SP members quit the AFL, seeking to take their locals into the IWW with them.

These shifts in affiliation helped strengthen the new formation. But the withdrawal of militants from the AFL also put Gompers in a better position to exert firm control over the federation. Through organizational infighting he stemmed the secessionist trend, and the AFL was kept largely intact.

By this time the syndicalists and De Leonists were pressing within the IWW for an advance beyond "pure and simple" trade unionism. Their aim was to speed its development in a revolutionary direction. Toward that end St. John and De Leon organized a campaign against Charles O. Sherman, a metal workers' leader who had been elected president of the IWW in 1905. Sherman, a nonpolitical figure interested only in building industrial unions, was accused of misconduct in office. But the main reason for opposing him was his failure to advocate a revolutionary course, which was construed to mean that he should be removed from high position. This objective was attained by the St. John–De Leon forces at a convention held in 1906. A majority voted to abolish the office of president, thereby automatically ousting Sherman from his post.

After the vote was taken the official delegation from the Western Federation of Miners, which supported Sherman, walked out of the convention. Haywood then took the lead in trying to prevent the rift from developing into a complete break between the WFM and the IWW. But he was in an Idaho prison at the time, where he awaited trial on a murder charge framed up by the mine owners. His intervention under those difficult circumstances proved unsuccessful, and before long all relations between the two organizations were severed.

St. John and his supporters among the hard-rock miners stayed with the IWW in the split, as did Haywood after he beat the murder charge and regained his freedom in 1907. That left the once-militant Western Federation of Miners in the hands of conservative leaders who steered it away from a class-struggle course. Removal of a "pure and simple" trade unionist from office had both stripped the IWW of its biggest affiliate and dealt a blow to the rank and file of the miners' union.

This turn of events caused many left-wing SP members to withdraw from the IWW. Among them was Debs, whose changed attitude stemmed in part from awareness that a number of socialist militants had become so preoccupied with the primary role he assigned to revolutionary unions that they were downgrading party building. The rise of such a trend—in an atmosphere of syndicalist propaganda against political action—had been enough in itself to disturb him. Then came Sherman's ouster and the break with the Western Federation of Miners. At that point Debs, who opposed both moves, left the IWW; but he continued to back it against the Gompersites.

After striving for two years to build a viable movement along industrial lines, the Socialist Party's left wing faced a negative balance sheet. Exaggeration of the role that revolutionary unions can play had caused political confusion. In the name of revolutionary unionism the syndicalists and De Leonists had thrust the IWW onto a sectarian course. Efforts to outflank the Gompersites through creation of a new union structure had miscarried, and prospects for renewal of an internal AFL struggle against the craft union hierarchy had been dampened by the previous removal of party cadres

Above, center figure is William D. Haywood. Below, an IWW rally during the Lawrence textile strike.

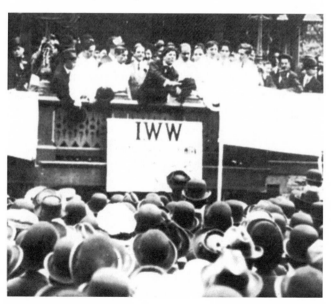

from that organization to help launch the IWW.

With the SP militants thus caught in a demoralizing bind, the opportunity was given for the Berger and Hillquit tendencies to launch a combined assault on the left wing. Their offensive began through criticisms leveled against the IWW. Facts were twisted to make the IWW appear a fomenter of class conflict, and advocate of revolutionary violence. The reformist and rightward-moving centrist tendencies then differentiated themselves from such alleged perspectives and united in calling for a peaceful transition from capitalism to socialism, stressing that it was to be achieved step by step through electoral and parliamentary activity. Their outlook was put forward, moreover, as though it accorded with the established party line.

Under cover of this propaganda barrage the right-wingers and centrists ganged up to initiate organizational reprisals against party members still active in the IWW. One of the first victims was Trautmann, who had been elected secretary-treasurer of the IWW and had espoused syndicalist views. He was expelled from the SP for "treasonable conduct."

Through such moves the reformists intended to give the party a "respectable" image. Once this was accomplished, they hoped it would become possible to win official AFL support of SP candidates for public office. To further enhance such a possibility they now abandoned their earlier pretense of "neutrality" concerning internal union disputes. Increasingly brazen support was given, instead, to the craft union, class-collaborationist line of the Gompersites.

Another goal in the drive for SP "respectability" was the widening of its influence in middle-class circles. Big capital's harsh exploitation of human and natural resources had continued to generate spontaneous waves of social protest. By 1906 this trend had given rise to a new upsurge of petty-bourgeois political movements, whose nomination of reform candidates in election campaigns had cut into the socialist vote. To counter this development right-wingers and centrists in the SP pressed for application of a line that would both attract middle-class support at the polls and facilitate recruitment of such elements into the party.

The revolutionary socialists warned against concentrating on efforts to win petty-bourgeois support. In general, they cautioned, political activists in that social layer were out to use the workers for their own ends; and if indiscriminately allowed to flood into the SP, they would programmatically disorient it. Socialists should, of course, cooperate in specific ways with those in the middle class who opposed the capitalists, especially in the case of working farmers. If ready to fight for socialism, such allies should be welcomed into the party. But it was imperative, the revolutionary militants added, that the SP remain an uncompromisingly working-class organization. Primary attention should be centered on supporting the workers in industrial struggles, advancing their political education, and drawing them into the party.

This clash over basic issues precipitated a factional struggle in which the left wing suffered from lack of competent guidance. Debs, the most outstanding of the revolutionary socialists, continued to refuse party leadership responsibilities commensurate with the workers' needs. His strategic political view of the road to socialism basically determined his attitude toward the party and its organizational character and norms. He saw no fundamental reason not to continue to foster the concept of an all-inclusive party, hoping that some way could be found to hold it together. This perspective led him to stand aloof from factional conflicts. If in disagreement with official party decisions, he set his own policies and counted on getting spontaneous backing in the ranks. For these reasons Debs refused to accept any post in the party or to attend its conventions.

Debs's political limits, which led to his failure to accept the necessary party leadership responsibility, gave the reformists a decided advantage. They were able to grab full control of the national party machinery and use it factionally in carrying out their policies. The SP was converted into little more than an electoral apparatus striving for votes on a reform program. Then, with the onset of a new economic crisis in 1907, the social unrest deepened. A big jump followed in socialist recruitment of petty-bourgeois members, many of whom were outright political opportunists. This inundation—together with the reformist line being followed—caused many revolutionary-minded workers to drop out of the party, and its social composition underwent substantial change.

At the Socialist Party's 1908 convention a majority of the delegates were petty bourgeois. They backed the Berger-Hillquit bloc in rejecting as "inexpedient" a left-wing proposal to support the industrial form of trade union organization. This move was accompanied by a decision restricting party membership to advocates of political action—as defined by the reformists. Berger then led an attempt to block nomination of Debs as the party's presidential candidate in the 1908 national elections. So great was Debs's prestige, though, that the convention overwhelmingly approved his nomination. Hanford, who had lined up with the centrists, was again named the vice-presidential choice.

During the election campaign right-wingers and centrists running on SP tickets at the state and city levels addressed themselves primarily to middle-class voters on the basis of their reformist line. Debs's supporters, in contrast, raised funds to provide him a campaign train called the "Red Special." Touring the country in this dramatic fashion, Debs presented a class-struggle program. He stressed labor issues, urged independent working-class political action through the Socialist Party, and underlined his support of revolutionary perspectives in the fight against capitalism.

In the balloting the SP's presidential slate received about 421,000 votes, a rise of only some 13,000 over the 1904 tally. This failure to register significant new gains at the polls was attributed by Berger and Hillquit to the "non-respectable" image given the party by the left wing, and they set out to purge the party entirely of those who opposed their reformist line.

Meanwhile, the relationship of forces had also been changing within the IWW. A general exodus of "pure and simple" trade unionists had resulted from the split with the Western Federation of Miners, and the departure of many Socialist Party members had followed. Even though a portion of the SP left wing led by Haywood had stayed with the IWW, alterations in the internal union situation had enabled the syndicalists to exert mounting influence over those who remained in the ranks. Then, with the unfolding of new events, their relative weight inside the organization had increased qualitatively.

In 1906 the IWW had opened a broad recruitment drive. Some progress ensued among workers neglected by the AFL, but this activity was suddenly cut short by the economic slump of 1907–8. At that point attention was turned to mobilization of the unemployed to fight for public relief. An especially big response came from the migratory workers in the West, who normally moved from one seasonal job to another as lumberjacks and harvest hands, in railroad construction, at whatever work they could find. Always badly underpaid, their plight rapidly became desperate when they were unemployed for an extended period. So they flocked into the IWW looking for a way to solve their problems, and as itinerants lacking residential qualifications needed to vote they had little interest in electoral activity. In the main these workers backed the syndicalist line of concentrating exclusively on direct economic action.

With this new support the St. John faction became the dominant force within the IWW, and it set out to block further attempts by De Leon to involve the ranks in political action through the Socialist Labor Party. An organizational maneuver was invoked for the purpose. De Leon's credentials as a delegate to the union's 1908 convention were challenged on technical grounds. A majority voted to deny him delegate status, and his followers immediately withdrew from the gathering.

De Leon then made the split definitive by drawing together such forces as he could to form a rival "IWW." This setup, which amounted to little more than a front for the SLP, was later reconstituted as the Workers' International Industrial Union. But it, too, failed to prosper, and any pretense of maintaining "socialist industrial unions" was eventually abandoned. The Socialist Labor Party itself degenerated into an utterly sterile sect. It dismissed mass efforts to win economic and social reforms as reactionary, contending that nothing other than explicit rejection of the capitalist system had meaning. Having lost all touch with the dynamics of class struggle, the SLP became a dogmatic observer scolding the workers from the sidelines.

A different situation evolved in what remained of the actual IWW. After the De Leonists left the 1908 convention, a narrow majority opted for elimination of all reference to political action from the general statement of policy. St. John was then elected general secretary, and under his guidance the syndicalist militants set out to convert the union into a mass revolutionary movement.

They functioned as a loosely coordinated vanguard that lacked concrete organizational form. Dangers were thereby heightened of individual militants, left too much on their own, losing revolutionary perspective through excessive adaptation in trade union activity to the limited class consciousness that prevailed in the IWW's ranks. These militants were further handicapped by a basic line that prevented them from combining economic and political actions in a manner that could raise the workers' consciousness transitionally to higher planes; and to make a bad matter worse, they were rendered incapable of combating the reformists politically.

While creating the foregoing difficulties, the syndicalist policies also generated ultraleftism. Efforts were made to combine struggles for limited economic gains with the parallel development of a forced march toward general acceptance of a revolutionary outlook among the workers. Syndicalist agitators conducted themselves as though the very fact of a strike implied rejection of the capitalist system by the union ranks. They sought to promote an uninterrupted fight with the boss class and were against signing union contracts with employers. Each work stoppage was viewed by them as a rehearsal for an ultimate general strike through which the workers were to seize power.

Objective reality made it necessary, though, to accept some form of compromise with the employers in settling a given strike. If this resulted in a victory for the workers, membership gains were registered by the union. But the IWW organizers failed to follow through with day-to-day enforcement of the strike settlement and with continued guidance of the workers in maintaining a stable organization. As a result the membership tended to dwindle after a time and in case after case became reduced to little more than the militants involved.

An irreconcilable contradiction thus resulted from application of the syndicalist line. The IWW remained too amorphous, in terms of the varying levels of class consciousness within its ranks, to play a vanguard role; and the revolutionary aims set by the leadership were too advanced for it to develop fully as a mass organization. As subsequent events were to demonstrate, it could serve neither as a substitute for a revolutionary party nor as an instrument for general mobilization of the workers at the trade union level.

By the end of 1908 an economic recovery was again under way in the country, and the syndicalist-led union was able to resume its organizing campaign. Much of the effort centered in the industrial East, with big steel quickly becoming a major target. In mid-1909 some 5,000 unorganized workers, both skilled and unskilled, engaged in a spontaneous walkout at a U.S. Steel subsidiary in McKees Rocks, Pennsylvania. When the company launched violent assaults on their picket lines, they fought back with grim determination. Then, at the strikers' invitation, the IWW signed them up as members. After that it backed them in mass picketing and protest demonstrations, a method of struggle that symbolized the union's strike techniques. In the end the steel employees won the battle, gaining company acceptance of almost all their demands.

This triumph for industrial unionism came at a time when the left wing of the Socialist Party found it difficult to conduct trade union work. Four years earlier many socialist militants had left the AFL to join the IWW. Although some of them had remained members of the federation, largely because of their trades, they were not very active in it since their interest focused mainly on the new union movement. These developments had given right-wing and centrist

SP members greater weight in the AFL, relative to that of the depleted left-wing forces. They had used this advantage to undermine the party's former class-struggle course in the craft unions. A shift had been made, one step after another, toward adaptation to Gompers's class-collaborationist policies. Such limited criticism as the reformists still directed at the federation president centered on his objections to official union support of socialist candidates for public office.

New handicaps were thereby imposed on the SP left wing when it sought to resume activity in the AFL after the rift with the IWW developed in 1906. Conservative SP members, who were now well entrenched in the craft unions, abetted the Gompers regime in resisting opposition from the left. This stab in the back from within their own party made it harder than ever for the socialist militants to advance industrial-union and class-struggle perspectives in the AFL; and the resulting sense of frustration—together with the strike victory at McKees Rocks—brought a revival of their interest in the IWW.

Matters were no better in the Socialist Party itself for workers who sought to promote revolutionary aims. Middle-class elements were now dominant in the party and its leadership, as were petty-bourgeois social concepts. The centrists were solidly aligned with the right wing on a program that envisaged the gradual evolution of capitalism into socialism through a series of reforms, and this line was put forward officially by the party in its electoral activity.

Campaigning on essentially local issues with little or no reference to socialist perspectives, the reformists made gains in the 1910 state and city elections. The main advance took place in Milwaukee, where SP candidates won several executive posts in the municipal government and got control of the city council. At the same time Victor Berger was elected to the U.S. Congress as a representative from Wisconsin. Additional successes were achieved the following year in another round of campaigns at the city level, and these developments emboldened the Berger-Hillquit gang to become more aggressive than ever in their drive to give the party an acceptable image among middle-class voters desiring improvement of their lot under capitalism.

To serve that end the attack on left-wing party members was further intensified. Their pro-IWW attitude was seized upon to denounce them as advocates of "revolutionary violence." They were accused of abandoning socialism on the premise that they rejected the "evolutionary process." Expulsions carried out on one or another pretext became increasingly common as the reformists undertook to drive the revolutionists from the party. This offensive precipitated a sharp internal conflict, and it became so bitter that in some instances dual state and local organizations were maintained by the contending factions.

The attempt to build an all-inclusive formation of revolutionists and reformists was coming to an end. Contradictions between their respective political outlooks, which had doomed the endeavor from the start, were now fully operative. One side or the other had to take decisive control of the party, and the odds favored the reformists, who had flooded it with petty-bourgeois elements. Modification of the membership composition in that manner was not in itself, however, the basic cause of the changed internal relationship of forces. More than anything else, the revolutionists were victims of their own ill-chosen policies.

They had subordinated programmatic clarity to the movement's rapid numerical growth. Reformists of every variety had been accepted into the ranks with freedom to promote whatever policies they favored. The proletarian left wing had failed to use its earlier majority to curb the wheeling and dealing that followed on the part of the reformist minority and as a consequence the party had become permeated with alien class influences.

In trade union activity the revolutionary socialists had tried to overleap the necessary transitional stages in advancing class consciousness among the workers as a mass. The fight for industrial unionism had been diverted from the realistic objective of better equipping the workers to force concessions from the employers and to learn political lessons in the process. It had been transformed, instead, into a sectarian attempt to immediately revolutionize the broad labor movement. The contemplated revolutionary unions had been assigned the main role in the anticapitalist struggle, with independent working-class political action relegated to second place; and that perspective made it hard for socialist militants to perceive the vital need for a revolutionary vanguard party.

These policies had put the SP left wing in sad straits. Within the party it was rapidly losing ground to the reformists. At the same time its adherents were becoming increasingly susceptible to the antipolitical line of the syndicalists who controlled the IWW, and the latter trend was now given further impetus by leading socialist militants.

Early in 1911 a pamphlet entitled *Industrial Socialism* was published under the joint authorship of Bill Haywood and another SP left-winger, Frank Bohn of Michigan. It presented the following basic line: Capitalist power rested on control of industry. The fight to break that control had to be waged in the workshops, with the general strike as the major weapon. To be effective, economic organization of the workers had to take place through industrial unions that would both unite them in their struggles against the capitalists and form the framework of the future socialist society. The Socialist Party's most important task was to aid in the organization of industrial unions. Its political functions had to be treated as secondary, as supportive of direct economic action in the sense that the winning of public office by socialists could obstruct capitalist use of the government against the workers.

Debs supported Haywood and Bohn on some points and differed with them on others. The party's immediate task was to help build industrial unions, he agreed, and revolutionary unions were essential to the overthrow of capitalism. His remarks on the latter subject reflected deepening thought, however, about the role of the state.

He no longer adhered to his earlier position (still advanced by Haywood and Bohn) that the role of socialist political action was mainly to hamper capitalist use of the government against revolutionary unions. Debs now called for election of an SP government to establish a socialist order, with the unions helping to force capitalist submission to the majority will expressed in the balloting. The proletariat, he was coming to understand, had to act politically to establish its own government and use that new state power to abolish capitalism.

The pro-syndicalist trend in the SP left wing had become too strong, though, for Debs's position to prevail. Most of the socialist militants supported the Haywood-Bohn line; and looking now mainly to Haywood for leadership, they managed late in 1911 to elect him to the party's National Executive Committee over vigorous opposition from the reformists.

Shortly thereafter, in January 1912, the IWW struck the textile mills at Lawrence, Massachusetts. The mill owners retaliated by having the strike leaders arrested, and Haywood stepped forward to fill the gap. With his help the workers defended their cause through various kinds of mass action. They also got assistance from foreign-language branches established somewhat earlier by the IWW, which played a part in drawing immigrant proletarians into the battle on the union's side. In doing so the IWW units were backed by language federations of foreign-born that had recently become affiliated to the Socialist Party. As mass support of the strike developed along increasingly broad lines, the reformists in the SP found it tactically advisable to lend a hand despite their hostility toward the IWW. All in all, the pressures on the employers became so great that they had to capitulate, and in March 1912 the conflict ended with a substantial union victory.

This accomplishment had the dual effect of drawing many left-wing socialists closer to the syndicalists and heightening the reformists' determination to drive these militants out of the Socialist Party. A new phase of internal party conflict ensued. It opened at an SP convention held two months later, where the Berger-Hillquit bloc won adoption of an amendment to the organization's constitution that disqualified from membership all who rejected their concept of "evolutionary" social change within the framework of bourgeois "law and order."

It read: "Any member of the party who opposes political action or advocates crime, sabotage, or other methods of violence as a weapon of the working class to aid in its emancipation, shall be expelled from membership in the party." Political action was officially defined as "participation in elections for public office and practical legislative and administrative work along the lines of the Socialist Party platform."

Berger and Hillquit also tried to prevent the naming of Debs as the SP's presidential candidate in the 1912 elections, but the convention nominated him over their objections. They did manage, though, to have a Milwaukee right-winger, Emil Seidel, chosen as the vice-presidential nominee.

During the campaign that followed Debs spoke out against the notion that capitalism could be reformed into socialism. He stressed the need for the workers to develop revolutionary perspectives as a class and to solidarize themselves with the working farmers, who were also victims of capitalist exploitation. This time Debs received about 900,000 votes, more than double his support at the polls in 1908. Of equal significance, party recruitment took a big leap and the SP membership rose to a record high of around 150,000.[*]

Party candidates who ran for various public offices on a reform program fared poorly in the balloting; so poorly, in fact, that Berger lost his congressional seat. This setback was interpreted by the reformists as decisive proof that left-wing "impossibilists" were scaring off potential middle-class votes for their candidates, and they cooked up a scheme to carry out the purge for which a basis had been laid in the constitutional amendment adopted at the recent convention.

Haywood was singled out as the initial target. He was accused of opposing "political action" and advocating "direct action and sabotage" in speeches made at public meetings. On those grounds Berger and Hillquit engineered his removal from the party's National Ex-

---

[*] Two articles by Lenin analyzing the results of the 1912 elections are contained in the appendix, pages 248–50 and 251–52.

ecutive Committee by a vote of about two to one in a membership referendum. This provocation had the effect they wanted. Haywood broke with the Socialist Party and became fully converted to syndicalism. Large numbers of workers in the left-wing emulated his example, and a good many others showed their disapproval of the reformists' policies and tactics by dropping out of the party.

In less than a year these defections reduced the SP membership to little more than half the 1912 figure. Since those who left the party were mostly workers, it now became overwhelmingly petty bourgeois in composition; and the revolutionary socialist members—polarized around Debs—had to function as a weak minority trapped in a stifling internal atmosphere.

While the reformists were splitting the SP, the syndicalist-led IWW expanded its organization drive among the industrial workers. Major strikes followed during 1913 in the auto, rubber, and silk industries. The workers, who had deep-seated grievances about the conditions of their employment, fought militantly. But they were unable to prevail against vicious strikebreaking tactics by the capitalists and disruption of labor solidarity on the part of AFL craft unions. In the end all the strikes were defeated.

This setback for the IWW was accompanied by yet another one, which had been largely self-inflicted. Applying syndicalist concepts, it failed to follow through after earlier strike victories with the consolidation of stable unions geared to serve the workers' day-to-day interests. In the case of the McKees Rocks local, for instance, the default had caused the disintegration of a once-viable formation, and an opportunity had been lost to use that base for a broader campaign in steel. By the end of 1913 a similar fate was befalling the strong textile union that emerged from the Lawrence strike. The IWW was thus left—after the defeats in auto, rubber, and silk—without any real foothold in the industrial East. Its chances of making a fresh start were further impaired, moreover, by an economic depression that was just setting in.

Now almost entirely frozen out of basic industry, the IWW shifted its main attention to organization of migratory workers who ranged the country from the Mississippi Valley to the West Coast. New successes were soon attained among itinerants working as harvest hands, lumber jacks, saw mill employees, etc. Then, after a time, the scope of organizational activity was broadened. This step led during 1916 to involvement in a strike of iron miners on the Mesabi Range in Minnesota, which saw a repetition of what had happened three years earlier in the East. Savage repressive measures were used by the ruling class to break the strike. The union ceased to be a factor on the Mesabi Range, and it remained incapable of making significant headway among industrial workers elsewhere.

Once again activity became focused primarily on organization of migrants. It was difficult to build a stable membership among these workers, however, since many of them entered and left the union ranks periodically according to the rhythms of their seasonal employment at one or another job. As this situation demonstrated, the IWW's incorrect policies had brought it to an impasse in which numerical growth and expanding influence commensurate with its aspirations had become impossible on a national scale.

The AFL, meantime, had developed as far the stronger of the two rival movements. This advantage occurred primarily from the recognition accorded to craft unions by the employers, who sought to encourage the federation in subordinating the needs of the proletarian masses to the special interests of the skilled trades. Through such means—together with the IWW's failure in basic industry—the boss class had got what it wanted. The great bulk of the industrial workers remained unorganized and completely at the mercy of the capitalist exploiters.

Since ascending capitalism was able to grant some concessions to the skilled crafts, the AFL officialdom had a material basis on which to maintain stable unions. Prospects of making gains a step at a time, along with the factor of relative job security, inculcated notions in the ranks that labor's needs could be taken care of and its problems solved gradually under the existing social order. Acceptance of such an outlook served, in turn, to promote acquiescence in the federation's class-collaborationist policies. The top hierarchy was thereby enabled to hold economic demands down to a level that minimized the provoking of sharp employer resistance, and it could manifest appreciation of economic favors the bosses were willing to concede by keeping the organization tied to capitalist politics.

Taking no chances about the enforcement of those policies, the Gompers regime had now firmly established itself as a ruling bureaucracy in the AFL. Basic decisions were made independently of control by the membership, and the top officials remained constantly on guard against threats to their usurped authority. Dissent in the ranks on policy matters was harshly attacked, as was any effort to block the usurpers' self-perpetuation in union office, with high salaries and generous expense accounts.

Consolidation of bureaucratic rule over the AFL had been preceded by a brief interlude of reformist opposition to the Gompers regime. That turn of events occurred during 1912 when the Socialist Party experienced a big upsurge in recruitment. Taking advantage of the party's new-found strength, the Berger-Hillquit bloc undertook a direct challenge to Gompers himself in an effort to promote official labor support of their candidates for public office. Max Hayes, a centrist moving to the right, was nominated for the presidency of the federation at its convention that year. But Gompers beat him by a vote of more than two to one and maintained a firm hold on the top union post.

After that the SP majority surrendered supinely to the craft union hierarchy. No further efforts were made to get official federation backing of socialist activity on the electoral plane, or to press the issue of socialism at national AFL conventions. The craft form of organization was supported publicly in the guise of repudiating industrial unionism on the grounds that its adoption by the IWW had proved ineffective. Concentration of trade union attention on the interests of the skilled trades was thereby endorsed in callous disregard of the unskilled and semiskilled workers' pressing needs. The imposition of bureaucratic control over the craft unions was likewise abetted in violation of the membership's democratic right to set policy.

Then, in 1916, Debs was bypassed in choosing the SP's presidential candidate. A right-winger, Allan Benson, got the nomination. The results far from met the expectations voiced that a reformist candidate would do better than a revolutionist. Benson received some 585,000 votes, which represented a steep decline from the ballots cast for Debs four years earlier.

By this time the party had completed its evolution from a revolutionary into an irredeemably reformist formation. The SP had become an integral part of the right-wing tendency in the Second International, which had thrust a self-defeating line upon the ranks everywhere.

With U.S. entry into the First World War impending, efforts to organize labor's main forces in basic industry had not succeeded. The IWW, which had tried to parlay the industrial form of organization into speedy establishment of revolutionary unions, was on the wane; and the AFL, representing a majority of organized workers, had become a bureaucrat-ridden, class-collaborationist setup tied to narrow craft union perspectives. Politically, no way had been found to help the great mass of workers out of entrapment in the capitalist two-party system. The Socialist Labor Party had fallen into sectarian abstention from the class struggle. Social Democrats in control of the Socialist Party had linked up with the AFL bureaucracy in counterposing reform to revolution. A big segment of the revolutionary vanguard had strayed onto the dead-end road of syndicalism, and those militants who came the closest to an understanding of revolutionary socialism were an isolated minority in the degenerated SP.

In sum, the labor movement was disoriented politically and fractured organizationally at a time when the U.S. ruling class was about to plunge the nation into the imperialist slaughter.

# 5

# *Supreme Test of War*

Toward the end of the nineteenth century, as the international capitalist system entered its imperialist stage, the working class was thrust into an acute crisis of leadership. The new economic situation resulted from the accelerated growth of monopoly and the domination of finance capital in the countries that had become most industrially advanced. While there were variations in the rate at which these characteristics were gaining ascendency, countries like Great Britain, France, Germany, Japan, and the United States shared these basic traits in common.

Within all the most advanced capitalist countries, small-scale competition was being supplanted by monopoly domination of the national economy. As concentrations of industrial capital grew larger, the robber barons behind the giant corporations and trusts hatched conspiracies to rig the economy for their private gain. Markets were divided among them. They limited production so as to create phony shortages, gouge consumers with exorbitant prices, and thus reap profit bonanzas. Alongside that trend, concentrations of money capital also increased, giving rise to the growth of monopoly in the banking sphere. The two forms of monopoly—in industry and banking—then began to merge into what is known as finance capital, owned by a small number of families who set out to manipulate the economic life of the nation.

They still had a problem, though, resulting from an unalterable aspect of the capitalist system. The workers got less pay in return for their labor power than the value it produced, and most of the surplus value in the products they turned out was expropriated as profits by the bourgeoisie in order to accumulate more capital. This inequity created a gap between the productive capacity of capitalist industry and the ability of the underpaid workers to absorb their rightful share of the potential output. With the domestic market thus increasingly restricted, the monopolists looked for a remedy that would serve their own narrow, greedy purposes. They aggressively sought new markets abroad for their goods in order to realize the highest profit returns on capital invested in industry.

A related situation arose concerning the mounting accumulations of money capital. Surpluses developed that could not be invested domestically with assurance of the monopoly profits the owners were accustomed to. So the finance capitalists looked elsewhere in the world for new fields of investment, and the export of capital increasingly became one of imperialism's distinctive features.

As production soared, the imperialist rulers' needs for raw materials increased. Thus controlling sources of raw materials worldwide, driving down the value of the labor power that produced them, and dividing the world among themselves as they divided markets at home, became permanent features of imperialism.

To attain these desired ends the imperialists used the capitalist governments of their respective countries to carve out spheres of influence in foreign lands for the purpose of converting them into colonies, or at least semicolonies. The job was done through diplomatic trickery and outright military force. Various religious groups were called upon to provide colonizing forces and ideological justification. Racism was promoted to new levels of virulence, at home and abroad, in order to help bolster imperialist aims. Domination was established over peoples in other lands where industrial development had often scarcely begun. The victims were put upon in countless ways, ranging from the plundering of natural resources to superexploitation of native labor power for the extortion of surplus value in order to accumulate still greater masses of capital.

Concession after concession was wrested from the enslaved countries. They were compelled to yield up raw material on imperialist-dictated terms. Agricultural production was disrupted, often leading to dependence on a single crop. Foreign entrepreneurs moved in on the railroad and mining industries, the one-crop agricultural economies often prevalent in such countries, and the building of industrial enterprises operated for private profit. The native workers were charged robber prices for goods shipped from imperialist nations or produced locally, which had to be met out of starvation wages. Similarly, the peasants were undercompensated for their agricultural products and overcharged for goods they purchased. The economies were warped to serve the needs of the foreign financiers and the door was closed to the kind of capitalist-led economic growth that had marked the industrial revolution and its aftermath in the metropolises.

While plundering the oppressed and exploited peoples in manifold ways, the imperialists gave scant heed to their human needs. The norm was miserable housing, little health care, and virtually no educational opportunities. Meager funds for social services in any form were provided only in the hope of keeping the super-exploited peoples from rebelling.

To maintain control under those harsh conditions, the imperialists relied on the collusion of the native bourgeoisie and petty bourgeoisie to the fullest extent possible. Their aim was to use class privilege as a buffer against potential rebellion on the part of the workers, lower peasantry, and impoverished artisans and independent producers. Whatever the specific form of governmental rule established in keeping with that approach, the object was always to impose the authority of the given set of exploiters. Open dictatorships were the norm. When necessary that authority was backed up by imperialist troops, often stationed at local military bases ceded in perpetuity to the foreign capitalist powers.

While the majority of peoples of the earth were thus being forced into imperialist bondage, the revisionists in the Second International still persisted in the illusion that capitalism could be reformed. In pursuing that goal they clung to the notion that "pure" democracy could be achieved; that advances could be made step by step along those lines not only to solve the workers' problems in the industrially advanced countries, but also to rectify imperialist injustices against peoples abroad. All this was to be accomplished, moreover, through utilization of the democratic capitalist state. In their view this state was an autonomous social instrument standing above the class struggle, and hence capable of being reformed to serve socialist rather than capitalist objectives.

They failed to perceive the essential character of the state as a tool of ruling-class oppression. The state apparatus in the industrially advanced countries was firmly in the hands of the capitalists, who were not about to let themselves be reformed out of that control. While bourgeois-democratic methods of rule generally prevailed in those countries, in no case was there any semblance of abstract democracy capable of being "purified." Each regime upheld private property in the means of production and distribution. Its overriding function was to advance capitalist interests, including the implementation of imperialist aims.

Despite this reality, the revisionists extolled reform of the capitalist state through bourgeois-democratic institutions—especially parliament—as the road to socialism. This caused them, in turn, to become more and more deeply mired in collaboration with the capitalist rulers. At the industrial level they helped limit organized labor to a quest for economic reforms under the existing system, abhorring the perspective of charting a class-struggle course to convert the trade unions into revolutionary instruments of the working class. Social change had to be initiated in the parliamentary sphere, they held, through a gradual process beginning within the framework of the capitalist political structure. The full implications of the latter view were graphically demonstrated in Europe, where the revisionists cooperated increasingly with bourgeois parties considered democratic. If in the meantime they expressed verbal opposition to imperialist depredations, it had no real meaning; for their class collaborationism in practice gave the ruling class adequate freedom of action to deepen oppression of the colonial peoples.

As against the revisionist course, revolutionists in the Second International reaffirmed the concepts set forth by Marx and Engels in the *Communist Manifesto*. Capitalism was pushing humanity toward a social catastrophe, they warned. To defend the workers and colonial victims against impending disaster, it was imperative to press for class-struggle action on all fronts. The fight against capitalist exploitation at home and imperialist expansion abroad had to be carried through to a definitive end; that is, capitalism had to be overthrown everywhere by revolutionary means and replaced by socialism on a world scale.

The Marxist line prevailed in the resolutions adopted at congresses of the Second International held during the early years of the twentieth century. To a growing extent, though, these strategic guidelines received backing that was more formal than real. In growing sections of the leadership a gap had developed between the word and the deed. And this contradiction within the movement steadily became more pronounced under the impact of events, especially on the heels of a new development in Russia.

The Russo-Japanese War broke out during 1904 in a dispute over imperialist control of Korea and Manchuria. Russia's armed forces suffered a series of defeats at the hands of the Japanese, and that precipitated a popular uprising against the tsarist government. It was the first major revolutionary outbreak in Europe since the Paris Commune of 1871. The uprising started early in 1905 in St. Petersburg (now Leningrad). The proletariat rapidly asserted its leadership. The immediate aim was to replace tsarist absolutism with a democratic republic. The peasant masses, along with sections of the armed forces, were drawn into the struggle for that objective and the land they hungered for. The revolutionary upsurge quickly became nationwide in scope. Spontaneous workers' councils, called *soviets*, became the main broad form of organization of the class struggle.

At the outset the Social Democratic cadres in Russia were rather small. Within a short time, however, their forces grew as they led the workers in applying proletarian methods of struggle. This demonstration of revolutionary vitality among the Russian Social Democrats, together with the impact of the mass uprising itself, inspired the ranks of the Second International everywhere. The revolutionary wing of the movement gained new followers, some of the centrists were pulled to the left, and the revisionists were dealt a setback.

At the end of 1905, the revolution was brought to a climax with the launching of an armed insurrection in Moscow. All the forces of reaction were rapidly mobilized against the Moscow rebels. The insurrection was suppressed before it could spread elsewhere; punitive measures followed against leading militants throughout the land; and the revolution was defeated.

As had occurred in the aftermath of the Paris Commune, the bourgeoisie of all Europe was thoroughly frightened by the revolutionary upsurge in Russia—especially by its culmination in an attempted insurrection spearheaded by the proletariat. In those circumstances its defeat gave reactionary trends new impetus on a continent-wide scale, while revolutionaries in the countries involved were forced to swim against the stream. This enabled revisionists in the European sections of the Second International to become more aggressive. They intensified their political collusion with bourgeois and petty-bourgeois democrats. Alien class pressures were thereby increased inside the socialist movement, with the result that the centrists were impelled more and more to the right.

To a greater degree than ever the International was breaking down into rival formations of revolutionists and revisionists whose contradictory programs made cohabitation in a single organization increasingly difficult. But that fact remained clouded over by the centrists' trick of voting for formal revolutionary declarations and then going right ahead and supporting the revisionists in most of their reformist practices. Tactics of that kind also served to obscure another reality. The revisionists were injecting a narrow spirit of imperialist nationalism into the world movement that gravely impaired its capacity to act in keeping with revolutionary internationalist principles.

A few years earlier the United States monopolists had entered the imperialist competition. They made the first big push by maneuvering the country into war against Spain in 1898, through which they aimed to grab control over several of its colonies. The U.S. imperialists emerged victorious and displaced the Spanish ruling class as the exploiters of Cuba, Puerto Rico, and the Virgin Islands in the Caribbean, and Guam and the Philippines in the Pacific as they expanded further toward Asia.

This act of aggression was denounced by Eugene V. Debs, speaking for the Social Democracy of America, which had recently been organized. The U.S. monopolists, he said in substance, were using armed force to open new markets for products made by half-paid labor in this country, and they were doing so at the expense of oppressed peoples abroad. Besides that, the conflict between the two imperialist powers violated the basic interests of both the U.S. and Spanish workers, who had identical class needs. The only just war for the working class was one to wipe out capitalism, which had become the common enemy of the exploited and downtrodden everywhere, Debs declared.

The socialist movement was unable, however, to arrive at a clear understanding of imperialism's full implications for the working class in the U.S. or internationally. This shortcoming was manifested during the campaign around the Debs-Harriman ticket in the presidential elections of 1900 and again in the line put forward within the Socialist Party after it was launched the following year. According to the views expressed, imperialism was not an urgent problem facing Socialists. It was a matter of concern primarily to small capitalists and the petty bourgeoisie who felt threatened by the monopolists' growing power, and the workers had no cause to side with those elements because they—like the monopolists—stood for preservation of the existing system. Hence, the real issue before the labor vanguard was not imperialism; it was socialism versus capitalism.

Further confusion about the essential character of the imperialist stage of capitalism and the new strategic tasks this imposed on Socialists arose during the ensuing years as the reformists became increasingly dominant within the Socialist Party. Their outlook on this subject was essentially the following: Central attention had to be concentrated on steps to gradually transform the existing order into a socialist society, and the change had to be brought about through legislative action. As progress was made in the parliamentary sphere, the monopolists' use of the state to carry out an imperialist foreign policy could in time be halted. But to accomplish the desired end the party had to focus its efforts on winning public office, and that need took precedence over everything else.

Before long, though, the attempt to put aside immediate problems caused by imperialism was frustrated.

In 1910 an uprising began in Mexico against the dictatorship of Porfirio Díaz, who had long ruled the country in the service of native landed interests and foreign imperialists. The revolutionary masses, whose most advanced leader was Emiliano Zapata, fought for land and for bourgeois-democratic reforms intended to improve their conditions of life and to give them a greater say in policy decisions. Frightened by the massive revolt at their border, the United States monopolists with large investments in Mexico urged the U.S. government to intervene militarily on their behalf. In doing so they had two central motives: protection of their property holdings; and outflanking rival British imperialists in a contest for control over Mexican affairs.

Thus confronted with a new war danger, the Socialist Party reacted through its National Executive Committee. That body issued a protest against U.S. intervention in Mexico. But when no immediate steps towards military action were taken—the U.S. monopolists having temporarily confined themselves to behind-the-scenes maneuvers—attention to the Mexican situation declined within the

SP. This complacent attitude, which reflected indifference toward the imperialist menace in general, seriously endangered the party, since a threat of war on an unprecedented scale was rapidly developing.

By now virtually the entire world had been partitioned into territories controlled by the rival imperialist powers. Little or no room was available for these predators to further expand their spheres of exploitation without coming into violent collision with one another. Yet the continued grabbing of new markets, sources of raw material, and fields of investment remained vital to all the monopolists and their drive to accumulate more and more capital. So they prepared to step up moves to muscle in on each other's territories. Large-scale militarization programs were launched by the European powers in preparation for a showdown to effect a redivision of the imperialist spoils.

Then, on August 4, 1914, open warfare began. At the outset England, France, and Russia lined up on one side, with Germany and Austria on the other. Thereafter the armed conflict gradually expanded on a global scale.

All organizations and tendencies in the world labor movement were now put to the supreme test of imperialist war. The European reformists adhering to the Second International responded by deepening their opportunism in the most criminal fashion. Country by country, with the support, in practice, of most centrists, they capitulated to their own capitalist class on a chauvinist basis. In each case the reformists called for "defense of the fatherland" and voted in parliament for military appropriations. At the same time they helped the bourgeoisie regiment the workers for war by urging abandonment of strikes, demonstrations, and other forms of the class struggle in the name of "national unity." This course demonstrated beyond debate that reformism had led to outright betrayal not only of the toilers in the embattled nations, but also of the colonial peoples victimized by imperialism.

Among the European masses there had long been widespread acceptance of reformist assurances that capitalism could slowly be transformed into socialism in an atmosphere of lasting peace. All of a sudden, however, everything was turned upside down. The reformist misleaders of the largest and most powerful workers' parties in the world capitulated to the imperialist warmakers without a struggle. That switch ruptured international labor solidarity; threw the workers into a state of political confusion; and facilitated their being drafted into military service to fight others of their own class for the sole benefit of "their own" capitalists. Thus caught helplessly in a murderous trap, millions of workers died before the bloodletting ended.

The reformist betrayal also took revolutionists in the Second International by surprise, causing many to flounder politically for a time. Only the clearest-thinking, most resolute of these cadres were able to step forward with a concrete antiwar line. The firmest of the latter were the Russian Bolsheviks, guided by V.I. Lenin from his place of exile in Switzerland. Others who differentiated themselves from the reformist capitulators and their centrist apologists included Leon Trotsky, a central leader of the 1905 Russian revolution who was living in France as an exile; a group of Social Democrats around Rosa Luxemburg and Karl Liebknecht in Germany; a wing of the Italian Socialist Party; and a scattering of small groups of militants elsewhere in Europe.

Denouncing the social reformists for their "defense of the fatherland," the revolutionists branded the war an interimperialist conflict. The workers' main enemy, they declared, was the bourgeoisie in their own respective countries. The only way to fight to end the war was to advance a course of action aimed at overthrowing bourgeois rule. For that purpose a genuine Marxist party had to be created in each of the warring nations. Its aim had to be revival of the revolutionary proletarian struggle at home and support of such struggles conducted by workers in other countries and the oppressed masses in the colonies.

It was necessary to recognize, the Marxists asserted, that reformist treachery had destroyed the Second International as a trustworthy leadership. The world socialist movement had to be reconstructed as a genuinely revolutionary formation. It had to reassert the common need of all workers and colonial peoples to liberate themselves from the horrors of imperialist war by abolishing capitalist oppression and exploitation.

In striving toward those ends the revolutionists faced considerable complications created by centrists within the socialist movement. Centrism's most influential exponent was Karl Kautsky, a central leader of the German Social Democracy. After Frederick Engels died in 1895 Kautsky had come to be regarded as foremost among Marxist theoreticians. Although more and more adapting to reformist practice, he had sought to justify this course from a revolutionary viewpoint. The latter factor had led those who opposed reformism to assume that he would make the necessary corrections when events disproved his theories. But with the outbreak of hostilities Kautsky and his ilk gave de facto support to their own national bourgeoisies, seeking to camouflage their renegacy and differentiate themselves from the most open revisionists by linking themselves to bourgeois and petty-bourgeois pacifist currents.

Bourgeois pacifism stemmed from tactical disagreements over foreign policy within the ruling class. While the monopolists in the warring nations generally favored military action to advance their aims, other sections of the bourgeoisie were in some instances opposed to such a course. Believing that continued peace would best serve their interests in the given circumstances, they wanted amicable relations among the imperialist powers. In opposition to the militarists, they advocated conciliation and arbitration to settle the international conflict.

Petty-bourgeois pacifists latched onto the line taken by their bourgeois counterparts, but their motives went beyond tactical differences with the monopolists. Perceiving no stake for their class in an aggressive foreign policy, this category of the petty bourgeoisie wanted the war brought to an end forthwith. After that, they naively hoped, capitalism could be reformed so as to bring lasting peace in international relations.

Adapting to the above currents, the centrists in the Second International followed a course defined by the revolutionists as "social pacifism"—that is, socialist in professed outlook and bourgeois pacifist in actual practice. Their line was distinctive only in the sense that a nuance was appended to petty-bourgeois notions about reforming capitalism: they persisted in claiming that socialism could be achieved by gradually transforming the outlived system which had given birth to imperialism. The social pacifists contended that the socialist movement was not strong enough to chart an independent working-class course of struggle to end the war. Socialists had to promote a multi-class alliance based on a petty-bourgeois program of mobilizing all those who wanted to end the fighting; all who were ready to demand peace without new annexations of territory, universal disarmament, and democratic control over foreign policy.

Many socialist militants were duped by the Kautskyist line. After the reformists capitulated to their respective bourgeoisies on one or the other side of the battle lines, these militants had become disoriented politically. They found it hard to develop united opposition to the war or see the road to class-struggle action against it, so support to a petty-bourgeois peace campaign seemed a useful and realistic course of action.

Addressing themselves to this problem, leading revolutionaries pointed out that the perspective of uniting socialist militants around the peace slogan could lead to the desired goal only under certain conditions. It had to be viewed as the first organized step in protest against the reformist betrayal of the workers in the war, and the demand for peace had to be advanced in a way that would help the masses perceive the responsibility of their own imperialist rulers for perpetuating the slaughter, and recognize the unbridgeable distinction between socialism and capitalism. Otherwise the antiwar militants would be adapting to reformism and class collaborationism, thereby playing into the hands of the centrists, a policy bound to maintain the imperialist warmakers in the saddle.

On the matter of calling for peace without new annexations of territory, the revolutionary leaders advised, the right of self-determination should be guaranteed for all countries; and imperialist violations of that right in the past should be rectified. The deceptive slogan of disarmament should also be rejected, they added. Revolutionists should advance, instead, the perspective of organizing and arming the workers, and winning the ranks of the armed forces to their side. The imperialist war should be transformed into a civil war against the bourgeoisie, the aim in each country being to establish a workers' state.

During the first period of the war the call for a Marxist course of action evoked only a limited response among socialist militants. Doubting the possibility of a successful proletarian revolution anywhere in Europe, most of them leaned toward support of pacifist campaigns for peace and were reluctant to make a clean break with the centrists. As a result the winning and shaping of revolutionary cadres advanced slowly. But time favored the left-wingers, whose line conformed with the objective needs of the working class and colonial peoples. As the war unfolded, reality made clear the trap the reformists and their centrist allies had led the workers into. The revolutionists were able to move gradually toward a definitive organizational polarization within the hitherto loosely constructed socialist movement. On one side there remained only a hollow shell of the Second International, which had been gutted by reformist capitulations to imperialism; and on the other a new International adhering to revolutionary principles was coming into being.

\*      \*      \*

Meanwhile the European war had precipitated new economic and political developments in the United States. Upon the opening of hostilities President Woodrow Wilson, a Democratic Party stooge for the U.S. ruling class, had issued a proclamation of neutrality. This move was supported by the capitalists because it served the immediate aims of the various contending factions among them.

Those in the lower echelons of the bourgeoisie, who felt they had little to gain by involving this country in the fighting, welcomed the government's neutral stance as a concession to their views. The industrial corporations and large banks, on the other hand, saw the nonbelligerent status as a preliminary device through which to advance imperialist aims. They began by selling war supplies and advancing high-interest loans to the countries opposing Germany, all at enormous profit for themselves. Support of this kind went mainly to Great Britain and France. As a cover for this partisanship in selecting customers, these countries were held to be "victims of German aggression." Such propaganda served the U.S. monopolists not only as a means of justifying their initial step, but also as the opening gambit for an eventual declaration of war against Germany.

The shipment of war goods to Europe started an industrial boom that soon overcame an economic depression which had begun in the United States at the end of 1913. During the slump unemployment had mounted, and the employers had taken advantage of the situation to impose wage cuts on workers still holding jobs. Things now began to change, however, as industrial production gained new momentum. Most of the unemployed again found work, and organized labor was able to win increases in pay.

Exceptional wage hikes were granted to the skilled trades by the war profiteers, enhancing the status of these workers as a labor aristocracy. These material inducements helped to convince them of the false and ultimately self-defeating course of identifying their own interests with imperialist interests, instead of those of the proletariat as a whole.

With economic conditions improving for the working class, the Gompers bureaucracy in the American Federation of Labor was able to develop its line on the war issue within the framework of a relatively stable internal union situation. Before 1914 Samuel Gompers had flirted with the pacifist movement, which lent itself to his nationalistic perspectives. But he now turned away from all that. Together with the rest of his bureaucratic clique, he undertook to assure the ruling class that the AFL would be reliable in matters of foreign policy. The Gompersites, who counted on backing from the skilled workers, intended to uphold the capitalist government in whatever foreign policy action it took. Yet they, too, found it necessary to proceed by devious means. Antiwar sentiment was widespread in the trade union ranks, and premature commitment to U.S. involvement in the European slaughter would have aroused strong opposition.

In those circumstances Wilson's neutrality proclamation was doubly advantageous to the AFL bureaucrats. By promptly endorsing it, they were able to assume what appeared to be an antiwar stand and yet demonstrate their readiness to back governmental policy. The latter intention was further emphasized by helping to justify arms shipments to England and France. Such action was proper, the Gompersites held, because those were the "most democratic" countries in Europe.

Unlike the class collaborationists heading the AFL, top leaders of the Industrial Workers of the World took a forthright antiwar position. They denounced the European parties of the Second International for capitulating to imperialism and warned that the U.S. capitalists would soon drag this country into the fighting. The IWW leaders did not appear to believe, however, that anything could be done to prevent the ruling class from achieving its objective. They advanced no perspective for working-class political action. Their proposals for action centered on maintaining a class-struggle line in industry and preparing for intensification of that course after the war ended.

An antiwar stand was also taken by the Socialist Party of America in a manifesto issued on August 12, 1914. Eugene V. Debs, especially, put his finger on the nature of the European antagonists. Each set of ruling capitalists had the same goal, he said; they were seeking by military force to redivide the colonial spheres of exploitation among themselves. He excoriated the misleaders of the European socialist movement. He insisted the United States should keep out of the imperialist slaughter. Most rank-and-file Socialists agreed with his view. This was shown in a referendum vote on an amendment to the party constitution ordering the expulsion of any member holding public office who voted for U.S. military appropriations. The amendment was adopted by an overwhelming majority.

Although the expulsion order differentiated the Socialist Party from the social reformists who had voted for war appropriations in European parliaments, the party leadership did not explicitly repudiate that piece of treachery. Instead, the National Executive Committee of the SP confined itself to a request that all affiliates of the Second International participate in a world congress with the aim of seeking an end to the fighting. As the nature of this request implied, a section of the leadership was introducing pacifist concepts into official party statements.

Bourgeois pacifism's most outstanding figure in the United States was William Jennings Bryan, a capitalist politician who had earlier gained wide popularity among workers and small farmers as a free-silver advocate. When the European conflict began, Bryan and his associates set out to bring antiwar sentiment in this country under their control. They propagated illusions that broad demonstrations for peace would in themselves offset pressures on the government—which they presented as above classes—from those capitalists who sought U.S. entry into the war. Mass hostility toward the imperialist plotters was channeled into support of a vaguely defined program—which made a basic concession to the militarists through advocacy of a "limited" arms buildup for "purposes of national defense"—and the workers and their allies were diverted from meaningful class-struggle action. The need for working-class initiative in militant opposition to the warmongers was thereby hampered and obscured.

Counting on the pacifists to keep the antiwar movement in safe bounds, Wilson speeded the implementation of U.S. imperialism's real policy. He began by calling for "preparedness" to assure an "adequate system of national defense." On that fake premise Congress appropriated huge sums for an armament program. Parallel with the arms buildup the president ordered the National Guard on a war footing in the "interests of national security" and made a plea for national unity behind the government.

Public demonstrations in favor of "preparedness" were also arranged. At one of these, held in San Francisco, California, during

1916, a bomb was exploded among the marchers, killing nine and wounding others. Two union organizers, Tom Mooney and Warren K. Billings, were then framed up on murder charges and imprisoned. Although the labor movement contended that agents provocateurs had done the bombing, Wilson turned a deaf ear to its plea for justice. His concern lay only in whipping up a pro-war spirit, no matter whose rights were violated.

With militarist propaganda beginning to have the desired effect at home, the U.S. imperialists moved against the Mexican revolution during 1916. An alleged border raid by Pancho Villa, the most outstanding leader of the revolutionary guerrilla forces in northern Mexico, was used as pretext. Pretending that the only objective was to capture Villa, Wilson ordered a military invasion of Mexico. The invading forces were then built up into an outright army of occupation.

Mass indignation among the Mexican people over the brutal intervention in their affairs forced President Venustiano Carranza, an agent of the native bourgeois and landed classes, to make a formal protest. Wilson, who did not want a complete break with the Mexican regime, withdrew his troops. He had to settle for something less than the swift crushing of the revolutionary threat to his imperialist masters, but in another respect the military action was of immediate benefit to the U.S. ruling class. It emboldened the pro-war forces and thus furthered the development of a militarist mentality in their own country.

At this juncture Wilson set up the Council of National Defense, staffed by capitalists and their lackeys. He also named an advisory commission to aid it. Gompers, who was already supporting the "preparedness" campaign, accepted nomination to the commission. In that capacity he helped promote acceptance of Wilson's military policy, telling the workers it was for purposes of national defense. Before long the AFL head also began to speak in favor of all-out support to England and France. If that led to involvement in the war, he argued, this country would only be defending its own freedom. His view was opposed, however, by many in the AFL, and a number of its units backed the pacifists in demanding that the U.S. remain neutral. So Gompers opened an attack on the peace movement with the aim of scaring off its labor supporters.

The IWW failed to link up with the antiwar movement developing in the AFL. Its attention still centered on union activity at the industrial level, which was now being conducted under a new central leader. Somewhat earlier Vincent St. John had declined, for personal reasons, to continue in the post of general secretary. He was then replaced in that office by William D. Haywood. With guidance from Haywood, the IWW took up the war issue at a convention held in the fall of 1916. The deliberations focused on what to do when the U.S. became involved in the fighting. When that happened, the gathering decided, organized labor should call a general protest strike throughout industry, and the unions should oppose the forcible conscription of workers into military service.

By this time external pressures had sown confusion inside the Socialist Party. A group of petty-bourgeois intellectuals in the ranks had abandoned their earlier antiwar position and were now backing Wilson's "preparedness" campaign. Their line was proving increasingly attractive to the general run of petty-bourgeois members, few of whom had actually become Marxists and fully adopted the proletarian point of view. Not being revolutionists, these elements saw little reason to maintain their former socialist pretenses in the reactionary political climate generated by imperialism; and they began to leave the party.

Right-wingers around Victor Berger in the SP were also adapting to certain aspects of the imperialist ploy. The broadest manifestation of this trend among them was endorsement of U.S. support to England and France. In addition some were going so far as to participate in "preparedness" demonstrations.

It was mainly among the workers in the party that an uncompromising antiwar stand remained prevalent. In keeping with their class instincts they were striving, especially, to mobilize opposition to Gompers's treacherous line in the AFL. The sentiments which motivated these militants had been articulated earlier by Debs in the September 11, 1915, issue of *Appeal to Reason,* a widely read socialist paper. "I am opposed to every war but one," he wrote. "I am for that war with heart and soul, and that is the worldwide war of the social revolution." Lenin frequently hailed this declaration by Debs, contrasting it to the capitulation by the majority of European Social Democratic leaders.

Like the IWW, Debs advocated a national protest strike if Congress declared war. Toward that end he proposed that some means be found to establish organizational unity among the antiwar forces within the working-class movement. A new trade union federation should be built, he suggested, through which class-conscious industrial unionists could prepare the workers for economic and political battle in the rapidly expanding war industries. Debs also recommended an organizational regroupment of all Marxist tendencies in order to take joint action against the war danger. Concerning the world socialist movement, he added, pro-war reformists should be purged from the European leadership to clear the way for reconstruction of the Second International as a revolutionary body.

As the rift over war policy developed in the SP, centrists led by Morris Hillquit moved to the right under cover of a continued anti-imperialist posture. In doing so they adapted Kautsky's social pacifism to the situation in this country, focusing on support of the Bryan campaign against U.S. involvement in the European hostilities. This line was nothing but a circuitous route to betrayal of the workers. It ensnared them in bourgeois pacifism—which opposed war only in peacetime—and steered them away from the revolutionary struggle needed to prevent their being dragged into the imperialist bloodbath.

All in all, much had changed inside the Socialist Party since it issued the 1914 manifesto against war. The right wing was developing a pro-war position, and the centrists were moving in the same direction. Only the left wing remained faithful to the 1914 stand. It was in those circumstances that a right-winger, Allan Benson, was chosen as the party's candidate for president in the 1916 elections. Those opposed to imperialist policy were able to insert a plank in the SP platform calling for a national referendum before war could be declared. But neither Benson nor other reformists among the party candidates for public office urged mass action to prevent U.S. involvement in the hostilities. They merely asked that all who wanted the nation to remain neutral express their wishes by voting Socialist.

The Democratic Party nominated Wilson for another term as president, using the deceitful slogan "He kept us out of war." Most pacifists went along with that line. Many others opposed to entering the war were also taken in by it, and Wilson was reelected by a narrow majority.

After being returned to office the president who "kept us out of war" moved rapidly toward U.S. entry into the imperialist conflict. Shipments of military hardware to England and France were sharply increased. When the German government reacted with a warning that all ships carrying supplies to its enemies would be subject to attack, Wilson severed diplomatic relations with Germany. He then asked Congress to authorize the arming of U.S. merchant vessels. Senator Robert M. La Follette of Wisconsin, a Progressive Republican leading a neutralist bloc in the Senate, managed to prevent action on the request before that body adjourned for its winter recess. But the maneuver proved meaningless. Wilson simply issued an executive order that the ships be armed forthwith.

His bellicose tactics alarmed the masses. Large numbers of people turned to the pacifist movement in the hope it could save the country from being plunged into the war; and many of them were trade unionists, who took a leading part in organizing protest demonstrations.

As mass opposition to Wilson's line gained increasing momentum, the Gompers hierarchy in the craft unions set out to help him stem the tide. It depicted the European conflict as a struggle between the "institutions of democracy and those of autocracy." If the U.S. entered into that struggle, the AFL hacks arbitrarily pledged, organized labor would recognize its obligation to serve in defense of the country.

Soon thereafter, on April 6, 1917, Congress declared war on Germany. A series of new political developments were thereby set into motion. Bourgeois pacifists put aside their tactical differences over foreign policy and lined up with the monopolists to present a solid ruling-class front in the "national emergency." Petty-bourgeois pacifists, demonstrating both fundamental support of capitalism and a purely nationalist outlook, followed suit. Within the labor movement every class-collaborationist tendency moved step by step, if not in one stride, toward capitulation to imperialism. It was a loathsome alliance, indeed, that now undertook to regiment the masses for a war "to make the world safe for democracy."

Wilson quickly set up the War Labor Board (WLB) to ride herd over the workers. Its members were employers, AFL officials, and pro-capitalist "public" representatives. The board's function was to freeze wages and job conditions, except for any change made with its approval. It was empowered to impose a settlement in labor disputes that arose and to move against strikes "arbitrarily" conducted by the workers.

The WLB directives brought a storm of criticism from trade unionists. The war was being used, workers protested, to hold down wages; but nothing was being done to freeze prices or to curb profiteering. This meant that labor, if denied the right to strike in self-protection, would suffer a drop in living standards. Here again, though, the Gompersites betrayed the union ranks. An official AFL stand was taken in support of WLB control over collective bargaining and in favor of a wartime no-strike policy.

On the heels of Wilson's direct attack on the trade unions, Congress passed a law imposing compulsory service in the imperialist armed forces. Many workers, who believed the war violated their class interests, were against being drafted to fight and die for the bosses. Yet the AFL officialdom failed to lift a finger in support of efforts to have the conscription law repealed.

In marked contrast to Gompers's collaboration with the ruling class, the Socialist Party officially reaffirmed its opposition to the imperialist plot. It did so at a special convention held in St. Louis,

Missouri, right after Congress declared war. Majority and minority resolutions were submitted to the gathering by party leaders.

The main points in the majority document included the following: The war resulted from imperialist rivalry for domination of world markets in order to amass greater profits. Entrance of the U.S. government into the conflict had been instigated by the capitalists, who were committing a crime against the people. The SP condemned that criminal act, reaffirmed its allegiance to working-class internationalism, and called upon the workers to withhold their support from the capitalist government. Organized labor was urged to demand the repeal of military conscription, oppose the raising of war funds, and continue the class struggle to free the toilers from economic exploitation and political oppression.

The other resolution, submitted by right-wingers in the leadership, advocated a pro-war line in the guise of emphasis on peace negotiations. It was necessary, they contended, for the party to recognize that U.S. involvement in the European hostilities had become a fact. The SP's former antiwar propaganda now had to be replaced by a new type of campaign. Public opinion should be mobilized to pressure the government into adoption of a "constructive" program for ending the conflict.

After extensive debate, the delegates voted about three to one in favor of the resolution calling for continued struggle against the war. A party referendum was then held in which a majority of the membership supported the convention decision.

The SP's official stand against the war precipitated a new internal party crisis. Petty-bourgeois members left its ranks in droves. The Bergerite right wing acted on its own to apply the minority line rejected by the St. Louis convention, a course that soon led to open support of U.S. imperialism—but for which they were not expelled. Reformists holding office in AFL unions knuckled under to pressures from Gompers and helped to carry out his policy.

As wartime pressures increased, these trends were accompanied by disintegration of the makeshift coalition—formed by leftwingers, centrists, and Christian pacifists—that had forced through the an-

In 1918 Debs was sentenced to prison for his opposition to the
war. Here he is dressed in a prison uniform.

tiwar declaration. The Christian pacifists had acted on the basis of moral opposition to all force and violence; that is, they were conscientious objectors to the war. As such, their main concern was to see the fighting ended. So, having no real perception of the class struggle, nor its stakes, they moved rapidly toward identification with the call for a negotiated peace on the basis of "democratic principles."

Centrists of the Hillquit stripe began to twist the St. Louis declaration in a way that served their social-pacifist concepts. Like the European Kautskyists, the Hillquit tendency combined advocacy of a negotiated peace with devious maneuvers toward an outright pro-war line. Moves in the latter direction were typified by the action of centrists holding public office. They backed a drive by the capitalist government to raise funds for military purposes through public sale of so-called Liberty Bonds.

As these developments unfolded within the SP, most of the leading figures lent themselves to a piece of trickery designed to reverse the line adopted at the St. Louis convention. The resolution approved by the convention—and supported in a membership referendum—stated that the capitalists had instigated U.S. entry into the war for profit motives. In outright violation of that position, the party officials now called upon the imperialist government for a clear statement of its war aims, as if their stated goals would be the real ones.

At this point the party's left wing stood virtually alone in fighting to uphold the previous antiwar stand. Although this made things rougher than ever, the native-born militants led by Debs found encouragement in the fact that they were gaining reinforcements from another quarter. By this time immigrant workers opposed to the war were joining the SP's language federations in large numbers. They readily entered into a bloc with the Debs group to shape a course of action. In choosing specific issues the bloc centered on a demand for repeal of military conscription, opposition to the sale of war bonds, and defense of free speech against growing violations of that constitutional right. A campaign was then launched to develop mass support around these issues, especially in the trade unions.

Initially, the left-wing campaign received substantial backing in the AFL ranks. This alarmed Gompers, who reacted by accusing the Socialists of undermining the trade unions. Seizing upon the circumstance that many foreign-born workers opposed the war, he demagogically launched a chauvinist call for "Americanization" of the labor movement and advocated governmental repression of the rebels.

Gompers's plea for repressive action coincided with imperialist preparations to launch a sweeping assault on the antiwar movement. Congress was in the process of amending the federal sedition laws in the form of the Espionage Act, purportedly directed against German spies. When the job was completed, however, the new act was found to focus primarily on restrictions of civil rights. It was made a crime to obstruct the draft, incite insubordination in the armed forces, interfere with the sale of war bonds, or use the mails for "subversive" propaganda. Freedom of speech was outlawed by prohibiting the utterance of "any disloyal, profane, scurrilous, or abusive language about the form of government of the United States, or the Constitution of the United States, or the military or naval forces of the United States."

Once the Espionage Act was passed, it served as the main instrument for a governmental attack on the antiwar militants. Federal agents seeking evidence of "disloyalty" made nationwide raids on headquarters of the SP and the IWW. Many were arrested for allegedly obstructing the draft, oftentimes to be tried in court and imprisoned. In addition to arrests, Socialist and syndicalist papers containing antiwar propaganda were stripped of their second-class mailing rights.

As the direct governmental attack gained momentum the capitalists incited an extralegal campaign against the peace movement. Police looked the other way as mobs, whipped into a frenzy by imperialist propaganda, terrorized Socialist, pacifist, and syndicalist opponents of the war. People were assaulted for refusing to buy Liberty Bonds. Books in the German language were taken from private homes and burned publicly by unlettered "patriots" who had no idea what they contained. A similar fate befell personal libraries of radicals.

The syndicalists—who had thought the capitalist state could be ignored and had rejected the concept of a political struggle to overturn it—and the workers they led bore the brunt of the state's repressive powers in the drive against the antiwar movement. U.S. troops crushed a strike of IWW lumber workers in the Northwest. Direct strike-breaking of that kind was accompanied by a federal assault in another harsh form. Haywood and ninety-four other leading militants in the union were arrested under the Espionage Act on charges of obstructing the war effort. Although they were not put on trial immediately, the mass arrest of outstanding leaders was enough in itself to deal the organization a crippling blow.

Criminal syndicalism laws, which had been enacted in several western states, were also used against the IWW. These laws proscribed alleged resort to violence by the syndicalists in economic conflicts. Under cover of propaganda denouncing opposition to the war as "treason," they were invoked for the purpose of conducting what was actually a union-busting attack. Hundreds upon hundreds of militant workers were arrested. Some were released after being held in jail for a time, but many others were sentenced to prison terms.

Extralegal assaults on the syndicalist movement were in some cases even more vicious. The employers used armed thugs masquerading as "patriots" to violently suppress a strike of Arizona miners led by the IWW. In a number of cities vigilantes ransacked and destroyed the union's headquarters. An IWW organizer, Frank Little, was hanged on August 1, 1917, by a Montana lynch mob.

The brutal steps taken to repress the antiwar movement not only played havoc with the syndicalists, but also created extreme adversities for left-wing Socialists in the AFL. As the hostile pressures mounted, those craft union leaders who had opposed the war capitulated, one after another, to the ruling class. Before long the Socialist militants found themselves almost entirely isolated. Few in the AFL outside their own limited numbers remained willing to continue antiwar activity.

Under those hard circumstances Debs groped for an effective policy in the fight against imperialism. Having abandoned his earlier adaptation to the syndicalist idea of overturning capitalism through a general strike, he had come to think in terms of a political struggle by the working class to establish a socialist order. But he still clung to the concept of acting solely within the confines of the capitalist-rigged electoral system. Debs did not appear to perceive that the war posed in sharpest form the need to project a revolutionary course toward the seizure of power by the workers and their allies; for his programmatic outlook on the war issue did not extend beyond urging continued protests against militarism.

In conducting protests of the kind the SP left wing now focused primary attention on opposition to military conscription. Party members were encouraged to resist the draft by declaring themselves conscientious objectors on an individual basis. In essence the socialist fight against the war had become downgraded to identification with what remained of the pacifist movement.

It is unlikely that Debs knew that Lenin had recently offered advice pertinent to the problem confronting the SP militants. At a meeting of revolutionists in Switzerland on January 22, 1917, the Bolshevik leader said: ". . . the history of the [1905] Russian revolution, like the history of the Paris Commune of 1871, teaches us the incontrovertible lesson that militarism can never and under no circumstances be defeated and destroyed, except by a victorious struggle of one section of the national army against the other section. It is not sufficient simply to denounce, revile, and 'repudiate' militarism, to criticize and prove that it is harmful; it is foolish peacefully to refuse to perform military service. The task is to keep the revolutionary consciousness of the proletariat tense and train its best elements, not only in a general way, but concretely, so that when popular ferment reaches the highest pitch, they will put themselves at the head of the revolutionary army" (V. I. Lenin, *Collected Works* [Moscow: Progress Publishers, 1964] vol. 23, p. 246).

This policy was soon verified in practice by the Russian Bolsheviks, and their dramatic success opened the way for new advances throughout the world socialist movement. It opened the door to solving the crisis of revolutionary leadership that had developed with the rise of imperialism and whose horrible results were demonstrated with the outbreak of the war. And it made possible reestablishment of the consciousness of revolutionary Marxist continuity on a world scale.

# 6

# *Bolshevik Revolution*

Russia entered the First World War as an imperialist power, with imperialist goals, but its class structure was marked by a semifeudal inheritance from the recent past. Serfdom, which held the peasants in bondage to the owners of large estates, had been annulled in 1861; but its abolition remained more juridical than real. A privileged aristocracy continued to monopolize the cultivable soil. Peasants having some form of land tenure on a small scale were still subjected to serflike exploitation by the big proprietors. Few among them had managed to climb out of crushing debt. An overwhelming majority of the rural toilers were pauperized small peasants and agricultural workers who labored on large farms for starvation pay.

Around 80 percent of the nation's population was engaged in agriculture. Capitalist industry, having undergone only limited development, had not absorbed much of the potential labor force. This industrial backwardness had at the same time restricted the growth of the native bourgeoisie, whose capacity to act as a social class was further hampered by the intervention of foreign imperialists with substantial investments in Russian enterprises.

The industrial workers, who had come mainly from the countryside, constituted a narrow layer of the total population. But they had exceptional social weight due to the relatively large size of factories for the times, their concentration in the large cities, and their strategic position in the national economy. Yet another factor served to augment their inherent class strength. As industry had slowly expanded, new labor forces were drawn to the industrial centers from rural areas. Lines of contact between the workers and peasants were thereby gradually broadened, and proletarians in the cities were able to exert leadership influence among toilers on the land in their common struggle against tsarist oppression.

A significant component of the petty bourgeoisie was also concentrated in the cities. It consisted of small merchants, educators, lawyers, doctors, government functionaries, etc. Apart from their specific economic and social functions, these elements—who stood in an intermediate class position between the industrialists and the proletariat—served as instruments for the propagation of bourgeois ideology among the workers.

In addition to the many contradictions in relations between the various social classes there were special problems involving oppressed nationalities. These were nations and peoples who had been forcibly incorporated into the Russian state and denied the right of self-government. As distinctive entities they were in each instance subjected to economic, social, and cultural discrimination. Victims of superexploitation, they were strongly impelled to struggle for national liberation, and this trend had persisted despite the setbacks experienced when the 1905 revolution was defeated. Because the subject nationalities were overwhelmingly peasant in composition, the national question and land question were closely interlinked.

This intricate combination of factors was thrusting Russia toward a social explosion. The bourgeoisie had failed to carry through a revolution against precapitalist property relations and methods of rule. As a result agrarian reform remained uncompleted. Industrialization still lagged badly. Bourgeois-democratic institutions such as the legislature, called the Duma, had a feeble existence and had not superseded feudal autocracy. The worker and peasant masses were growing increasingly rebellious against the harsh economic exploitation to which they were subjected by the privileged classes with the aid of a tyrannical government; and the oppressed nationalities were becoming more insistent about their right to self-determination.

State power, which was used in brutal fashion to repress all manifestations of mass struggle, remained in the hands of the landed nobility. This class ruled through the medium of the tsar, who exercised total control over the state machinery. Although opposed to that absolutist form of rule, the liberal bourgeoisie could not act to overturn tsarism. It was afraid to risk any weakening of the repressive apparatus used against the rebellious masses, let alone make any moves that could set the toilers in motion. So the bourgeoisie aspired to nothing more than a subordinate share of state power with the landed nobility through establishment of a constitutional monarchy subject to control by the Duma.

Such was the situation when Russia declared war on Germany and Austria in 1914. Confronted with military and technical deficiencies resulting from lack of industrial development, the imperialist government tried to compensate through use of human cannon fodder on a vast scale. By the end of 1916 an army of some 15 million had been conscripted. Out of this number around one-third had been killed, wounded, or captured; desertions from the army were growing rapidly as it suffered one defeat after another.

On the home front prices were rising at an increasing rate, and there were growing shortages of consumer goods. This was most acute in the large cities, where bread and fuel became increasingly scarce. Meanwhile, war profiteers were amassing huge fortunes. The bloody interimperialist conflict was imposing terrible hardships on the Russian masses.

Early in 1917 popular indignation over these injustices broke through to the surface. In the industrial centers workers gathered in factory meetings called to discuss the problems imposed upon them by the war. Protest demonstrations, along with strikes over various issues, took place with increasing frequency. Extensive fraternization developed between the workers and the discontented soldiers that the government depended on as a repressive force. Signs of growing unrest appeared in the provinces as well. Everywhere in the country the masses showed mounting readiness to fight for peace, liberty, bread, and—in the case of the peasants—land.

The developing struggle assumed an overtly revolutionary character in mid-February (by the old calendar then used in Russia; early March by the modern calendar). This stage opened with a strike of women textile workers in Petrograd (formerly St. Petersburg and today Leningrad). Other walkouts quickly followed, and the strike movement became city-wide in scope. Broader sections of the urban masses were simultaneously drawn into the fight on labor's side, as were most of the soldiers in the local garrison. An armed insurrection resulted, and the rebellious masses seized power in Petrograd, the national capital, on February 27 (March 12), 1917. Popular support of the insurrection was manifested throughout Russia—in other cities, on the land, and among the troops at the front. Tsarist rule had been overturned.

During the insurrection soviets (councils), which had first arisen spontaneously in the 1905 revolution, again sprang up, largely on the initiative of the masses. The popular composition and democratic character of these bodies was without precedent. Direct, comprehensive representation was provided, through freely elected delegates, for all who toiled. In that way the popular masses were able to organize themselves on a wide scale, through these organs of struggle, with the prospect of taking full control over their social destiny.

Formation of the soviets began in the largest factories. Workers generally, in all occupations, quickly followed suit; and from there the creation of these organs spread into the military forces and among the peasants. The key body of elected representatives from various soviets—the General, or All-Russian, Soviet of Workers' and Soldiers' Deputies—was organized in Petrograd. Since most soldiers were peasants in uniform, this formation constituted a direct link between the proletariat and the peasantry. In addition to that vital factor the Petrograd soviet functioned in the national capital, which was also a major industrial center. For these reasons that body was able to play a decisive political role in the ongoing revolutionary struggle.

The soviets from the first constituted an overwhelming force in Russian society, but they were handicapped in making full use of their strength. These bodies embraced masses among whom there were widely divergent levels of political consciousness. This rendered them incapable, in their majority, of immediately developing the program that pointed out the necessary line of march of the proletariat to power. Mistakes would have to be made and lessons learned in the experiences of the next stages of class struggle before a majority could become fully revolutionary in political understanding as well as in spirit. In the test of events the various political tendencies within the soviets would have to compete for decisive leadership authority. At the beginning, however, the Marxist tendency was at a great disadvantage in this respect. Some of its most outstanding leaders—especially Lenin and Trotsky—who were driven into exile after the 1905 revolution had not yet been able to return.

As the insurrection reached its climax, the Duma, a parliamentary body that had previously been subject to tsarist control, stepped to the fore. Duma members from the bourgeois Cadet Party (Constitutional Democrats) took the lead in rushing to form a new, provisional government. Top positions in this government were filled mainly by capitalists and big landowners, with one notable exception. A cabinet post was accepted by the lawyer Alexander Kerensky, who was prominent in the Petrograd soviet and belonged to the Social Revolutionaries, an anti-Marxist populist party rooted in the peasantry.

The Cadets represented the liberal bourgeoisie and some landlords who, having also become factory owners, had adopted a bourgeois outlook. These elements were ready to accept creation of a constitutional republic, but only if the state apparatus could still be used to uphold capitalist and landed property rights at the expense of the exploited masses, and to preserve and extend the Russian Empire.

Others among the privileged classes, including most landowners and the conservative section of the bourgeoisie, were opposed to the setting up of a parliamentary republic. They wanted tsarism rehabilitated in the form of a constitutional monarchy. For the time being, though, they supported the Cadet government as the only mechanism capable then and there of safeguarding their vested interests, and a similar view was taken by foreign imperialists with holdings in Russia. All these reactionary forces brought pressure to keep the new regime as far to the right as possible.

The Provisional Government was a class organ of bourgeois-landowner-foreign imperialist domination, and this was reflected through its policies. Russia was kept in the imperialist war with the tsar's generals still in command. An effort was made, moreover, to revive a martial spirit on the false premise that the change in government justified continuation of the fighting in the name of "revolutionary defensism" against the German Kaiser. The new regime also showed great zeal in protecting the capitalist and landowning interests, but it took an opposite attitude toward the claims of the workers, peasants, and oppressed nationalities. Their rights, aspirations, and just demands were ignored.

While pursuing these reactionary and delaying policies, the Provisional Government announced that it would soon convene a constituent assembly. Such a political instrument, formed through a democratized election process, had appeared in several of the bourgeois-democratic revolutions before the rise of imperialism. Its function was to draft a constitution and reconstruct a social order after feudalism, absolutism, and foreign domination had been overthrown. The promise to follow a similar course in Russia of 1917 helped ease mass pressure on the current government by raising expectations that all difficulties could be ironed out through the convocation of such an assembly.

The promise was made tongue in cheek, however, for the privileged classes were opposed to any policy-making agency that could not be rigged in their favor. They had no intention of entrusting their fate to a body that might favor the workers over the capitalists and the peasants over the landed nobility. So their Provisional Government kept postponing the convening of a constituent assembly, hoping it could first manage to dissolve the soviets, which stood in the way of the vested interests grabbing uncontested power. (Elections to the Constituent Assembly were not held until November, after the Bolshevik-led workers and peasants had toppled the Provisional Government and established soviet power.)

Weaknesses inside the soviets made them vulnerable to the conspiracy of the owning classes. Great numbers of people who were experiencing political life for the first time had been drawn into the movement. Most were petty bourgeois—rural or urban—whose outlook was characterized by naive trust in the liberal bourgeoisie. Their attitude infected the proletariat, moreover, which lacked adequate consciousness of its own potential role as a class. Under those conditions a big majority supported the soviet parties of compromise and reform, the Mensheviks and Social Revolutionaries. The proletarian revolutionists were thrust into a minority.

The Social Revolutionaries, a petty-bourgeois party based on the peasantry, rejected the Marxist goal of a proletarian dictatorship. Its ally in the soviets, the Menshevik Party, represented the reformist wing of the Russian Social Democrats. Both parties insisted that the democratic revolution would be led by the liberal capitalists and that the proletariat dare not overstep the bourgeois tasks tolerable to the liberals. They favored establishment of a parliamentary republic, assuring the workers and peasants that it would serve their needs. Although the soviets represented a decisive majority and had armed strength at their command, these parties voluntarily handed power to the Provisional Government, which was nothing more than an agency of the privileged classes. The soviets, they held, should concentrate on supervising the convocation of a constituent assembly by the bourgeois Provisional Government.

Accepting the myth of "revolutionary defensism," the compromisers in the leadership of the soviets backed Russia's continued involvement in the imperialist war. They opposed the spontaneous peasant seizures of landed estates until the issue of ownership could be decided by a constituent assembly; failed to press the workers' demand for an eight-hour day; double-talked about the right of oppressed nationalities to self-determination; and asked little more of the Provisional Government than freedom for the soviet parties to conduct propaganda and agitation.

This was the way matters stood when Lenin, in April, and Trotsky, in May, arrived in Petrograd from their places of exile abroad. Up to then they had differed over the basic political question of how to build the proletarian vanguard party.

During the 1890s the Social Democratic Party had been organized in Russia as an affiliate of the Second International. Its right wing was led by petty-bourgeois reformists who held that the revolution had to be consolidated as a bourgeois-democratic republic for a prolonged interval; that the workers should subordinate themselves to the representatives of the employing class in fighting tsarism; and that such a revolutionary victory would enable the masses to win reforms under capitalism. Organizationally the right wing shared the view prevalent in the Second International, that the party should be all-inclusive, a formation embracing socialist members with diverse and contradictory views about basic program expressing the strategic line of march of the proletariat. As later events were to show, this was an overall prescription for a disoriented, amorphous, vacillatory movement utterly incapable of leading decisive proletarian action when the hour struck.

Lenin counterposed the perspective of shaping a revolutionary combat party, and he described how that should be done. To accomplish this, the revolutionary party had to continually strive to be a politically homogeneous formation, based on membership adherence to Marxist principles. That in turn would provide an internal framework of mutual loyalty to the party built on these principles in which episodic political disagreements over matters of program, strategy, and tactics could be discussed and decided on the democratic basis of majority rule and all members could then be expected to unite in carrying out majority decisions. This revolutionary centralism would enable the party to present a solid front in the workers' movement and further test and adjust its tactics.

It was also imperative, Lenin stressed, for the party to become mainly proletarian in composition as well as in program. Toward that end revolutionists should become totally integrated in mass organizations, go through the workers' experiences with them, win their respect for the party, and recruit them into its ranks.

Following the experiences of Marx and Engels, Lenin taught that the revolutionary workers' party took part in and explained—from the point of view of the line of march of the proletariat and in light of its historic experiences—the political meaning of all the social conflicts in the country. Only this generalized experience and program, brought into the broad workers' movement by the revolutionary party, could chart the transitional steps that lay along the road to the conquest of power, its defense, and its extension.

To the extent that this was understood, more and more proletarian militants could be educated as revolutionary politicians and prospective leaders of mass actions; and they could be assimilated into every aspect of the party's functioning, including participation in its leading staff. (This transitional method and Leninist strategy of party building, whose organizational norms are often called democratic centralism, will be taken up more extensively in the next volume.)

The dispute over these principles came to its first climax in the 1903 convention of the Russian Social Democratic Labor Party. A split occurred between the revolutionary supporters of Lenin, the Bolsheviks (the Russian term meaning "majority"), and a bloc of reformists and centrists, the Mensheviks ("minority"). After this the two factions developed further through various forms until, in 1912, they became two definitively separate parties. Following the 1903 split Trotsky, who favored retention of an all-inclusive formation, briefly maintained ties with the Mensheviks. Then he established a centrist current around the particular issue of advocating reunification of the warring factions in a single party. Trotsky did

Left, V.I. Lenin. Right, Leon Trotsky.

not entirely shed this centrist stance until the opening of the Russian revolution in early 1917.

With the outbreak of World War I in 1914, however, there was a convergence of Lenin's and Trotsky's views. Both condemned the social-patriotic response by the majority of European Social Democratic leaders, as well as the pacifist cover provided for this betrayal by the centrist Kautsky and his followers. As patriotic sentiments infected growing layers even among those who had initially aligned themselves with the revolutionary antiwar current in Europe, Trotsky drew closer and closer to Lenin's firm rejection of conciliation with any wing of the Mensheviks.

This convergence was accelerated by the broad agreement on the part of Lenin and Trotsky concerning the tasks of the Russian working class following the February 1917 revolution. The political basis for this agreement had been laid twelve years earlier following the defeat of the 1905 revolution in Russia. Whereas the events of 1905 deepened the Mensheviks' conviction that the liberal bourgeoisie must be at the helm of the revolution, Lenin and Trotsky drew the opposite conclusion. They both argued that the working class, in alliance with the peasantry, would be the leading force in making a revolution that could begin to solve the tasks facing the Russian toilers. Disagreements between Lenin and Trotsky over the method to advance this revolution, as well as how it would unfold and how to knit the necessary worker-peasant alliance, were transcended in 1917, as they drew virtually identical conclusions following the overthrow of the tsar.

Both Lenin and Trotsky recognized the revolutionary significance of the soviets of workers', peasants', and soldiers' representatives that had arisen during the February insurrection. Both argued that the revolution could succeed only along the lines of a fight for all power to be taken by the soviets, no support to the bourgeois Provisional Government, and political opposition to any soviet party that compromised on this question. To achieve their immediate goals—peace, land, bread, liberty—the workers and peasants needed to replace the Provisional Government. The soviets had to take power, instead of voluntarily ceding it to the privileged classes represented by the Provisional Government, as the Mensheviks and leaders of the peasant-based Social Revolutionaries had done. The leadership in carrying through the revolution would be the industrial workers, in alliance with the peasants, especially the poor peasants, and the rural laborers. Under the guidance of the workers' vanguard party, the revolution could then move in transitional stages from the solution of immediate democratic, social, and economic tasks toward the founding of a socialist order in cooperation with the toilers of the world.

Since 1914 Trotsky, who had been president of the St. Petersburg soviet in 1905, had seen the Bolshevik Party stand firm in opposition to the imperialist war. The worker members, who constituted its mass base, had played a decisive role in the February insurrection.

Bolshevik leaders inside Russia had initially adopted a conciliatory stance toward the Provisional Government. Thanks to the entire course of the Bolshevik Party since the break with the Mensheviks in 1903, however, Lenin's efforts to correct this political orientation following his return in April did not require a struggle against a large class-collaborationist wing of an all-inclusive party. A staunch proletarian revolutionary formation already existed whose leadership was being reoriented politically and which was openly confronting the Menshevik and Social Revolutionary misleaders within the soviets. Hence, there could no longer be any doubts about the correctness of Lenin's intransigent, fifteen-year battle against the Mensheviks and for a politically homogeneous combat party.

Lenin had already won a majority on all the key questions under dispute in the Bolshevik leadership when Trotsky arrived back from exile in May, a month after Lenin. Trotsky's return had been delayed by his detention in a Canadian concentration camp by British authorities—an act vigorously denounced by Lenin and one which forced even the new Provisional Government to lodge a formal protest.

Trotsky—who led the Mezhrayontsi (interdistrict organization), which he had formed several years earlier—did not proceed at once to join the Bolshevik Party as an individual. He had the responsibility of bringing the rest of the Mezhrayontsi group, 4,000 revolutionists, into the Bolshevik ranks with him. This process was facilitated by the growing practical collaboration between members of the Bolsheviks and the Mezhrayontsi, especially in Petrograd. As this cooperation advanced, a solid foundation already existed for Lenin and Trotsky to cooperate politically on the same course as co-leaders of the workers' vanguard. Going ahead along those lines, they first assessed the current state of the revolution and on that basis charted a new course whereby the masses could attain progressive goals.

Lenin explained that the revolution had rapidly arrived at a situation of dual power, which nobody had foreseen. A bourgeois government controlled the organs of state power, and it was trying to strengthen the repressive apparatus for use against the masses. But another government, a government of the workers and peasants, also existed in the form of soviets. Although these bodies lacked direct command of the state machinery, they rested on the support of the popular masses—including armed workers and soldiers—and thus held de facto power in their hands. Lenin pointed out that the defeat of the Paris Commune had already demonstrated that such an interlocking of two powers could not exist indefinitely, however. One of them had to establish its supremacy and dispose of its rival. If the workers failed to act decisively, they would be crushed.

A bourgeois-landowner conspiracy was being hatched, Lenin and Trotsky warned, to break the deadlock through a counterrevolution organized under cover of the Provisional Government. To block that move, the two Marxist leaders hammered away at the following themes—for a transfer of state power to the soviets; for creation of a soviet republic; for replacement of the standing army and police by the arming of the whole people; and for workers' control of industry.

In an immediate sense, Lenin and Trotsky noted, such a transfer of power would merely place it in the hands of the Mensheviks and Social Revolutionaries. That contradiction could be resolved, though, by taking advantage of the twofold nature of these compromisist parties. It was primarily their petty-bourgeois leaders who had close ties with the bourgeoisie and feared the idea of taking power in their own right. At the moment they could influence most of the rank-and-file workers, soldiers, and peasants who also entertained illusions about the bourgeoisie. But a vast majority in the ranks were loyal above everything else to the soviets, through which they hoped to win their just demands. That fact opened the way to influence them on programmatic issues. Thus, the fight for soviet power was at the same time a battle to loosen the hold of the compromisers over the soviets.

To acquire such influence, the Bolsheviks and Mezhrayontsi launched a joint propaganda offensive calling for major changes in soviet policy. They made the slogan "All power to the soviets" the key point in a program of concrete immediate, democratic, and transitional demands shaped roughly as follows:

An immediate end to Russia's involvement in the imperialist war. Confiscation of landed estates and institution of sweeping agrarian reform by peasant soviets. An eight-hour day in industry. Workers' control of industry. Nationalization of the banks and industrial syndicates, together with seizure of capitalist profits reaped from the war. Self-determination for all oppressed nations and peoples, including the right to secession, and guarantees of full rights for national minorities. Speedy convocation of a constituent assembly, with the necessary soviet measures to assure democratic representation of the toilers.

As this propaganda offensive began, Lenin outlined the manner in which it should be conducted. To be most effective, he cautioned, the vanguard forces had to keep in mind that they were as yet able to influence only a minority within the soviets. To win a majority they had to wage an irreconcilable struggle against the petty-bourgeois parties; help the people learn to distrust the bourgeoisie; and clearly explain the socialist alternative to capitalism. In doing so, adaptation was required to special conditions of work among unprecedentedly large masses who were just awakening to political life. They needed to have the errors in program, strategy, and tactics by the reformist-led soviets patiently explained to them, again and again, so they could overcome these mistakes in the course of their own further experience.

As gains were made through such efforts, Lenin stressed, the Bolsheviks and their allies could become the majority force in the soviets. These bodies would then be freed from petty-bourgeois timidity. They would be able to act in a bold, determined manner. The revolution could then advance toward establishment and consolidation of a proletarian dictatorship.

By this time objective developments were preparing the way for open-minded consideration of revolutionary socialist views among the masses. In the industrial centers workers' demands for wage hikes to offset skyrocketing prices were resisted by the bosses. Food shortages were becoming more acute. The conditions of life generally were deteriorating, and no end was in sight to the war that brought such hardships.

Toward the end of April, the mounting discontent led to spontaneous flare-ups of mass protest in cities all over Russia. The main action took place in Petrograd, where an armed demonstration was organized. It was supported by many soldiers in the local garrison, a development that reflected growing dissatisfaction among peasants who had been drafted into the army. Demands raised by the Petrograd demonstrators included removal from government office of the most notorious pro-war figures, but they did not yet perceive the need to replace the Provisional Government itself with soviet power.

The Mensheviks and Social Revolutionaries on the soviet executive committee reacted to the mass pressure by entering more deeply into collusion with the bourgeoisie. At the beginning of May they helped to form a new coalition government. The change involved removal of the most outspoken imperialist agents from the Provisional Government and their replacement by representatives of the soviet. These representatives, however, being petty-bourgeois compromisers, agreed to retention of a capitalist majority in the reconstituted government, whom they served as a loyal opposition—that is, as little more than a screen for deception of the masses, while the privileged classes tried to consolidate their position.

During these events the Bolsheviks' influence among the masses increased significantly, especially in Petrograd. But they remained a minority in the soviets, where most leaders of the workers, soldiers, and peasants had been taken in by the shift to a coalition government. This situation was soon to undergo further change, however, as new developments presented both fresh opportunities and complex problems.

After the tsar was overthrown, the Russian soldiers had grown more reluctant than ever to fight. Their feelings had been communicated to the German troops and fraternization had developed quite extensively. This had led in turn to a virtual armistice at the front when the German commanders accepted the situation for their own reasons. Meantime, Russia's imperialist allies had been pressing the Russian bourgeoisie to get the country back on a war footing, and the coalition government now made the try. An offensive was launched in mid-June. The Germans responded with a counterattack in which the Russian forces, upon whom heavy casualties were inflicted, suffered a catastrophic defeat.

The resumption of military hostilities aroused popular indignation throughout Russia. Once again the main protest actions took place in Petrograd. Armed workers and soldiers in the capital initiated big demonstrations demanding that the soviet executive committee seize power and end the war. As this step revealed, the revolution was reaching a turning point; many in the ranks of Russia's toilers were ready to take the struggle for peace into their own hands.

The demand that power be transferred to the soviets was rejected, however, by the compromisers on the soviet executive committee who had become part of the Provisional Government.

Under those circumstances, resort to an armed insurrection

would have been premature. There were no widespread vacillations within the owning classes or among the petty-bourgeois misleaders of the workers' movement. Instead, the bourgeoisie was preparing a counterrevolutionary offensive and the petty-bourgeois compromisers were providing a cover for the plot. Therefore, the test of further events was necessary. Before the required changes in policy and leadership could be made, the task remained one of patiently explaining, of winning a majority in the soviets.

For an insurrection to succeed, Lenin and Trotsky warned, the workers had to be ready as a class to make the move; the revolutionary upsurge of the people as a whole had to be at a high point; and vacillations in the ranks of the enemy had to be most pronounced. At that moment, they explained, the prerequisites for a successful insurrection did not exist. Even in Petrograd a majority belonged to the petty-bourgeois parties. Many workers still cherished illusions about the compromisers, to whom they were ready to offer power. The proletariat did not have the bulk of the soldiers on its side. A new revolutionary upsurge had not yet developed among the peasants.

Besides all these factors, it was not enough merely to seize power. The revolutionary forces had to be able to hold it against counterattacks by the privileged classes; otherwise reaction would in the end prevail in an even more bloody manner.

Most of the Petrograd rebels were unwilling to heed such advice. They felt an urge to push all the soviet parties toward decisive action, and they were determined to proceed accordingly. If at that juncture the Marxists had turned their backs on the rebel masses because they were acting prematurely, the movement would have fallen under the influence of ultraleftism, which had arisen in various forms during earlier struggles against tsarism. That could only have led to disastrous adventurism. So Lenin and Trotsky had no alternative but to lead the Marxist forces to place themselves at the head of the movement with the aim of preventing the mass protest from turning into an ill-conceived and premature test of armed strength.

Early in July the Petrograd workers, acting with extensive support from soldiers garrisoned in the city, conducted what were and could be no more than armed demonstrations that reconnoitered the relationship of forces between the contending classes. The movement had at most a semi-insurrectionary character in the sense that the masses adopted the Bolshevik slogans: "Down with the capitalist ministers!" and "All power to the soviets!"

Pointing to these demands as a pretext, both the government and the compromisers in the official soviet leadership claimed that the Bolsheviks and their allies had started an insurrection. Reliable military units were called in. They opened fire on the demonstrators, and in the encounters that followed there were a number of casualties. The protest movement was suppressed, striking a heavy blow at the masses. But thanks to the revolutionary Marxist intervention, which kept the conflict from escalating into an all-out armed confrontation, the blow was not a decisive one. The future of the revolution was safeguarded, and it would henceforth unfold in the atmosphere of civil war that had now been created by the bourgeoisie.

The July defeat temporarily altered the relationship of class forces to the disadvantage of the revolutionary vanguard. Mass resistance having been weakened, the government was able to disarm the Petrograd workers and weed out rebel units in the local garrison. Menshevik and Social Revolutionary proletarians, who had moved to the left during the upsurge, turned back to their own parties—a trend that strengthened the compromisers in the soviet leadership.

Grabbing the opportunity thus created, the bourgeois government took reprisals against the Bolshevik Party and the Mezhrayontsi. Both organizations were outlawed. Their press was banned, and they were subjected to extralegal raids by counterrevolutionary gangs. Many of their leaders, including Trotsky, were jailed by the authorities, but a few managed to go underground before they could be arrested. Lenin was among the latter, and that enabled him to continue providing active guidance in a restricted way.

At this juncture the Mezhrayontsi fused with the Bolshevik Party—which between April and July had grown from 80,000 to 240,000 proletarian members—at a joint congress that was held clandestinely in late July. Although neither Lenin nor Trotsky could attend, their policies were adopted by the gathering and both were elected to the central committee of the expanded party. From then on their political collaboration was reinforced by close organizational ties as official Bolshevik leaders.

About the same time further changes were made in the Provisional Government. When the Petrograd demonstrations were broken up by armed force, the adverse consequences extended beyond the blows rained upon the revolutionary vanguard. The soviets themselves were placed at a disadvantage by the defeat, and that emboldened the possessing classes to strive more aggressively for definitive control over the country. The Cadet leaders of the liberal bourgeoisie made the opening move by withdrawing from their cabinet posts. In doing so, they confronted the petty-bourgeois compromisers with an ultimatum: either accept major changes in the form of rule, or face an open confrontation with the capitalists. As usual, the compromisers knuckled under to the Cadet demands.

Toward the end of July a new type of government was formed with Kerensky as the prime minister. His cabinet was composed of other Social Revolutionaries, together with Mensheviks and Cadets. As had been the case in the previous cabinet, the Cadets retained the upper hand. All involved agreed that the new regime should function as an arbiter between the contending social classes. More than ever, as this concept showed, the soviets were being relegated to the role of mere appendages to a bourgeois ruling structure.

Kerensky's government had a Bonapartist character. As a modern phenomenon, Bonapartism has tended to appear in revolutionary confrontations when the capitalists and workers find themselves stalemated in a struggle for power. Basing itself on the state's repressive apparatus, Bonapartism assumes the guise of a central authority standing impartially above the contending classes. It poses as the guardian of abstract "national interests" allegedly involving the common welfare of the entire population. But such a government's real function is to consolidate the victory of reaction, or to end the revolutionary upsurge before capitalist property relations can be upset.

This was the basic task assigned to Kerensky by the Russian bourgeoisie. In striving to comply, he planned to use false promises about ultimate concessions to the exploited classes as a means of warding off major confrontations with the masses until the soviets could be dissolved. He assumed that once these troublesome formations disappeared the repressive apparatus could be used to consolidate bourgeois power. This clever scheme had a fundamental flaw; it was based on a wrong judgment of objective reality. The revolution had not yet exhausted its forces. Hence, no basis existed through the use of political trickery for class equilibrium to prevail.

Although the Mensheviks and Social Revolutionaries had crippled the soviets, these democratic organs of struggle continued to survive, and a developing resurgence of mass activity threatened to breathe new life into them. This trend caused panic among the owning classes, who soon realized that the Cadet-manipulated Kerensky government was incapable of warding off the soviet threat to their special privileges.

The big landowners began to clamor for more decisive measures to block expropriation of their estates. This impatience with the Cadet line was shared by much of the bourgeoisie, who had become closely tied up with the landed nobility and recognized that abolition of private land ownership would inevitably propel the revolution toward nationalization of the banks and other measures against capital itself. So they wanted sterner repressive action to preserve capitalism. Harsher steps were also demanded by the British, French, and U.S. imperialists. They were concerned both to protect their investments in Russian enterprises and to keep the war going on Germany's eastern front.

This cabal set out to break the dual-power deadlock by means of a military coup. General Lavr Kornilov, a monarchist who remained supreme commander of the army, was chosen to head the conspiracy. His main target was Petrograd, where the workers had been disarmed and where the more revolutionary troops had been re-moved from the city. With the immediate means of armed opposition thus impaired, all the military factors seemed in readiness for the counterrevolution to succeed.

Political preparations for the move also appeared favorable. Under pressure from the reactionary bloc, the Cadets had lined up in support of Kornilov. As is always the case with liberals, when the chips were down their main concern was preservation of the capitalist system; and to gain that end they had no scruples against imposition of a police state upon the masses. Besides that, Kerensky, who had linked his political career with maintenance of bourgeois rule, stood ready to connive with the plotters behind the backs of the Russian masses. All in all, the privileged classes felt the time had come to make their bid for undisputed control over the country.

On August 26 (September 8) the capitalist ministers resigned once more from the Provisional Government. Kornilov then launched the military rebellion, seeking to disguise it as a campaign directed only against the Bolsheviks. The most reliable detachments were withdrawn from the front and ordered to march on Petrograd. Once the capital had been taken, Kornilov aimed to crush the soviets and set up a military dictatorship.

But the anti-Bolshevik propaganda gimmick didn't work. Bitter experience had taught the masses that a tsarist general meant them no good, and their angry reaction to the military threat showed that it was likely to fail. Confronted with that probability, Kerensky dissociated himself from the attack by ordering Kornilov removed from command of the army. Kornilov disregarded the order, and at that point responsibility for defense of the capital was formally assumed by the government, which was compelled to act in cooperation with the soviet executive committee.

With their own necks at stake, the compromisers in the soviet leadership now found it expedient to shift their policy to the left, at least temporarily, so as to appeal for mass backing against Kornilov. Promises were made to press the government for immediate establishment of a democratic republic and speedy implementation of agrarian reforms. The soviet executive committee then held a joint meeting with special representatives chosen by the Petrograd workers and soldiers at which an ad hoc committee was formed to organize the defense of the capital. From the outset of the crisis, though, the compromisers tended to be pushed aside by militants in the soviet ranks. The Provisional Government was similarly bypassed, and the main activities were carried out through unofficial channels.

Special committees of defense appeared spontaneously as the innate capacity of the soviets to mobilize great masses was again demonstrated. These vital organizations of mass struggle that the compromisers had sought to liquidate were being resuscitated through initiative in the ranks. The resistance movement spread into the countryside and to the front-line trenches, where most of the troops were against the officer corps. In fact the soldiers and sailors had even more at stake than identification with progressive social aims. If the forces of reaction won out, they faced the danger of bloody reprisals because of their past revolutionary conduct.

The Bolshevik Party played a key role in organizing the defense. Its cadres were extremely active everywhere. Under their pressure the defense committees decided to arm the workers. Red Guard units were formed in the factories, and the capital was quickly transformed into a military stronghold of the revolution.

As it turned out, however, Petrograd didn't have to be defended in battle. Kornilov never got there. His army, which found itself faced with universal hostility, disintegrated while still on the march. The counterrevolutionary attempt had met with ignominious defeat.

By now the Bolshevik Party had become widely respected among the workers. While consistently supporting their struggles, it had methodically analyzed the political mistakes of their misleaders and patiently advocated policies conforming with the laws of proletarian revolution. Changing objective trends had been examined in detail, always with care not to underestimate capitalist strength in assessing the current relationship of class forces. In this way the party had been able—at each stage of developments—to project a course of action that squared with existing reality and what was needed. Through firm measures taken accordingly, it had managed to prevent an untimely armed uprising by the workers and then to mobilize and arm these workers and their allies in an effective defense against a military attack from the right.

Concrete experiences during both these phases of the unfolding class showdown had caused many workers to reject the Menshevik-Social Revolutionary line and become more attentive to Bolshevik advice. Their shift in attitude was reflected in the mushrooming of Bolshevik influence throughout industry. Party recruitment also rose at a quickening pace, and the ranks gained increased confidence in their ability to win leadership of the substantial majority of the working class.

The workers' changing political consciousness soon found expression in the broad membership of the soviets. A campaign was launched for release of the imprisoned Bolshevik leaders, and the government was compelled to free them, if not unconditionally at least on bond. Before long the Bolsheviks won a majority in the executive committee of the Petrograd soviet. Trotsky was then chosen as its new president, and under his leadership the compromisers were pushed aside. Thus having become more homogeneous in revolutionary outlook, the Petrograd body set the pace in arming the workers on an extensive scale through expansion of the Red Guard. It also voted for replacement of the Kerensky regime with a soviet government.

Concerning the latter question, the Bolshevik leaders cautioned, the slogan "All power to the soviets" had undergone a change in meaning since it was raised back in April. At that time the people were fully armed; the propertied classes had no way to take repressive action; and this made it possible for the soviets to take power peacefully. Since then, however, the Mensheviks and Social Revolutionaries had not only weakened the soviets, but also strengthened the Provisional Government, which would stop at nothing to maintain continued bourgeois rule.

Under these conditions, they pointed out, the Kerensky regime could be overturned only by revolutionary means. Toward that end the workers' vanguard had to prepare an armed uprising to put the soviets in power. But the final step could be taken only if and when objective developments made it possible to act with sufficient support on a national scale.

It didn't take long for the masses to reach the point where they were ready for decisive revolutionary measures. The industrial workers conducted protest demonstrations and strikes at an accelerated tempo. Peasant committees which had already seized some of the landed estates clamored for all of them to be confiscated and placed under their control. Ferment mounted among oppressed nationalities seeking the right of self-determination. The army, which now understood that it was still being used to serve imperialist ends, resumed fraternization with the German troops; and desertions began to disintegrate the Russian front. An overwhelming majority of the population became united around a central demand for immediate peace.

Goaded by a deepening sense of frustration, the masses everywhere were turning away from the compromisers. The soldiers themselves helped the Bolsheviks brush aside government attempts to isolate them from the front. Many peasants were beginning to see that the proletariat had to replace the bourgeoisie at the head of the state, and they were tending accordingly to emulate the workers in looking to the Bolsheviks for leadership.

The contest between the proletariat and bourgeoisie for influence over the petty-bourgeois masses grew sharper by the day. Less and less room existed for a straddling position between the two basic classes. Deep rifts developed within the Menshevik Party, which began to lose its worker members to the Bolsheviks. The Social Revolutionary Party, to which Kerensky formally adhered, underwent a different type of split. Its peasant members began to side with the Bolsheviks against the SR leaders who held posts in the government. After trying in vain to mend this rupture, a radical intellectual wing broke away from the main party and set up an independent Social Revolutionary formation with a leftist tinge. Like most of the intelligentsia, this petty-bourgeois grouping proved incapable of coming all the way over to the proletarian vanguard.

The extremely concentrated developments since February had prepared the way for a proletarian-led revolution such as the world had never seen. In the factories, on the land, and at the front the masses were simply waiting for the Petrograd soviet to take the initiative. The time had come to act.

At this point Lenin—who had become the central target of bourgeois hatred and still had to remain underground or face the danger of physical removal from all contact with the revolutionary cadres—summoned the Bolsheviks to insurrection. A small minority in the party's central committee opposed such a move, and their hesitations reflected the existence to some extent of similar vacillations in the party cadres. So Lenin, with Trotsky's support, undertook to clarify the question.

The acute nature of the developing struggle created renewed danger, Lenin explained in sum, that the government would again use troops against the people. A showdown was, therefore, at hand to determine whether a proletarian revolution or a military dictatorship would prevail. The proletariat now had a good chance to resolve the issue in its favor. It had the support of a national majority; the forces of reaction had fallen momentarily into a state of confusion; and the compromisist parties had become disorganized. If action was delayed, however, this opportunity would be lost. The petty-bourgeois elements had little staying power. If their expectations were not realized then and there a drift would begin toward renewed support of bourgeois efforts to resolve the crisis in a counterrevolutionary manner.

To prevent an assault from the right, he urged, the Bolsheviks had to lead an immediate soviet attack on the government. This could be done successfully through use of the armed workers and revolutionary soldiers in Petrograd. Strong backing of the Petrograd action could be mobilized in Moscow. Initiative taken in these major cities was bound to receive massive support nationally. The

Kerensky government could be overthrown, the capitalist state machine smashed, and the soviet apparatus put in its place. No less important, state power could most likely be held until reinforcement came through the proletarian revolutions maturing elsewhere in Europe.

Most of the Bolsheviks agreed with Lenin. At the party's initiative, with the coming insurrection in mind and in the face of the Kornilov offensive, a Military Revolutionary Committee was formed by the Petrograd soviet in early October. An all-Russian congress of soviets had been scheduled to convene in the capital at the end of October. It had become evident to all that the government was preparing new counterrevolutionary measures. This circumstance provided an ideal opening to force a quick showdown. (As Trotsky observed later in writing about October, a revolution can win only on the offensive; but the more the tasks are posed in terms of self-defense, the better the revolution develops.) With little bloodshed the insurrectionary forces swept aside such military units as the government had at its disposal, and Kerensky took flight.

Dual power had definitively come to an end. On October 25 (November 7), 1917, the Military Revolutionary Committee issued a proclamation that the Provisional Government had been deposed; that power was in the hands of the Petrograd soviet. Eight months after tsarism was overthrown the workers had come to the head of the country.

# 7

# First Workers' State

After seizing power the Petrograd workers and soldiers handed it over to the All-Russia Congress of Soviets then in session. The various bodies represented at the congress thereby assumed a changed role as the supreme authority in the land. Broader layers of the nation's toilers were rapidly drawn into the existing formations. Parallel with that advance, newly created soviets began to spring up, especially among the peasants as they now prepared to carry out the agrarian reforms so long denied them. Mass participation in organized political life thus took an immense leap forward, and the Bolshevik Party had to guide these forces step by step from the achievement of immediate, limited objectives to a basic transformation of the entire social structure.

Policy decisions were made and carried out by the soviets on the basis of full internal democracy. All political tendencies loyal to the revolution had complete freedom to advance their views. They could function in an organized manner, publish their own newspapers, and nominate their own candidates for election to soviet office.

Democracy was not, however, elevated to an abstract principle standing above the imperative requirements of the class struggle.

The tiny minority of exploiters were denied their customary use of the press, which they had previously monopolized through their wealth and power to deceive and cheat the exploited majority. Acts of sabotage against the revolution by the propertied classes or their agents brought severe punishment.

As the main safeguard against counterrevolution the old state machine was completely dismantled. The capitalist police apparatus, which had been used primarily to uphold bourgeois property rights, was replaced by a new, revolutionary police force designed to protect human rights and defend the revolution against its enemies. Maintenance of a standing army for the purpose of repressing unarmed masses was ended. Instead, the soviets created a military force of workers and peasants having close ties with all who engaged in productive labor. In making this change the huge army that had been mobilized during the imperialist war—and remained deployed at the front—was democratized. The rank-and-file soldiers were authorized to elect the officers, supervise their conduct, and displace them as needed.

At the governmental level the new regime developed as the most democratic and progressive structure ever created. Power was vested in representatives elected by the people. The soviets to which they were elected carried out both legislative and executive functions. There was no artificial separation of powers between different branches of government, a bourgeois method used to block measures opposed by the propertied classes. The advantages of representative democracy over autocratic rule were combined with those of immediate and direct democracy—all within the framework of the rule of the toilers, not the exploiters.

Control over administrative work was taken away from highly paid specialists beholden to the bourgeoisie for their sinecures. It was allotted to agencies run by the toilers. Salaries received by those engaged in such activity were no higher than the wage rate of a skilled worker. All elected representatives and appointed personnel were subject, moreover, to recall at any time.

The Bolsheviks, who were now the majority party in the soviets, gave all worker and peasant political tendencies an opportunity to participate in the government. In the existing circumstances, however, this policy could be applied only to a limited degree. On the eve of the October insurrection the leading Mensheviks and Social Revolutionaries had proposed that the Kerensky regime be replaced through changes in the governmental coalition with the bourgeoisie. When their line was rejected they bolted the soviet congress. The left Social Revolutionaries acted otherwise. They supported the insurrection, and the Bolsheviks invited them to become part of the government.

But the group's petty-bourgeois leaders refused to go all the way in collaborating with the proletariat. They declined nomination to the Council of People's Commissars, which the soviets formed as the government's executive body. So all council posts had to be filled by the Bolsheviks, and Lenin was elected to serve as the presiding officer.

Despite their strategic position at the head of the country, it was not possible at this juncture for the Bolsheviks to fully develop the dictatorship of the proletariat. Only the first moves could be initiated toward the creation of a workers' state in whose hands all major means of production and distribution would be concentrated. In doing so, moreover, power had to be shared for an indefinite period with the peasantry, and the peasants—especially the more prosperous ones—did not attach much importance to socialist objectives. The ruling structure thus remained at the preliminary stage of a workers' and farmers' government.

Even though the propertied classes had been superseded politically, the new regime's freedom of action was still restricted by continued prevalence of capitalist property relations. To overcome this obstacle the bourgeoisie had to be expropriated economically. But a majority of all toilers had first to become convinced of the need for such action; in addition, the ground had to be prepared for them to carry out the task when they were ready. For these reasons only partial measures of workers' control could initially be introduced in the spheres of industry and trade—measures that cut into the capitalists' special privileges, undermined their economic power, and simultaneously brought immediate benefits to the masses and initial experience in managing the economy.

Still another matter figured prominently in developments at this point. The peasants and oppressed nationalities were pressing the government to concentrate on fulfillment of their demands. A quick response was required, and a combined character was thereby imparted to the next phase of the revolution. While preparing to eradicate bourgeois property relations in order to consolidate a workers' state, other economic and political actions had to be taken at once to meet the needs of the insurgent peasants and oppressed nationalities.

Although these combined tasks presented many difficulties, the proletariat had an enormous stake in devoting major attention to these problems, unsolved because there had never been a bourgeois-democratic revolution in Russia. The welfare of the peasants and oppressed nations was bound up with the fate of the unfolding of the socialist revolution. As concrete action was taken to meet their needs, they could be induced to support broader measures required to safeguard these gains. To assure such an advance in fundamental outlook, however, these sections of the population had to be drawn into all aspects of the continuing struggle on an extensive scale against the exploiters and conditions of life they had created. This could be accomplished only in a manner permitted by the given economic reality and state of mass political consciousness.

Proceeding accordingly, the Bolsheviks outlined the initial course of government policy. It involved prompt measures to take Russia out of the imperialist war; abolition of landed proprietorship and direct participation by the peasants in agrarian reform; guarantees of self-determination for national minorities; and complete workers' control over industrial production and the distribution of commodities.

Longer-term soviet perspectives were also projected. Acting with the consent of the masses and in keeping with their accumulating experiences, the Bolsheviks advocated that the government should transform the whole state system along socialist lines. Capitalism should be done away with entirely. Class exploitation and inequality could then be ended; a higher form of economic relations, based on collective ownership of industry and the land, could be developed and the products of labor made available to all in a just manner. With the Russian soviets setting an example of this nature, they emphasized, strides could be made toward a world socialist victory that would be sealed by the advanced workers of other countries.

Action began forthwith on the most pressing matters. The soviet government publicized secret treaties found in the tsarist archives that exposed the imperialist character of the war. Russia's involvement in predatory alliances with foreign powers was repudiated. Immediate negotiations were proposed to conclude a democratic peace with self-determination guaranteed to every nationality, including the restoration of self-government in territories annexed by the imperialists in the past. This proposal was addressed not only to the governments, but also to the workers, soldiers, and farmers in the warring countries. The masses everywhere were urged to unite with the soviets in revolutionary opposition to continuation of the world slaughter.

In the existing international situation, however, the ruling classes of Britain, France, and the United States were able to ignore the Russian call for a prompt end to the war. So the soviet government initiated its own separate peace talks with the Germans. A temporary cease fire was arranged on December 15 (28), 1917, and a peace conference opened soon thereafter. There was no secret diplomacy in the negotiations; they were conducted openly, in full view of the masses.

Meantime, there was urgent need for expanded agricultural production, and it had to take place along lines acceptable to the peasants. Hence the government's chief role was to encourage peasant initiatives in agrarian reform, taking care to set equal standards for all. A start had already been made in changing the relations between land ownership and agriculture. Although the basic aim was to establish public ownership and move toward collective tillage of the soil, this could not be done in a single leap. It would have been self-defeating to deny the peasants access to land taken from the big proprietors, or to undertake forced collectivization of small, individually owned plots. The peasants demanded the right to have farms of their own. If such a diffused ownership structure remained a far cry from the advantages of collectivization, it was on the road toward socialist collectives.

Landed estates were expropriated with government authority and parceled under management of the peasants themselves. Primary responsibility for redistribution of such holdings was assigned to soviets of poor peasants, which were organized separate and apart from units representing better-off peasants. All categories of small farmers were encouraged to help increase the total agricultural output, and industrial aid was extended in the form of implements, fertilizer, etc., to help them do so.

While concentrating on the foregoing measures, a first step was taken toward development of a transition from small-peasant farming to socialization of the land. Where feasible, model collective farms were established and operated by soviets of agricultural laborers. Even though these units could as yet constitute only a minor part of the economic complex, it was expected that they would increase as the farm equipment and supplies necessary for collectivization were produced, and the example they set would contribute to ultimate peasant recognition of the advantages inherent in mechanized, socialist agriculture.

High priority was also given to the exercise of self-determination by oppressed nationalities. This question involved a democratic right, not a principle of socialist organization. These nations had been denied the elementary democratic right of self-government by the Russian bourgeoisie after it took power in February 1917, and the violation could be corrected only under proletarian leadership. This is true with many democratic rights in the epoch of imperialist decay. But there were two sides to the solution of the nationalities problem.

In laying the foundations for a socialist order, the working class needed to economically and socially reorganize the largest area possible. Under the inherited conditions, that of the tsarist "prison house of nations," this could be done only by erecting a new, federated structure of individual soviet republics embracing various nationalities. A compromise thus had to be reached between centralization needed to shape a planned economy, and decentralization required for the free development of nations previously oppressed by the imperialists. It would take more time to convince the workers and peasants of these nations—through further experiences in economic, political, and cultural collaboration within the soviet federation—that fuller centralization was in the best interests of all toilers.

Even a viable federated structure could exist, moreover, only through voluntary acceptance of fraternal association by the nations involved; the right of self-determination had to remain fully operative. For these reasons, the new Bolshevik-led government extended freedom of choice to all nationalities. They could either remain part of the Soviet Union with broad local autonomy, or peacefully secede from it should they so desire. In most cases they joined the federation of soviets.

Concerning the situation in industry, changes had already begun concurrent with the reappearance of soviets when the tsar was dethroned. Organization of factory committees was initiated by the Petrograd workers and gradually extended elsewhere. These committees went beyond actions to improve wages, hours, and job conditions. They also took measures to alleviate shortages of goods and curb price gouging. Factory owners were forced to open their books for inspection by the workers. Capitalist profiteering was exposed. Supervision was expanded step by step over factory operations and the distribution of products.

Dual power of an economic character began to develop, with neither the workers nor the bosses having total control. It was not possible, though, to resolve this contradiction in the workers' favor at the factory level. A political obstacle had to be removed. At every turn the bourgeois Provisional Government sided with the bosses.

The compromisers in the soviet leadership backed the government, and the workers found themselves stalemated.

Although the October insurrection ended capitalist use of the government against the workers, it did not follow that they could achieve full economic supremacy in one stroke. More was involved than the seizure of capitalist industry by the soviet regime. For this step to become practical, the workers first needed to gain experience in administering the national economy while most factories remained temporarily capitalist owned.

To carry out the desired measures in the industrial sphere, Lenin explained, revolutionary democracy had to be applied so the masses could develop confidence in their own strength. In addition to their other functions, the trade unions had to become schools for managing the economy. The workers had to be schooled in the art of administration in handling overall management of production and distribution. Toward that end their control over the bosses had to be extended at once to every facet of industry and trade. Knowledge acquired through such activities would prepare them to administer the whole economic structure, and all capitalist enterprises could then be expropriated.

Quick action was taken by the soviet government to set this process into motion. By official decree workers' control was established over all industrial, commercial, banking, and agricultural enterprises employing five or more people. Committees elected by the workers in these enterprises were authorized to keep a constant eye on company books, records, inventories, etc.; ferret out secrets kept from them by the bosses; and see that all operations were conducted in the public interest.

Factory committees of this kind constituted the organizational nuclei for state regulation of the industrial economy. They became part of and subordinate to the trade unions in the various branches of industry. The unions, while independent, were in turn responsible to the soviets, and subordinate to them on matters of planning and state policy. By means of this overall structural form, the workers in each factory could defend their immediate interests.

Actions they took could be coordinated with the general policies required for the given branch of production, and all this could be done in a way that served the broad objectives of the working class as a whole.

Disputes with individual employers were handled by the factory committees. Where necessary they conducted strikes to enforce their demands. It was no longer possible, though, for the bosses to retaliate by using lockouts as a punitive weapon against the workers. The capitalists could do no more than appeal their cases to higher workers' bodies.

The bourgeoisie tried to resist imposition of workers' control by disruption of industrial production, openly or covertly. The government retaliated by confiscating the property holdings of the most incorrigible capitalist saboteurs. At the same time a law was enacted making it obligatory for all citizens to perform work assigned to them by the soviets. This measure was used not only to break passive resistance on the part of individual capitalists, but also to draw upon the services of trained specialists—administrators, engineers, accountants, etc.

Wartime controls over necessities, such as bread rationing, served as a means of compulsion. Those who refused to work found it hard to get food. To further assure full compliance with the law, workers' organizations verified the quantity and quality of services performed by the capitalists and their trained specialists.

Measures were also taken by the new regime to eradicate bourgeois financial domination over the country. A state bank—designed to provide a means for national accounting of production and distribution—was organized under government control. The private banking system was then nationalized as the first step to absorb it into the new financial structure. Directors and shareholders belonging to the wealthy classes were required to keep the nationalized enterprises functioning in good order, doing so in compliance with the law on workers' control.

As a safeguard against undercover financial manipulations, members of the wealthy classes were ordered to keep their assets in the state bank. Limited withdrawals for living expenses were allowed. In the case of funds intended for use in production and trade, however, withdrawals had first to be approved by the organizations of workers' control. Persons who deceived the state had all their property confiscated, and they were made liable to imprisonment, military service at the front, or hard labor.

Special attention was also given to the question of summoning the Constituent Assembly. This body's traditional functions of eradication of precapitalist property relations and establishment of a representative political structure, were already being handled effectively by the soviets; and the soviets were advancing simultaneously toward an unprecedented historic leap through preparations to abolish capitalism. But mass consciousness lagged behind changing reality. Most workers and peasants remained unaware of the October revolution's full scope and significance. They still looked upon the Constituent Assembly—which could have played a progressive role under the bourgeois republic set up after the February uprisings—as the key instrument for social reorganization, and they wanted it convened.

Delegates to the assembly had been elected after the October revolution, but on the basis of slates that had been presented before then, in mid-October. At that point, the Kerensky regime had yielded to mass pressure on the issue, in hopes of using the step as a means of warding off the impending workers' insurrection. Nominees were chosen at a time of great political confusion brought about by Menshevik and Social Revolutionary collusion with the liberal bourgeoisie, and the selection of candidates did not reflect the anticapitalist mood and orientation rapidly developing among the toilers.

On top of that the peasants, who comprised a big majority of the population, had been subjected to entrapment in the elections. In the main they supported the Social Revolutionary Party. But no provision had been made for them to choose between the party's right-wing supporters of the bourgeoisie and its left-wing backers of the proletariat; they could vote only for a party slate rigged by the compromisers. Through this piece of trickery, the right Social Revolutionaries had won a majority in the assembly, where they would be further strengthened by support from their Menshevik allies.

It thus became possible for the bourgeoisie and the compromisers to use the Constituent Assembly as a means of undermining soviet rule, and the Bolsheviks alerted the masses to the danger. Broad alignments in the political sphere, they pointed out, had undergone a qualitative change since mid-October. A contradiction resulted in the composition of the assembly, and it should be resolved through new elections; that is, by exercising the electorate's democratic right to recall those elected. Otherwise the Mensheviks and right Social Revolutionaries could use the assembly to promote their policy of capitulating to the bourgeoisie. They could again betray the revolutionary cause of the working and exploited classes.

The compromisers responded with a propaganda campaign around the slogan "All power to the Constituent Assembly!" This demand was supported by the propertied classes. They had no intention, though, of reverting to pre-October collaboration with a compromisist wing in the soviets. Their aim was to use the assembly issue as the opening gambit in a counterrevolutionary offensive; for only by crushing the soviets, one way or another, could they halt agrarian reform, protect capitalist property, and keep Russia in the imperialist war.

Since illusions among the masses could be overcome only when the Constituent Assembly was seen in action, the soviet government convened it on January 18 (31), 1918. The Bolshevik delegation in attendance moved at once to expose the compromisers' opposition to basic soviet policy. This was accomplished by submitting for adoption by the gathering a declaration on the rights of workers, peasants, and oppressed nationalities.

All power, the declaration asserted in substance, shall be vested in a federation of soviet national republics democratically established as a free union of nations. The fundamental soviet aims shall be to abolish exploitation of the toilers, eliminate the division of society into classes, and achieve socialism. Landed estates shall be proclaimed the property of the entire working people. Workers' control shall be authorized to guarantee their power over the exploiters and as the first step toward full conversion of industry into national property. All banks shall be taken over by the state. The working people shall be armed, an army of workers and peasants created, and the propertied classes completely disarmed. A democratic peace between the countries now at war shall be urged, without indemnities or annexations of territory, and on the basis of free self-determination for all nations.

When a motion was made to open discussion on the declaration, the compromisist majority voted it down. At this point the Bolshevik delegation walked out in protest, after first announcing that the majority's counterrevolutionary stand would be referred to the soviet power for appropriate action. The left Social Revolutionaries then called for adoption of the soviet peace policy. Their motion, too, was summarily rejected, whereupon they also withdrew from the gathering. With these developments the masses were able to perceive the real nature of the Constituent Assembly, and they backed the government in dissolving it the next day.

Having been frustrated in their attempt to use the Constituent Assembly as a counterrevolutionary instrument, the propertied classes now staked their all on overturning the soviet power by force and violence. They resorted to full-scale civil war. The governments of Britain, France, and the United States gave them material support, and a bloody struggle broke out.

When the civil war erupted, the German imperialists sought to gain direct advantage from the internal Russian conflict. They confronted the beleaguered soviet government with an ultimatum: either cede some parts of the Soviet Union to German capitalism and its Austro-Hungarian allies, or face an immediate resumption of hostilities.

Differences then arose within the Bolshevik leadership over the manner in which the Council of People's Commissars should respond to the ultimatum. Some advocated the waging of revolutionary war against the attempt to annex soviet territory. Trotsky called for opposition to the imperialists through a policy of "neither war nor peace." By resorting to either active or passive resistance, Trotsky argued, the Russians could seek to hold out until an aroused German working class halted the aggression. Lenin disagreed with both tactical proposals. The soviets had no alternative, he contended, but to conclude peace on the predatory imperialist terms. His argument in support of that view can be summed up as follows:

If the concessions demanded were refused, a revolutionary war would have to be conducted against the imperialist attack. A struggle of that nature could not necessarily be expected to quickly trigger a working-class uprising in Germany, given the character of the misleadership of the German workers. The soviets would have to rely entirely on their own resources for a considerable time before proletarian support could be mustered internationally. Under such circumstances, resumption of the fighting could prove fatal. The lower peasantry was capable of supporting a socialist revolution led by the working class, but it was not ready at that juncture to carry on a revolutionary war against Germany. The peasants in uniform, who made up the greater part of the army, were fatigued after nearly four years in battle. A majority of them would favor the ceding of territory to the enemy in order to gain peace. So if hostilities began again and defeats were suffered, they might decide to overthrow the soviet government because of its responsibility in the matter.

Military setbacks would have to be expected, he stressed, because the army was in no condition to beat off a German offensive. It lacked adequate equipment for battle against an enemy using advanced weaponry. To make things worse, the soviet forces had now become involved in a civil war, and that conflict was already causing economic dislocations that further magnified the military difficulties. Hence, peace had to be concluded on the harsh terms offered by the German regime. Time had to be bought in order to build up the soviet power, defeat the bourgeois counterrevolution, and solve the problems involved in carrying out the complete expropriation of the capitalists.

When Lenin's proposal to comply with the ultimatum was put to a vote in the Bolshevik central committee, a narrow majority rejected it. He then reformulated the question. If the offensive became a fact, it was now phrased, and there was no revolutionary upsurge of the German workers, should peace be concluded? This time a majority, in which both Lenin and Trotsky were included, answered in the affirmative. It didn't take long after that for the matter to be settled definitively in the way Lenin envisaged.

The German imperialists soon broke the truce established in December 1917, and launched an offensive along the whole front. This atrocity provoked no significant opposition from the German workers, whose mass organizations remained under the control of social-patriotic misleaders. The soviet army suffered one reverse after another. No room was left for doubt about the need for the Council of People's Commissars to seek an end to the fighting on imperialist terms. A message to that effect was sent to the German government, and a formal peace treaty was signed without further negotiations on March 3 (16), 1918.

Undivided attention could now be centered on developments in the civil war. At this point the soviet regime benefited greatly from the progressive measures already taken to serve the needs of the masses. Workers, peasants, and formerly oppressed nationalities came to its support in vast numbers. Their strong backing enabled the government to speedily build up the Red Army; Trotsky was designated its commander in chief, and the full Soviet power was brought to bear against the reactionary assault.

By this time former tsarist generals, commanding a counterrevolutionary army mobilized by the landed aristocracy, had set out to seize control in the countryside as the first step toward overthrow of the soviet regime. The Red Army had immediately joined battle with them, and the fighting that followed gradually broadened in scope.

The bourgeoisie supported the counterrevolutionary military offensive in diverse ways. Provocateurs and assassins were used to disrupt the soviets internally. Inventories of military supplies, food, and civilian goods were falsified to conceal their availability. Shipments intended for the Red Army at the scene of battle were misrouted. Industrial production was sabotaged, and this particular disruptive action forced an immediate change in soviet economic policy. It became necessary to end dual worker-capitalist power in large sections of industry and accelerate the advance toward establishment of a full dictatorship of the proletariat, acting in alliance with the peasantry.

As the incidence of industrial sabotage became widespread the soviet government had to nationalize more and more capitalist enterprises in self-defense. A shift in priorities followed. Further development of workers' control over capitalist industrial management was made secondary to rapid preparations for direct workers' management of the enterprises being taken over. In addition, workers' committees in many enterprises had already become involved in conflicts with employers that resulted in takeovers on the workers' own initiative.

Experience gained from previous exercise of control over the bosses had done much to ready the workers for assumption of this responsibility through their factory committees and trade unions. But it did not follow that the time had come for such measures to be applied throughout industry and trade. A sweeping action of that nature involved additional problems related to management of the overall economic structure.

Since the Red Army was immersed in beating off the counterrevolutionary assault on all fronts, the Bolsheviks thought it possible to complete expropriation of the capitalists at a tempo slow enough to be most practical for the soviets. If so, gains already achieved could be more securely consolidated. Advances still to be made could be accomplished with less difficulty, and the country's internal equilibrium could gradually be restored on a sound basis within the framework of the new order.

As things developed politically, though, little time remained in which to wind up the eradication of capitalism. With the native counterrevolutionaries facing defeat, foreign imperialists came to their support. The ruling cliques in Britain, France, Japan, and the United States led the way. The real aims behind their official rhetoric were to preserve bourgeois property relations in Russia and to drag it back into the imperialist war as an ally. But to befuddle the workers and farmers in their own countries, the imperialists lied about the actual purposes of the intervention. Strong measures had to be used, they claimed, to "protect" Russia from the Germans.

These hypocrites had been parties to the launching of a reactionary war—in which millions had already been maimed and slaughtered—to determine which predatory gang would dominate the world. Yet they brazenly accused the Bolsheviks of using "terrorism" against the counterrevolutionaries. Under cover of this vicious propaganda barrage, the imperialists intervened militarily in the civil war in opposition to the soviet power. The opening move was made in the summer of 1918 by British and Japanese troops, who received material backing from the United States government.

Powerful forces were now joining in the attempt to throttle the soviet republic, and the native bourgeoisie grew bold enough to openly defy the Bolshevik government. Under these circumstances there was no alternative to swift completion of the expropriations that had already begun to be carried out by the government or by the workers. The tempo of soviet action was stepped up accordingly, and within the next few months, by the end of 1918, almost every capitalist enterprise of decisive economic importance had been nationalized and placed under administration of the workers, who schooled themselves for the task at a forced pace.

With this step bourgeois property relations were definitively abolished. All key instruments of production were now centralized in the hands of the state—that is, in the hands of the proletariat organized as the ruling class. In addition a state monopoly was imposed over international trade to prevent capitalist infiltration of the soviet economy.

\*      \*      \*

Seventy years after publication by Marx and Engels of the *Communist Manifesto,* the October revolution had brought a government to power that led the workers in establishing the world's first workers' state. Its appearance introduced qualitatively new dimensions into the class struggle internationally. For the first time in history a state without exploiters was being founded. The old bourgeois society—in which a privileged minority used its control of the economy to rule over and plunder the toiling masses—had been displaced. The means of production and distribution were now collectively owned by the working people.

A viable structure already existed for the organization of mass action to achieve new social advances made possible by the changed property relations. The soviets served that purpose admirably. These bodies provided a vehicle for establishment of a higher form of democracy than had ever existed in any bourgeois republic. The soviets personified the Marxist concept of a self-conscious movement representing the immense majority, acting in the interests of the immense majority, and doing so in keeping with the democratic principle of conscious development of society by majority decision. They served as dynamic instruments through which to extend the rights and ensure the welfare of the working people.

Once in full control over industry and commerce, the soviet leadership made economic planning to serve social aims the keystone of the new society. Under the old bourgeois order, in which the coining of capitalist profits was the main goal, social relations had been conditioned by the blind play of economic forces. As a result downturns, if not deep economic depressions, had followed inevitably after periods of relative prosperity. In sharp contrast to the economic anarchy that had previously prevailed in production and distribution under capitalism, the soviets were given the chance to demonstrate the intrinsic value of a planned economy.

Such planning, carried out in a society where capitalist expro-priators of the surplus social product had themselves been expro-priated laid the basis for rapid development of the productive forces. The available social wealth could thus be increased apace, and means provided to make a better life for all.

Appropriation of the surplus social product by the proletariat through its government opened the way to new cultural advances. It became possible not only to reduce scarcities in living necessities and eventually eliminate them, but also to widen the vistas of the future. The door was opened to begin eradicating the crushing in-equalities due to class, race, and sex oppression that had been rein-forced by centuries of exploitation and rule by the privileged classes.

Together with the new social potential that had been created, the soviet triumph gave powerful impetus to proletarian struggles go-ing on elsewhere in the world. A concrete demonstration had been seen of the manner in which the working class internationally could take steps to end the imperialist war, abolish capitalism, and move toward construction of a socialist order.

In the process of reaching these goals through their own revolu-tionary struggles, the Bolsheviks had also shown in practice how the workers elsewhere could build a vanguard party capable of lead-ing the exploited masses in battle against the capitalists. The con-crete results obtained in Russia by the methods used made a deep impression on all militants, and the proletarian vanguard in other countries, including the United States, set out to emulate the Bol-shevik Party.

The impact of these historic events on the socialist-minded work-ers of the United States, and how Lenin and Trotsky, through the Communist International, sought to help them develop a revolu-tionary strategy and forge a proletarian Marxist party, will be the opening theme of the second volume of this narrative.

# *Appendix*

## Marx to Friedrich Bolte in New York

The *International* was founded in order to replace the socialist or semisocialist sects by a really militant organisation of the working class. The original Rules and the Inaugural Address show this at a glance. On the other hand the International could not have stood its ground if the course of history had not already smashed sectarianism. The development of socialist sectarianism and that of the real working-class movement always stand in inverse proportion to each other. Sects are (historically) justified so long as the working class is

This excerpt is from a November 23, 1871, letter from Karl Marx to Friedrich Bolte, who became the secretary of the Federal Council of the North American Sections of the International in 1872. The resolutions Marx refers to were adopted at the September 1871 London conference of the International. They deal with the strengthening and centralization of the International, emphasizing the leading role of the General Council and the necessity of creating an independent party of the proletariat; and with the abolishing of the Bakuninist faction, the Alliance of Socialist Democracy.

The letters of Marx and Engels reprinted here are available in *Letters to Americans 1848–1895* (New York: International Publishers, 1953), *Marx and Engels on the United States* (Moscow: Progress Publishers, 1979), and *Selected Correspondence* (Moscow: Progress Publishers, 1975).

not yet ripe for an independent historical movement. As soon as it has attained this maturity all sects are essentially reactionary. But the features displayed by history everywhere are repeated in the history of the International. Antiquated aspects attempt to reestablish and to assert themselves within the newly acquired form.

And the history of the International was a *continual struggle of the General Council* against the sects and amateur experiments, which sought to assert themselves within the International against the real movement of the working class. This struggle was conducted at the *Congresses,* but to a far greater extent in private negotiations between the General Council and individual sections.

Since in Paris, the Proudhonists (Mutualists) were cofounders of the Association, they naturally held the reins there for the first few years. Later, of course, collectivist, positivist, etc., groups arose there in opposition to them.

In Germany—the Lassalle clique. I myself corresponded with the notorious Schweitzer for two years and proved to him irrefutably that Lassalle's organisation was a mere sectarian organisation and, as such, hostile to the organisation of the real workers' movement propagated by the International. He had his "reasons" for not understanding.

At the end of 1868 the Russian Bakunin joined the *International* with the aim of forming inside it a second International called *"Alliance de la Démocratie Socialiste", with himself as leader.* He—a man devoid of all theoretical knowledge—claimed to represent the *scientific* propaganda of the International in that separate body, and wanted to make such propaganda the special function of that second *International within the International.*

His programme was a hash superficially scraped together from the Right and from the Left—*equality of classes* (!), *abolition of the right of inheritance* as the *starting point* of the social movement (St.-Simonist nonsense), *atheism* as a *dogma* dictated to the members, etc., and as the main dogma (*Proudhonist*): *abstention from political action.*

This puerile myth found favour (and still has a certain hold) in

Italy and Spain, where the material conditions for the workers' movement are as yet little developed, and among a few vain, ambitious, and empty doctrinaires in the French-speaking part of Switzerland and in Belgium.

To Mr. Bakunin his doctrine (the rubbish he borrowed from Proudhon, St.-Simon, and others) was and is a secondary matter — merely a means to his personal self-assertion. Though a nonentity as a theoretician he is in his element as an intriguer.

For years the General Council had to fight against this conspiracy (supported up to a certain point by the French Proudhonists, especially in the *South of France*). At last, by means of Conference Resolutions I: 2 and 3, IX, XVI, and XVII, it delivered its long-prepared blow.

It goes without saying that the General Council does not support in America what it combats in Europe. Resolutions I: 2 and 3, and IX now give the New York committee the legal means with which to put an end to all sectarianism and amateur groups, and, if necessary, to expel them. . . .

The ultimate object of the political movement of the working class is, of course, the conquest of political power for this class, and this naturally requires that the organisation of the working class, an organisation which arises from its economic struggles, should previously reach a certain level of development.

On the other hand, however, every movement in which the working class as a *class* confronts the ruling classes and tries to constrain them by pressure from without is a political movement. For instance, the attempt by strikes, etc., in a particular factory or even in a particular trade to compel individual capitalists to reduce the working day, is a purely economic movement. On the other hand the movement to force through an eight-hour, etc., *law* is a *political* movement. And in this way, out of the separate economic movements of the workers there grows up everywhere a *political* movement, that is to say, a *class* movement, with the object of enforcing its interests in a general form, in a form possessing general, socially coercive force. While these movements presuppose a certain degree of previous organisation, they are in turn equally a means of developing this organisation.

Where the working class is not yet far enough advanced in its organization to undertake a decisive campaign against the collective power, i.e., the political power, of the ruling classes, it must at any rate be trained for this by continual agitation against this power and by a hostile attitude toward the policies of the ruling classes. Otherwise it remains a plaything in their hands, as the September revolution in France showed, and as is also proved to a certain extent by the game that Mr. Gladstone & Co. have been able to play in England up to the present time.

# Engels to Friedrich Adolph Sorge in Hoboken

With your resignation the *old* International is anyhow entirely wound up and at an end. And that is well. It belonged to the period of the Second Empire, during which the oppression reigning throughout Europe prescribed unity and abstention from all internal polemics to the workers' movement, then just reawakening. It was the moment when the common cosmopolitan interests of the proletariat could come to the fore. Germany, Spain, Italy, and Denmark had only just come into the movement or were just coming into it. In 1864 the theoretical character of the movement was still very vague everywhere in Europe, that is, among the masses—in real life. German communism did not yet exist as a workers' party. Proudhonism was too weak to be able to trot out its particular hobbyhorses, Bakunin's new rubbish did not even exist in his own head, and even the leaders of the English Trade Unions thought they could

This excerpt is from a September 12–17, 1874, letter from Frederick Engels to Friedrich Adolph Sorge, a friend and associate of Marx and Engels and the secretary of the General Council of the International (1872–74). On August 14, 1874, Sorge informed Engels that he had resigned from the General Council.

join the movement on the basis of the programme laid down in the Preamble to the Rules. The first great success was bound to explode this naive conjunction of all factions. This success was the Commune, which was undoubtedly the child of the International intellectually—although the International did not lift a finger to produce it—and in this respect the International was quite properly held responsible for it.

When, thanks to the Commune, the International had become a moral force in Europe, the row began at once. Every trend wanted to exploit the success for itself. Disintegration, which was inevitable, set in. Jealousy of the growing power of the only people who were really ready to continue working along the lines of the old comprehensive programme—the German Communists—drove the Belgian Proudhonists into the arms of the Bakuninist adventurers. The Hague Congress was actually the end—and for both parties. The only country where something could still be accomplished in the name of the International was America, and by a happy instinct the executive was transferred there. Now its prestige is exhausted there, too, and any further effort to galvanise it into new life would be folly and a waste of energy. The International dominated one side of European history—the side on which the future lies—for ten years and can look back upon its work with pride. But in its old form it has outlived its usefulness. In order to produce a new International after the fashion of the old, an alliance of all proletarian parties of all countries, a general suppression of the labour movement, like that which prevailed from 1849–64, would be necessary. For this the proletarian world has now become too big, too extensive. I believe the next International—after Marx's writings have exerted their influence for some years—will be directly communist and will candidly proclaim our principles. . . .

# Engels to Sorge in Hoboken

The Henry George boom has of course brought to light a colossal mass of fraud, and I am glad I was not there. But in spite of it all it was an epoch-making day. The Germans have not understood how to use their theory as a lever which could set the American masses in motion; they do not understand the theory themselves for the most part and treat it in a doctrinaire and dogmatic way as something that has to be learned by heart, which then will satisfy all requirements forthwith. To them it is a credo and not a guide to action. What is more, they learn no English on principle. Hence the American masses had to seek out their own path and seem to have found it for the time being in the K[nights] of L[abor], whose confused principles and ludicrous organization seem to correspond to their own confusion. But from all I hear, the K of L are a real power, especially in New England and the West, and are becoming more so every day owing to the brutal opposition of the capitalists. I think it is necessary to work inside them, to form within this still quite plastic mass a core of people who understand the movement and its aims

This excerpt is from a November 29, 1886, letter from Engels to Sorge.

and will therefore take over the leadership, at least of a section, when the inevitably impending breakup of the present "order" takes place. The rottenest side of the K of L was their political neutrality, which has resulted in sheer trickery on the part of the Powderlys, etc.; but the edge of this has been taken off by the behavior of the masses in the November elections, especially in New York. The first great step of importance for every country newly entering into the movement is always the constitution of the workers as an independent political party, no matter how, so long as it is a distinct workers' party. And this step has been taken, much more rapidly than we had a right to expect, and that is the main thing. That the first program of this party is still confused and extremely deficient, that it has raised the banner of Henry George, these are unavoidable evils but also merely transitory ones. The masses must have time and opportunity to develop, and they can have the opportunity only when they have a movement of their own—no matter in what form so long as it is *their own* movement—in which they are driven further by their own mistakes and learn through their mistakes. The movement in America is at the same stage as it was with us before 1848; the really intelligent people there will first have to play the part played by the Communist League among the workers' associations before 1848. Except that in America now things will proceed infinitely faster; for the movement to have gained such election successes after scarcely eight months of existence is wholly unprecedented. And what is still lacking will be set going by the bourgeoisie; nowhere in the whole world do they come out so shamelessly and tyrannically as over there, and your judges brilliantly outshine Bismarck's pettifoggers in the Reich. Where the bourgeoisie wages the struggle by such methods, the struggle comes to a decision rapidly, and if we in Europe do not hurry up the Americans will soon outdistance us. But just now it is doubly necessary to have a few people on our side there who are thoroughly versed in theory and well-tested tactics and can also speak and write English; because, for good historical reasons, the Americans are worlds behind in all theoretical questions, and while they did not bring over any medieval institutions from Europe, the did bring over masses of medieval traditions, religion, English common (feudal) law, superstition, spiritualism, in short, every kind of imbecility which was not directly harmful to business and which is now very serviceable for stupefying the masses. If there are people at hand there whose minds are theoretically clear, who can tell them the consequences of their own mistakes beforehand and make clear to them that every movement which does not keep the destruction of the wage system constantly in view as the final goal is bound to go astray and fail—then much nonsense can be avoided and the process considerably shortened. But it must be done in English; the specific German character must be laid aside, and for that the gentlemen of the *Sozialist* hardly have the qualifications, while those of the *Volkszeitung* are cleverer only where *business* is involved.

In Europe the effect of the American elections in November was tremendous. That England, and America in particular, had no labor movement up to now was the big trump card of the radical republicans everywhere, especially in France. Now these gentlemen have been utterly contradicted; on November 2 the whole foundation, especially of Mr. Clemenceau's policy, collapsed. "Look at America," was his eternal motto; "where there is a real republic, there is no poverty and no labor movement!" And the same thing is happening to the liberals and "democrats" in Germany and here—where they are also witnessing the beginnings of their own movement. The very fact that the movement is so sharply accentuated as a labor movement and has sprung up so suddenly and forcefully has stunned the people completely. . . .

# Engels to Florence Kelley-Wischnewetzky in New York

Of course the appendix is now a little out of date, and as I anticipated something of the kind, I proposed that it should be written when the book was ready through the press. Now a preface will be much wanted, and I will write you one; but before, I must await the return of the Avelings to have a full report of the state of things in America; and it seems to me that my preface will not be exactly what you desire.

First, you seem to me to treat New York a little as the Paris of America, and to overrate the importance, for the country at large, of the local New York movement with its local features. No doubt it has a great importance, but then the Northwest, with its background of a numerous farming population and its independent movement, will hardly accept blindly the George theory.

Secondly, the preface of *this* book is hardly the place for a thor-

---

This excerpt is from a December 28, 1886, letter from Engels to Florence Kelley-Wischnewetzky, American socialist and translator of Engels's *Condition of the Working Class in England in 1844.*

oughgoing criticism of that theory, and does not even offer the necessary space for it.

Thirdly, I should have to study thoroughly Henry George's various writings and speeches (most of which I have have not got) so as to render impossible all replies based on subterfuges and side-issues.

My preface will of course turn entirely on the immense stride made by the American workingman in the last ten months, and naturally also touch H. G. and his land scheme. But it cannot pretend to deal extensively with it. Nor do I think the time for that has come. It is far more important that the movement should spread, proceed harmoniously, take root, and embrace as much as possible the whole American proletariat, than that it should start and proceed from the beginning on theoretically perfectly correct lines. There is no better road to theoretical clearness of comprehension than to learn by one's own mistakes, *"durch Schaden klug werden."* And for a whole large class, there is no other road, especially for a nation so eminently practical and so contemptuous of theory as the Americans. The great thing is to get the working class to move *as a class*; that once obtained, they will soon find the right direction, and all who resist, H. G. or Powderly, will be left out in the cold with small sects of their own. Therefore I think also the K of L a most important factor in the movement which ought not to be pooh-poohed from without but to be revolutionized from within, and I consider that many of the Germans there have made a grievous mistake when they tried, in the face of a mighty and glorious movement not of their own creation, to make of their imported and not always understood theory a kind of *alleinseligmachendes* [it alone bringing salvation] dogma, and to keep aloof from any movement which did not accept that dogma. Our theory is not a dogma but the exposition of a process of evolution, and that process involves successive phases. To expect that the Americans will start with the full consciousness of the theory worked out in older industrial countries is to expect the impossible. What the Germans ought to do is to act up to their own theory—if they understand it, as we did in 1845 and 1848—to go in for any real general working-class movement, accept its *faktische* [actual] starting point as such, and work it gradually up to the theoretical level by pointing out how every mistake made, every reverse suffered, was a necessary consequence of mistaken theoretical orders in the original program; they ought, in the words of the *Communist Manifesto: in der Gegenwart der Bewegung die Zukunft der Bewegung repräsentieren* [To represent the future of the movement in the present of the movement]. But above all give the movement time to consolidate; do not make the inevitable confusion of the first start worse confounded by forcing down people's throats things which, at present, they cannot properly understand but which they soon will learn. A million or two of workingmen's votes next November for a *bona fide* workingmen's party is worth infinitely more at present than a hundred thousand votes for a doctrinally perfect platform. The very first attempt—soon to be made if the movement progresses—to consolidate the moving masses on a national basis will bring them all face to face, Georgeites, K of L, trade unionists, and all; and if our German friends by that time have learnt enough of the language of the country to go in for a discussion, then will be the time for them to criticize the views of the others and thus, by showing up the inconsistencies of the various standpoints, to bring them gradually to understand their own actual position, the position made for them by the correlation of capital and wage-labor. But anything that might delay or prevent that national consolidation of the workingmen's party—on no matter what platform—I should consider a great mistake, and therefore I do not think the time has arrived to speak out fully and exhaustively either with regard to H. G. or the K of L. . . . .

# Appendix to the American Edition of
## *The Condition of the Working Class in England*

But while England has thus outgrown the juvenile state of capitalist exploitation described by me, other countries have only just attained it. France, Germany, and especially America, are the formidable competitors who at this moment—as foreseen by me in 1844—are more and more breaking up England's industrial monopoly. Their manufactures are young as compared with those of England, but increasing at a far more rapid rate than the latter; but curious enough, they have at this moment arrived at about the same phase of development as English manufacture in 1844. With regard to America, the parallel is indeed most striking. True, the external surroundings in which the working class is placed in America are very different, but the same economical laws are at work, and the results, if not identical in every respect, must still be of the same order. Hence we find in America the same struggles for a shorter work-

This article is excerpted from the appendix written by Engels for the first American edition of his *Condition of the Working Class in England in 1844*, published in 1887. Engels subsequently included much of this appendix in his preface to the 1892 English edition of this work.

ing-day, for a legal limitation of the working time, especially of women and children in factories; we find the truck-system in full blossom, and the cottage-system, in rural districts, made use of by the "bosses" as a means of domination over the workers. At this very moment I am receiving the American papers with accounts of the great strike of 12,000 Pennsylvania coal-miners in the Connellesville district, and I seem but to read my own description of the North of England colliers' strike of 1844. The same cheating of the workpeople by false measure; the same truck-system; the same attempt to break the miners' resistance by the capitalists' last, but crushing resource, the eviction of the men out of their dwellings, the cottages owned by the companies.

There were two circumstances which for a long time prevented the unavoidable consequences of the capitalist system from showing themselves in the full glare of day in America. These were the easy access to the ownership of cheap land, and the influx of immigration. They allowed, for many years, the great mass of the native American population to "retire" in early manhood from wage-labor and to become farmers, dealers, or employers of labor, while the hard work for wages, the position of a proletarian for life, mostly fell to the lot of immigrants. But America has outgrown this early stage. The boundless backwoods have disappeared, and the still more boundless prairies are fast and faster passing from the hands of the nation and the states into those of private owners. The great safety-valve against the formation of a permanent proletarian class has practically ceased to act. A class of life-long and even hereditary proletarians exists at this hour in America. A nation of sixty million striving hard to become—and with every chance of success, too—the leading manufacturing nation of the world—such a nation cannot permanently import its own wage-working class; not even if immigrants pour in at the rate of half a million a year. The tendency of the capitalist system towards the ultimate splitting-up of society into two classes, a few millionaires on the one hand, and a great mass of mere wage-workers on the other, this tendency, though constantly crossed and counteracted by other social agencies, works nowhere with greater force than in America; and the result has been the production of a class of native American wage-workers, who form, indeed, the aristocracy of the wage-working class as compared with the immigrants, but who become conscious more and more every day of their solidarity with the latter and who feel all the more acutely their present condemnation to life-long wage-toil, because they still remember the bygone days, when it was comparatively easy to rise to a higher social level. Accordingly the working-class movement in America has started with truly American vigor, and as on that side of the Atlantic things march with at least double the European speed, we may yet live to see America take the lead in this respect too.

# The Labour Movement in America

Ten months have elapsed since, at the translator's wish, I wrote the appendix to this book; and during these ten months, a revolution has been accomplished in American society such as, in any other country, would have taken at least ten years. In February 1885, American public opinion was almost unanimous on this one point; that there was no working class, in the European sense of the word, in America; that consequently no class struggle between workmen and capitalists, such as tore European society to pieces, was possible in the American republic; and that, therefore, socialism was a thing of foreign importation which could never take root on American soil. And yet, at that moment, the coming class struggle was casting its gigantic shadow before it in the strikes of the Pennsylvania coal-miners, and of many other trades, and especially in the preparations, all over the country, for the great Eight Hours' movement which was to come off, and did come off, in the May follow-

<hr>

This article was written by Engels on January 26, 1887, as the preface to the American edition of his *Condition of the Working Class in England in 1844,* published in 1887.

ing. That I then duly appreciated these symptoms, that I anticipated a working-class movement on a national scale, my Appendix shows; but no one could then foresee that in such a short time the movement would burst out with such irresistible force, would spread with the rapidity of a prairie fire, would shake American society to its very foundations.

The fact is there, stubborn and indisputable. To what an extent it had struck with terror the American ruling classes, was revealed to me, in an amusing way, by American journalists who did me the honor of calling on me last summer; the "new departure" had put them into a state of helpless fright and perplexity. But at that time the movement was only just on the start; there was but a series of confused and apparently disconnected upheavals of that class which, by the suppression of Negro slavery and the rapid development of manufactures, had become the lowest stratum of American society. Before the year closed, these bewildering social convulsions began to take a definite direction. The spontaneous, instinctive movements of these vast masses of working people, over a vast extent of country, the simultaneous outburst of their common discontent with a miserable social condition, the same everywhere and due to the same causes, made them conscious of the fact that they formed a new and distinct class of American society; a class of—practically speaking—more or less hereditary wage-workers, proletarians. And with true American instinct this consciousness led them at once to take the next step towards their deliverance: the formation of a political workingmen's party, with a platform of its own, and with the conquest of the Capitol and the White House for its goal. In May the struggle for the Eight Hours' working-day, the troubles in Chicago, Milwaukee, etc., the attempts of the ruling class to crush the nascent uprising of Labor by brute force and brutal class-justice; in November the new Labor Party organized in all great centers, and the New York, Chicago and Milwaukee elections. May and November have hitherto reminded the American bourgeoisie only of the payment of coupons of U.S. bonds; henceforth May and November will remind them, too, of the dates on which the American working class presented *their* coupons for payment.

In European countries, it took the working class years and years before they fully realized the fact that they formed a distinct and, under the existing social conditions, a permanent class of modern society; and it took years again until this class-consciousness led them to form themselves into a distinct political party, independent of, and opposed to, all the old political parties formed by the various sections of the ruling classes. On the more favored soil of America, where no mediaeval ruins bar the way, where history begins with the elements of modern bourgeois society as evolved in the seventeenth century, the working class passed through these two stages of its development within ten months.

Still, all this is but a beginning. That the laboring masses should feel the community of grievances and of interests, their solidarity as a class in opposition to all other classes; that in order to give expression and effect to this feeling, they should set in motion the political machinery provided for that purpose in every free country—that is the first step only. The next step is to find the common remedy for these common grievances, and to embody it in the platform of the new Labor Party. And this—the most important and the most difficult step in the movement—has yet to be taken in America.

A new party must have a distinct positive platform; a platform which may vary in details as circumstances vary and as the party itself develops, but still one upon which the party, for the time being, is agreed. So long as such a platform has not been worked out, or exists but in a rudimentary form, so long the new party, too, will have but a rudimentary existence; it may exist locally but not yet nationally; it will be a party potentially but not actually.

That platform, whatever may be its first initial shape, must develop in a direction which may be determined beforehand. The causes that brought into existence the abyss between the working class and the capitalist class are the same in America as in Europe; the means of filling up that abyss are equally the same everywhere. Consequently, the platform of the American proletariat will in the long run coincide, as to the ultimate end to be attained, with the one which, after sixty years of dissensions and discussions, has become the adopted platform of the great mass of the European militant proletariat. It will proclaim, as the ultimate end, the conquest of political supremacy by the working class, in order to effect the direct appropriation of all means of production—land, railways, mines, machinery, etc.—by society at large, to be worked in common by all for the account and benefit of all.

But if the new American party, like all political parties everywhere, by the very fact of its formation aspires to the conquest of political power, it is as yet far from agreed upon what to do with that power when once attained. In New York and the other great cities of the East, the organisation of the working class has proceeded upon the lines of the Trades' societies, forming in each city a powerful Central Labor Union. In New York the Central Labor Union, last November, chose for its standard-bearer Henry George, and consequently its temporary electoral platform has been largely imbued with his principles. In the great cities of the Northwest the electoral battle was fought upon a rather indefinite labor platform, and the influence of Henry George's theories was scarcely, if at all, visible. And while in these great centers of population and of industry the new class movement came to a political head, we find all over the country two widespread labor organizations: the Knights of Labor and the Socialist Labor Party, of which only the latter has a platform in harmony with the modern European standpoint as summarised above.

Of the three more or less definite forms under which the American labor movement thus presents itself, the first, the Henry George movement in New York, is for the moment of a chiefly local significance. No doubt New York is by far the most important city of the States; but New York is not Paris and the United States are not France. And it seems to me that the Henry George platform, in its present shape, is too narrow to form the basis for anything but a local movement, or at best for a short-lived phase of the general movement. To Henry George, the expropriation of the mass of the people from the land is the great and universal cause of the splitting up of the people into rich and poor. Now this is not quite correct historically. In Asiatic and classical antiquity, the predominant form of class oppression was slavery, that is to say, not so much the expropriation of the masses from the land as the appropriation of their persons. When, in the decline of the Roman Republic, the free Italian peasants were expropriated from their farms, they formed a class of "poor whites" similar to that of the Southern slave states before 1861; and between slaves and poor whites, two classes equally unfit for self-emancipation, the old world went to pieces. In the Middle Ages, it was not the expropriation of the people *from*, but on the contrary, their appropriation *to* the land which became the source of feudal oppression. The peasant retained his land, but was attached to it as a serf or villein, and made liable to tribute to the lord in labor and in produce. It was only at the dawn of modern times, towards the end of the fifteenth century, that the expropriation of the peasantry on a large scale laid the foundation for the modern class of wage-workers who possess nothing but their labor-power and can live only by the selling of that labor-power to others. But if the expropriation from the land brought this class into existence, it was the development of capitalist production, of modern industry and agriculture on a large scale which perpetuated it, increased it, and shaped it into a distinct class with distinct interests and a distinct historical mission. All this has been fully expounded by Marx (*Capital*, Part VIII: "The So-Called Primitive Accumulation"). According to Marx, the cause of the present antagonism of the classes and of the social degradation of the working class is their expropriation from *all* means of production, in which the land is of course included.

If Henry George declares land-monopolization to be the sole cause of poverty and misery, he naturally finds the remedy in the resumption of the land by society at large. Now, the Socialists of the school of Marx, too, demand the resumption, by society, of the land, and not only of the land but of all other means of production likewise. But even if we leave these out of the question, there is another difference. What is to be done with the land? Modern Socialists, as represented by Marx, demand that it should be held and worked in common and for common account, and the same with all other means of social production, mines, railways, factories, etc.; Henry George would confine himself to letting it out to individuals as at present, merely regulating its distribution and applying the rents for public, instead of, as at present, for private purposes. What the Socialists demand, implies a total revolution of the whole system of social production; what Henry George demands, leaves the present mode of social production untouched, and has, in fact, been anticipated by the extreme section of Ricardian bourgeois economists who, too, demanded the confiscation of the rent of land by the State.

It would of course be unfair to suppose that Henry George has said his last word once and for all. But I am bound to take his theory as I find it.

The second great section of the American movement is formed by the Knights of Labor. And that seems to be the section most typical of the present state of the movement, as it is undoubtedly by far the strongest. An immense association spread over an immense extent of country in innumerable "assemblies," representing all shades of individual and local opinion within the working class; the whole of them sheltered under a platform of corresponding indistinctness and held together much less by their impracticable constitution than by the instinctive feeling that the very fact of their clubbing together for their common aspiration makes them a great power in the country; a truly American paradox clothing the most modern tendencies in the most mediaeval mummeries, and hiding the most democratic and even rebellious spirit behind an apparent but really powerless despotism—such is the picture the Knights of Labor offer to a European observer. But if we are not arrested by mere outside whimsicalities, we cannot help seeing in this vast agglomeration an immense amount of potential energy evolving slowly but surely into actual force. The Knights of Labor are the first national organisation created by the American working class as a whole; whatever be their origin and history, whatever their short-comings and little absurdities, whatever their platform and their constitution, here they are, the work of practically the whole class of American wage-workers, the only national bond that holds them together, that makes their strength felt to themselves not less than to their enemies, and that fills them with the proud hope of future victories. For it would not be exact to say that the Knights of Labor are liable to development. They are constantly in full process of development and revolution; a heaving, fermenting mass of plastic material seeking the shape and form appropriate to its inherent nature. That form will be attained as surely as historical evolution has, like natural evolution, its own immanent laws. Whether the Knights of Labor will then retain their present name or not, makes no difference, but to an outsider it appears evident that here is the raw material out of which the future of the American working-class movement, and along with it, the future of American society at large, has to be shaped.

The third section consists of the Socialist Labor Party. This section is a party but in name, for nowhere in America has it, up to now, been able actually to take its stand as a political party. It is, moreover, to a certain extent foreign to America, having until lately been made up almost exclusively by German immigrants, using their own language and for the most part little conversant with the common language of the country. But if it came from a foreign stock, it came, at the same time, armed with the experience earned during long years of class struggle in Europe, and with an insight into the general conditions of working-class emancipation, far superior to that hitherto gained by American workingmen. This is a fortunate circumstance for the American proletarians who thus are enabled to appropriate, and to take advantage of, the intellectual and moral fruits of the forty years' struggle of their European class-mates, and thus to hasten on the time of their own victory. For, as I said before, there cannot be any doubt that the ultimate platform of the American working class must and will be essentially the same as that now adopted by the whole militant working class of Europe, the same as that of the German-American Socialist Labor Party. In so far this party is called upon to play a very important part in the movement. But in order to do so they will have to doff every remnant of their foreign garb. They will have to become out and out American. They cannot expect the Americans to come to them; they, the minority and the immigrants, must go to the Americans, who are the vast majority and the natives. And to do that, they must above all things learn English.

The process of fusing together these various elements of the vast moving mass—elements not really discordant, but indeed mutually isolated by their various starting-points—will take some time and will not come off without a deal of friction, such as is visible at different points even now. The Knights of Labor, for instance, are here and there, in the eastern cities, locally at war with the organized trades unions. But then this same friction exists within the Knights of Labor themselves, where there is anything but peace and harmony. These are not symptoms of decay, for capitalists to crow over. They are merely signs that the innumerable hosts of workers, for the first time set in motion in a common direction, have as yet found out neither the adequate expression for their common interests, nor the form of organization best adapted to the struggle, nor the discipline required to insure victory. They are as yet the first levies en masse of the great revolutionary war, raised and equipped locally and independently, all converging to form one common army, but as yet without regular organization and common plan of campaign. The converging columns cross each other here and there: confusion, angry disputes, even threats of conflict arise. But the community of ultimate purpose in the end overcomes all minor troubles; ere long the straggling and squabbling battalions will be formed in a long line of battle array, presenting to the enemy a well-ordered front, ominously silent under their glittering arms, supported by bold skirmishers in front and by unshakable reserves in the rear.

To bring about this result, the unification of the various independent bodies into one national labor army, with no matter how inadequate a provisional platform, provided it be a truly working-class platform—that is the next great step to be accomplished in America. To effect this, and to make that platform worthy of the cause, the Socialist Labor Party can contribute a great deal, if they will only act in the same way as the European Socialists have acted at the time when they were but a small minority of the working class. That line of action was first laid down in the *Communist Manifesto* of 1847 in the following words:

"The Communists"—that was the name we took at the time and which even now we are far from repudiating—"the Communists do not form a separate party opposed to other working-class parties.

"They have no interests separate and apart from the interests of the whole working class.

"They do not set up any sectarian principles of their own, by which to shape and model the prolitarian movement.

"The Communists are distinguished from the other working-class parties by this only: 1. In the national struggles of the proletarians of the different countries they point out, and bring to the front, the common interests of the whole proletariat, interests independent of all nationality; 2.In the various stages of development which the struggle of the working class against the capitalist class has to pass through, they always and everywhere represent the interests of the movement as a whole.

"The Communists, therefore, are on the one hand, practically the most advanced and resolute section of the working-class parties of all countries, that section which ever pushes forward all others; on the other hand, theoretically, they have, over the great mass of the proletarians, the advantage of clearly understanding the line of march, the conditions, and the ultimate general results of the proletarian movement.

"Thus they fight for the attainment of the immediate ends, for the enforcement of the momentary interests of the working class; but in the movement of the present, they represent and take care of the future of the movement."

That is the line of action which the great founder of modern socialism, Karl Marx, and with him, I and the Socialists of all nations who worked along with us, have followed for more than forty years, with the result that it has led to victory everywhere, and that at this moment the mass of European Socialists, in Germany and in France, in Belgium, Holland and Switzerland, in Denmark and Sweden as well as in Spain and Portugal, are fighting as one common army under one and the same flag.

# Engels to Kelley-Wischnewetzky

The movement in America, just at this moment, is I believe best seen from across the ocean. On the spot personal bickering and local disputes must obscure much of the grandeur of it. And the only thing that could really delay its march would be the consolidation of these differences into established sects. To some extent that will be unavoidable, but the less of it the better. And the Germans have most to guard against this. Our theory is a theory of evolution, not a dogma to be learnt by heart and to be repeated mechanically. The less it is drilled into the Americans from the outside and the more they test it through their own experience—with the help of the Germans—the deeper will it pass into their flesh and blood. When we returned to Germany, in spring 1848, we joined the Democratic Party as the only possible means of gaining the ear of the working class; we were the most advanced of that party, but still a wing of it. When Marx founded the International, he drew up the General Rules in such a way that all working-class socialists of

---

This excerpt is from a January 27, 1887, letter from Engels to Kelley-Wischnewetzky.

that period could join it—Proudhonists, Pierre Lerouxists, and even the more advanced section of the English trade unions; and it was only through this latitude that the International became what it was, the means of gradually dissolving and absorbing all these minor sects, with the exception of the anarchists, whose sudden appearance in various countries was but the effect of the violent bourgeois reaction after the Commune and could therefore safely be left by us to die out of itself, which it did. Had we from 1864 to 1873 insisted on working together only with those who openly adopted our platform, where should we be today? I think all our practice has shown that it is possible to work along with the general movement of the working class at every one of its stages without giving up or hiding our own distinct position and even organization, and I am afraid that if the German-Americans choose a different line they will commit a great mistake.

# Engels to Hermann Schlüter in Hoboken

The fact that things are going downhill with the Socialist Labor Party is quite evident from its fraternisation with the Nationalists, compared to whom English Fabians—likewise bourgeois—are radicals. I should have thought that the *Sozialist* would scarcely be able to produce increased boredom by cohabitating with the *Nationalist*. Sorge sends me the *Nationalist*, but despite all my efforts I cannot find anyone who is willing to read it.

Nor do I understand the quarrel with Gompers. His federation is, as far as I know, an association of trade unions and nothing but trade unions. Hence they have the *formal right* to reject anyone coming as the representative of a labour organisation that is *not* a trade union, or to reject delegates of an association to which such organisations are admitted. I cannot judge from here, of course, whether it was *propagandistically* advisable to expose oneself to such

---

This excerpt is from a January 29, 1891, letter from Engels to Hermann Schlüter, a German Social Democrat who emigrated to the U.S. in 1889. The Nationalists mentioned by Engels were a group of bourgeois and petty-bourgeois intellectuals who supported the nationalization of property. *Sozialist* was the SLP's paper.

a rejection. But that it had to come was beyond all doubt and I, for one, cannot blame Gompers for it.

But when I think of the next international congress in Brussels, I should have thought it would have been advisable to keep on good terms with Gompers, who at any rate has more workers behind him than the Socialist Labor Party, and to ensure as big a delegation from America as possible, including *his* people. They would see many things there that might cause them to revise their narrow-minded trade union standpoint—and besides, where do you want to find a recruiting ground if not in the trade unions?. . . .

# Engels to Schlüter in New York

Your great obstacle in America, it seems to me, lies in the exceptional position of the native workers. Up to 1848 one could only speak of the permanent native working class as an exception: the small beginnings of it in the cities in the East could always hope to become farmers or bourgeois. Now a native working class has developed and is also to a large extent organised in trade unions. But it still assumes an aristocratic posture and wherever possible leaves the ordinary badly paid occupations to the immigrants, of whom only a small section enter the aristocratic trades. These immigrants however are divided into different nationalities and understand neither one another nor, for the most part, the language of the country. And your bourgeoisie knows much better even than the Austrian government how to play off one nationality against the other: Jews, Italians, Bohemians, etc., against Germans and Irish, and each one against the other, so that differences in the living standard of the workers exist, I believe, in New York to an extent unheard-of

This excerpt is from a March 30, 1892, letter from Engels to Schlüter.

elsewhere. And added to this is the total indifference of a society which has grown up on a purely capitalist basis, without any genial feudal background, towards the human beings who succumb in the competitive struggle: "there will be plenty more, and more than we want, of these damned Dutchmen, Irishmen, Italians, Jews, and Hungarians"; and, to cap it all, John Chinaman stands in the background, who far surpasses them all in his ability to live on next to nothing.

In such a country, continually renewed waves of advance, followed by equally certain setbacks, are inevitable. But the advancing waves are always becoming more powerful, the setbacks less paralysing, and on the whole things are nevertheless moving forward. But this I consider certain: the purely bourgeois basis, with no pre-bourgeois humbug behind it, the corresponding colossal energy of the development, which manifests itself even in the mad excesses of the present protective tariff system, will one day bring about a change that will astound the whole world. Once the Americans get started it will be with an energy and vehemence compared with which we in Europe shall be mere children.

# Engels to Sorge in Hoboken

There is no place yet in America for a *third* party, I believe. The divergence of interests even in *the same* class stratum is so great in that tremendous area that wholly different strata and interests are represented in each of the two big parties, depending on the locality, and to a very large extent each of the two parties contains representatives of nearly every particular section of the possessing class, though *today* big industry on the whole forms the core of the Republicans, just as the big landed property of the South forms that of the Democrats. The apparent haphazardness of this jumbling together provides the splendid soil for the corruption and the exploitation of the government that flourish over there so extensively. Only when the land—the public lands—is completely in the hands of the speculators and settlement on the land thus becomes more and more difficult or becomes the subject of trickery—only then, I think, with *tranquil* development, will the time for a third party come. *Land* is the basis of speculation, and the mania and opportu-

This excerpt is from a January 6, 1892, letter from Engels to Sorge.

nity for speculation in America are the chief levers that keep the native-born worker under the sway of the bourgeoisie. Only when there is a generation of native-born workers that can no longer expect *anything* from speculation will we have a solid foothold in America. But of course who can count on *tranquil* development in America? There are economic leaps over there like the political ones in France, and they do indeed produce the same temporary retrogressions.

The small farmers and the lower middle class will hardly ever succeed in forming a strong party: they consist of elements that change too rapidly—the farmer moreover is often migratory, working two, three, and four farms in succession in different states and territories; immigration and bankruptcy promote change in personnel in the two groups, and economic dependence upon the creditor also impedes independence—but on the other hand they are a splendid element for politicians, who speculate on their discontent in order to sell them out to one of the big parties afterward.

The "tenacity" of the Yankees, who are even rehashing the greenback humbug, is a result of their theoretical backwardness and their Anglo-Saxon contempt for all theory. They are punished for this by a superstitious belief in every philosophical and economic absurdity, by religious sectarianism, and idiotic economic experiments, which however are profitable to certain bourgeois cliques. . . .

# The Results and Significance of the U.S. Presidential Elections

Wilson, a "Democrat", has been elected President of the United States of America. He has polled over six million votes, Roosevelt (the new National Progressive Party) over four million, Taft (Republican Party) over three million, and the Socialist Eugene Debs 800,000 votes.

The world significance of the U.S. elections lies not so much in the great increase in the number of Socialist votes as in the far-reaching *crisis* of the *bourgeois* parties, in the amazing force with which their decay has been revealed. Lastly, the significance of the elections lies in the unusually clear and striking revelation of *bourgeois reformism* as a means of combating socialism.

In all bourgeois countries, the parties which stand for capitalism, i.e., the bourgeois parties, came into being a long time ago, and the greater the extent of political liberty, the more solid they are.

---

This article by V. I. Lenin is from the November 9, 1912, issue of *Pravda* and was printed in Lenin's *Collected Works*, vol. 18, pp. 402–4. It and the following article are also available in *Lenin on the United States* (New York: International Publishers, 1970).

Freedom in the U.S.A. is most complete. And for a whole *half-century*—since the Civil War over slavery in 1860–65—*two* bourgeois parties have been distinguished there by remarkable solidity and strength. The party of the former slave-owners is the so-called Democratic Party. The capitalist party, which favoured the emancipation of the Negroes, has developed into the Republican Party.

Since the emancipation of the Negroes, the distinction between the two parties has been diminishing. The fight between these two parties has been mainly over the height of customs duties. Their fight *has not had* any *serious* importance for the mass of the people. The people have been deceived and diverted from their vital interests by means of spectacular and meaningless duels between the two bourgeois parties.

This so-called bipartisan system prevailing in America and Britain has been one of the most powerful means of preventing the rise of an independent working-class, i.e., genuinely socialist, party.

And now the bipartisan system has suffered a fiasco in America, the country boasting the most advanced capitalism! What caused this fiasco?

The strength of the working-class movement, the growth of socialism.

The old bourgeois parties (the "Democratic" and the "Republican" parties) have been facing towards the past, the period of the emancipation of the Negroes. The new bourgeois party, the National Progressive Party, is facing towards the *future*. Its programme turns entirely on the question whether capitalism is to be or not to be, on the issues, to be specific, of protection for the workers and of "trusts", as the capitalist associations are called in the U.S.A.

The old parties are products of an epoch whose task was to develop capitalism as speedily as possible. The struggle between the parties was over the question *how* best to expedite and facilitate this development.

The new party is a product of the present epoch, which raises the issue of the very existence of capitalism. In the U.S.A., the freest and most advanced country, this issue is coming to the fore more clearly and broadly than anywhere else.

The entire programme and entire agitation of Roosevelt and the Progressives turn on how to *save capitalism* by means of *bourgeois reforms.*

The bourgeois reformism which in old Europe manifests itself in the chatter of liberal professors has all at once come forward in the free American republic as a party four millions strong. This is American style.

We shall save capitalism by reforms, says that party. We shall grant the most progressive factory legislation. We shall establish state control over *all* the trusts (in the U.S.A. that means over *all* industries!). We shall establish state control over them to eliminate poverty and enable everybody to earn a "decent" wage. We shall establish "social and industrial justice". We revere *all* reforms—*the only "reform"* we don't want is *expropriation of the capitalists!*

The national wealth of the U.S.A. is now reckoned to be 120 billion (thousand million) dollars, i.e., about 240 billion rubles. Approximately *one-third* of it, or about 80 billion rubles, belongs to *two* trusts, those of Rockerfeller and Morgan, or is subordinated to these trusts! Not more than 40,000 families making up these two trusts are the masters of 80 million wage-slaves.

Obviously, so long as these modern slave-owners are there, all "reforms" will be nothing but a deception. Roosevelt has been *deliberately* hired by the astute multimillionaires to preach this deception. The "state control" they promise will become—if the capitalists keep their capital—a means of combating and crushing strikes.

But the American proletarian has already awakened and has taken up his post. He greets Roosevelt's success with cheerful irony, as if to say: You lured four million people with your promises of reform, dear impostor Roosevelt. Very well! Tomorrow those four million will see that your promises were a fraud, and don't forget that they are following you *only* because they feel that it is *impossible* to go on living in the old way.

# After the Elections in America

We have already pointed out in *Pravda* the great importance of the Republican Party split in America and the formation of Roosevelt's Progressive Party.

Now the elections are over. The Democrats have won, and at once the consequences predicted by the Socialists are beginning to tell. Roosevelt's Progressive Party, with its 4.5 million votes, is a specimen of the broad bourgeois-reformist trend which has come on the scene in sweeping American fashion.

What happens to this trend is of general interest because, in one form or another, it exists *in all* capitalist countries.

In any bourgeois-reformist trend there are two main streams: the bourgeois bigwigs and politicians, who deceive the masses with promises of reform, and the cheated masses, who feel that they cannot go on living in the old way, and follow the quack with the loudest promises. And so we find the brand-new Progressive Party in America splitting at the seams right after the elections.

This article was written by Lenin sometime before November 25 (December 6), 1912, and was printed in Lenin's *Collected Works*, Vol. 36, pp. 204–5.

The bourgeois politicians who made use of Roosevelt's quackery to dupe the masses are already yelling about a *merger* with the Republican Party. What's the idea? It is simply this: the politicians want the cushy jobs which the victorious party in America hands out to its supporters with especial brazenness. The Republican split gave the victory to the Democrats. These are now ecstatically sharing out the luscious public pie. Is it surprising that their rivals are prepared to renounce the Progressive Party and return to the *consolidated* Republican Party, which has every chance of defeating the Democrats?

Indeed, this looks very much like a cynical cheap sale of "party loyalties". But we see exactly the same thing in all capitalist countries; and the *less* freedom there is in a country, the dirtier and fouler is the sale of party loyalties among the bourgeois sharks, and the greater is the importance of backstairs intrigues and private connections in procuring concessions, subsidies, bonanza legal cases (for the lawyers), etc.

The other wing of any bourgeois-reformist trend—the cheated masses—has now also revealed itself in the highly original, free and lucid American style. "Scores who had voted for the Progressive Party," writes *Appeal to Reason,* the New York workers' paper, "now come to socialist editorial offices and bureaux for all kinds of information. They are mostly young people, trusting, inexperienced. They are the sheep shorn by Roosevelt, without any knowledge of politics or economics. They instinctively feel that the Socialist Party, with its one million votes, is a more serious proposition than Roosevelt's 4.5 million, and what they want to know most is whether the minimum reforms promised by Roosevelt can be implemented."

"Needless to say," the paper adds, "we are glad to give every one of these 'progressives' *any* information, and never let any of them leave without Socialist literature."

The lot of capitalism is such that its sharpest operators cannot help "working"—for socialism!

# Index

# BASIC WORKS OF MARXISM

## The Communist Manifesto
KARL MARX, FREDERICK ENGELS
Founding document of the modern working-class movement, published in 1848. Explains why communism is derived not from preconceived principles but from *facts* and the actual dynamics of the class struggle. $3.95 Also in Spanish.

## Imperialism: The Highest Stage of Capitalism
V.I. LENIN
"The income of the bonholders is *five times greater* than the income obtained from the foreign trade of the greatest 'trading' country in the world," wrote Lenin in this 1916 booklet. "This is the essence of imperialism and imperialist parasitism." $3.95

## Collected Works of Karl Marx and Frederick Engels
The writings of the founders of the modern revolutionary working-class movement. Vols. 1–47 of 50-volume set are now available. Each volume contains notes and index. Progress Publishers, cloth only.
Set (47 vols.), $1,185. Write or call for prices of individual volumes.

## Collected Works of V.I. Lenin
The writings of the central leader of the Bolshevik Party, the October 1917 Russian revolution, the young Soviet workers and peasants republic, and the early Communist International.
45-volume set, plus 2-volume index. $500

WRITE FOR A CATALOG.

# The Communist International in Lenin's Time

## Workers of the World and Oppressed Peoples, Unite!
*Proceedings and Documents of the Second Congress, 1920*
The debate among delegates from 37 countries
takes up key questions of working-class strategy
and program and offers a vivid portrait of social
struggles in the era of the October revolution.
2-vol. set $65

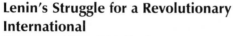

## To See the Dawn
*Baku, 1920—First Congress of the
Peoples of the East*
How can peasants and workers in the colonial
world achieve freedom from imperialist
exploitation? By what means can working people
overcome divisions incited by their national ruling
classes and act together for their common class
interests? These questions were addressed by 2,000
delegates to the 1920 Congress of the Peoples of the
East. $19.95

## Lenin's Struggle for a Revolutionary International
*Documents,1907–1916; The Preparatory Years*
The debate among revolutionary working-class
leaders, including V.I. Lenin and Leon Trotsky, on a
socialist response to World War I. $32.95

## The German Revolution and the Debate on Soviet Power
*Documents, 1918–1919; Preparing the
Founding Congress*
$31.95

## Founding the Communist International
*Proceedings and Documents of the
First Congress, March 1919*
$27.95

Available from Pathfinder

# THE TEAMSTER SERIES

## FARRELL DOBBS

Four books on the 1930s
strikes and organizing drive
that transformed the Teamsters
union in Minnesota and much
of the Midwest into a fighting
industrial union movement.
Written by a leader of the
communist movement in the U.S.
and organizer of the Teamsters
union during the rise of the CIO.

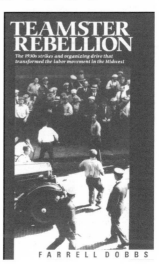

### Teamster Rebellion
Tells the story of the 1934 strikes
that built a fighting union
movement in Minneapolis. $16.95

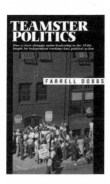

### Teamster Power
The 11-state Midwest over-the-road
organizing drive. $18.95

### Teamster Politics
Rank-and-file Teamsters lead the fight
against antiunion frame-ups and assaults by
fascist goons; the battle for jobs for all; and
efforts to advance
independent labor
political action. $18.95

### Teamster Bureaucracy
How the rank-and-file Teamsters leadership
organized to oppose World War II, racism,
and government efforts—backed by the
international officialdom of the Teamsters, the
AFL, and the CIO—to gag class-struggle-
minded workers. $18.95

# New International
### A MAGAZINE OF MARXIST POLITICS AND THEORY

## U.S. Imperialism Has Lost the Cold War

... That's what the Socialist Workers Party concluded at the opening of the 1990s, as regimes and parties across Eastern Europe and in the USSR that claimed to be communist collapsed. Contrary to imperialism's hopes, the working class in those countries had not been crushed. It remains an intractable obstacle to reimposing and stabilizing capitalist relations, one the exploiters will have to confront in class battles—in a hot war.

Issue no. 11 of *New International* analyzes the propertied rulers' failed expectations, assesses the weight of the Cuban Revolution in world politics, and explains why the odds in favor of the working class have increased, not diminished, at the opening of the 21st century. $14.00

## Imperialism's March toward Fascism and War

### Jack Barnes

"There will be new Hitlers, new Mussolinis. That is inevitable. What is not inevitable is that they will triumph. The working-class vanguard will organize our class to fight back against the devastating toll we are made to pay for the capitalist crisis. The future of humanity will be decided in the contest between these contending class forces."— Jack Barnes, "Imperialism's March toward Fascism and War." In *New International* no. 10. $14.00

## Opening Guns of World War III
### Washington's Assault on Iraq
### Jack Barnes

The U.S. government's murderous assault on Iraq heralded increasingly sharp conflicts among imperialist powers, the rise of rightist and fascist forces, growing instability of international capitalism, and more wars. In *New International* no. 7. Also includes "1945: When U.S. Troops Said, No!" by Mary-Alice Waters. $12.00

## The Second Assassination of Maurice Bishop
### Steve Clark

The lead article in *New International* no. 6 reviews the accomplishments of the 1979–83 revolution in the Caribbean island of Grenada. Explains the roots of the 1983 coup that led to the murder of revolutionary leader Maurice Bishop, and to the destruction of the workers and farmers government by a Stalinist political faction within the governing New Jewel Movement.

Also in *New International* no. 6: "Washington's Domestic Contra Operation" by Larry Seigle. $15.00

## The Rise and Fall of the Nicaraguan Revolution

Lessons for revolutionists from the workers and farmers government that came to power in Nicaragua in July 1979. Based on ten years of socialist journalism from inside Nicaragua, this special issue of *New International* no. 9 recounts the achievements and worldwide impact of the Nicaraguan revolution. It then traces the political retreat of the Sandinista National Liberation Front leadership that led to the downfall of the revolution in the closing years of the 1980s. Documents of the Socialist Workers Party by Jack Barnes, Steve Clark, and Larry Seigle. $14.00

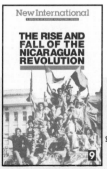

Many of the articles above can be found in *New International*'s sister publications in Spanish, French, and Swedish

# Unions Their past, present, and future

## The Eastern Airlines Strike

ACCOMPLISHMENTS OF THE
RANK-AND-FILE MACHINISTS

*Ernie Mailhot, Judy Stranahan, and Jack Barnes*
The story of the 686-day strike in which a
rank-and-file resistance by Machinists
prevented Eastern's union-busting onslaught
from becoming the road toward a profitable
nonunion airline. $9.95

## The 1985–86 Hormel Meat-Packers Strike in Austin, Minnesota

*Fred Halstead*
The hard-fought strike against Hormel opened a round of battles
by packinghouse workers that—together with strikes by paper
workers, cannery workers, and western coal miners—marked a
break in the rout of U.S. unions that began during the 1981–82
recession. $5.00

## Trade Unions in the Epoch of Imperialist Decay

*Leon Trotsky*
FEATURING "TRADE UNIONS: THEIR PAST, PRESENT,
AND FUTURE" BY KARL MARX
The trade unions must "learn to act deliberately as organizing centers of the working class [and] convince the world at large that
their efforts, far from being narrow and selfish, aim at the emancipation of the downtrodden millions." *—Karl Marx, 1866.*
In this book, two central leaders of the modern communist
workers movement outline the fight for this revolutionary
perspective. $14.95

## Labor's Giant Step

*Art Preis*
THE FIRST TWENTY YEARS OF THE CIO: 1936–55
The story of the explosive labor struggles and political battles in the
1930s that built the industrial unions. And how those unions
became the vanguard of a mass social movement that began
transforming U.S. society. $28.95

From Pathfinder

# THE FIGHT AGAINST FASCISM AND WAR

## THE STRUGGLE AGAINST FASCISM IN GERMANY
Leon Trotsky

Writing in the heat of struggle against the rising Nazi movement, a central leader of the Russian revolution examines the class roots of fascism and advances a revolutionary strategy to combat it. $28.95

The Struggle Against Fascism in Germany by Leon Trotsky
introduction by Ernest Mandel

## THE SOCIALIST WORKERS PARTY IN WORLD WAR II
WRITINGS AND SPEECHES, 1940–43
James P. Cannon

Preparing communist movement in the United States to stand against the patriotic wave inside the workers movement supporting the imperialist slaughter and to campaign against wartime censorship, repression, and antiunion assaults. $22.95

James P. Cannon
WRITINGS AND SPEECHES, 1940-43
The Socialist Workers Party in World War II

## THE JEWISH QUESTION
A MARXIST INTERPRETATION
Abram Leon

Traces the historical rationalizations of anti-Semitism to the fact that Jews—in the centuries preceding the domination of industrial capitalism—were forced to become a "people-class" of merchants and moneylenders. Leon explains why the propertied rulers incite renewed Jew-hatred today. $17.95

## WHAT IS AMERICAN FASCISM?
James P. Cannon and Joseph Hansen

Analyzing examples earlier in the 20th century—Father Charles Coughlin, Jersey City mayor Frank Hague, and Sen. Joseph McCarthy—this collection looks at the features distinguishing fascist movements and demagogues in the U.S. from the 1930s to today. $8.00

# Also from Pathfinder

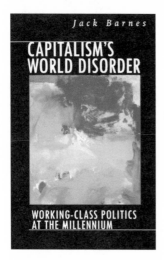

## Capitalism's World Disorder
Working-Class Politics at the Millennium
JACK BARNES

The social devastation and financial panic, the coarsening of politics and politics of resentment, the cop brutality and acts of imperialist aggression accelerating around us—all are the product of lawful forces unleashed by capitalism. But the future the propertied classes have in store for us can be changed by the united struggle and selfless action of workers and farmers conscious of their power to transform the world. Also available in Spanish and French. $23.95

## The Changing Face of U.S. Politics
Working-Class Politics and the Trade Unions
JACK BARNES

A handbook for the new generations coming into the factories, mines, and mills, as they react to the uncertain life, ceaseless turmoil, and brutality of capitalism. It shows how millions of working people, as political resistance grows, will revolutionize themselves, their unions and other organizations, and their conditions of life and work. Also available in Spanish and French. $19.95

## The Struggle for a Proletarian Party
JAMES P. CANNON

Cannon and other leaders of the Socialist Workers Party defend the centrality of proletarianization within the political and organizational principles of Marxism in a polemic against a petty-bourgeois current in the party. The debate unfolded as Washington prepared to drag U.S. working people into the slaughter of World War II. $21.95

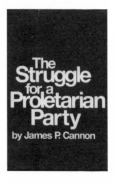

*Write for a catalog. See front of book for addresses.*

## Malcolm X Talks to Young People

"I for one will join in with anyone, I don't care what color you are, as long as you want to change this miserable condition that exists on this earth."—Malcolm X, December 1964. Also includes his 1965 interview with the *Young Socialist* magazine. $10.95

## The Working Class and the Transformation of Learning

The Fraud of Education Reform under Capitalism
JACK BARNES

"Until society is reorganized so that education is a human activity from the time we are very young until the time we die," says Barnes, "there will be no education worthy of working, creating humanity." Also in Spanish and French. $3.00

## Puerto Rico: Independence Is a Necessity

RAFAEL CANCEL MIRANDA

Puerto Rican independence leader Cancel Miranda —one of five Puerto Rican Nationalists imprisoned by Washington for more than 25 years until 1979— speaks out on the brutal reality of U.S. colonial domination, the campaign to free Puerto Rican political prisoners, the example of Cuba's socialist revolution, and the resurgence of the independence movement today. Also in Spanish. $3.00

## Fertile Ground: Che Guevara and Bolivia

A Firsthand Account by Rodolfo Saldaña

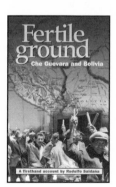

Told by one of the Bolivians who joined ranks with Guevara, Saldaña talks about the unresolved battles of the tin miners, peasants, and indigenous peoples of his country that created "fertile ground" for Guevara's revolutionary course and mark out the future of Bolivia and the Americas. $9.95

## Socialism on Trial

JAMES P. CANNON

The basic ideas of socialism, explained in testimony during the trial of 18 leaders of the Minneapolis Teamsters union and the Socialist Workers Party framed up and imprisoned under the notorious Smith "Gag" Act during World War II. $15.95

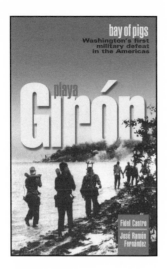

## Playa Girón/Bay of Pigs

Washington's First Military Defeat in the Americas

FIDEL CASTRO, JOSE RAMON FERNANDEZ

In less than 72 hours of combat during April 1961 near the Bay of Pigs, Cuba's revolutionary militias, police, and Rebel Army forces defeated an invasion by 1,500 mercenaries armed, trained, supported, and deployed by Washington. In the process, the Cuban people not only transformed their country and themselves, but set an example for workers and farmers across the Americas and the world. Also available in Spanish. $20.00

## The History of the Russian Revolution

LEON TROTSKY

The social, economic, and political dynamics of the first socialist revolution as told by one of its principal leaders. 3 volumes in 1. $35.95

## The Politics of Chicano Liberation

OLGA RODRIGUEZ

Lessons from the rise of the Chicano movement in the United States in the 1960s and 1970s, which dealt lasting blows against the oppression of the Chicano people. Presents a fighting program for those determined to combat divisions within the working class based on language and national origin. $15.95

## The Jewish Question

A Marxist Interpretation

ABRAM LEON

Traces the historical rationalizations of anti-Semitism to the fact that Jews—in the centuries preceding the domination of industrial capitalism—emerged as a "people-class" of merchants and moneylenders. Leon explains why the propertied rulers incite renewed Jew-hatred today. $17.95

## To Speak the Truth

Why Washington's 'Cold War' against Cuba
Doesn't End

FIDEL CASTRO AND CHE GUEVARA

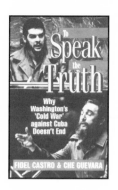

In historic speeches before the United Nations and
UN bodies, Guevara and Castro address the
workers of the world, explaining why the U.S.
government so hates the example set by the
socialist revolution in Cuba and why Washington's
efforts to destroy it will fail. $16.95

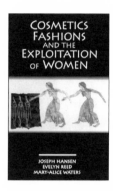

## Cosmetics, Fashions, and the Exploitation of Women

JOSEPH HANSEN, EVELYN REED,
AND MARY-ALICE WATERS

How big business promotes cosmetics to generate
profits and perpetuate the oppression of women.
The introduction by Waters explains how the entry
of millions of women into the workforce during and
after World War II irreversibly changed U.S.
society and laid the basis for a renewed rise of
struggles for women's equality. $14.95

## Communist Continuity and the Fight for Women's Liberation

Documents of the Socialist Workers Party 1971–86

EDITED WITH AN INTRODUCTION BY MARY-ALICE WATERS

How did the oppression of women begin? Who benefits? What social
forces have the power to end the second-class status of women? This
three-part series helps politically equip the generation of women and men
joining battles in defense of women's rights today. 3 volumes, $30.00

## Lenin's Final Fight

Speeches and Writings, 1922–23

V.I. LENIN

In the early 1920s Lenin waged a political battle in
the leadership of the Communist Party of the USSR
to maintain the course that had enabled the
workers and peasants to overthrow the tsarist
empire, carry out the first successful socialist
revolution, and begin building a world communist
movement. The issues posed in Lenin's political fight
remain at the heart of world politics today. $19.95

### Revolutionary Continuity

FARRELL DOBBS

How successive generations of fighters took part in the struggles of the U.S. labor movement, seeking to build a leadership that could advance the class interests of workers and small farmers and link up with fellow toilers around the world. In 2 volumes.

**The Early Years, 1848–1917.** $16.95
**Birth of the Communist Movement, 1918–1922.** $18.95

### Thomas Sankara Speaks

The Burkina Faso Revolution, 1983–87

Peasants and workers in the West African country of Burkina Faso established a popular revolutionary government and began to combat the hunger, illiteracy, and economic backwardness imposed by imperialist domination. Thomas Sankara, who led that struggle, explains the example set for all of Africa. $19.95

### Fighting Racism in World War II

C.L.R. JAMES, GEORGE BREITMAN, EDGAR KEEMER, AND OTHERS

A week-by-week account of the struggle against racism and racial discrimination in the United States from 1939 to 1945, taken from the pages of the socialist newsweekly, the *Militant*. $20.95

### John Coltrane and the Jazz Revolution of the 1960s

FRANK KOFSKY

An account of John Coltrane's role in spearheading innovations in jazz that were an expression of the new cultural and political ferment that marked the rise of the mass struggle for Black rights. Also contains the best-known interview with Coltrane—recorded in 1966, a year before his death. $23.95

### Socialism: Utopian and Scientific

FREDERICK ENGELS

Modern socialism is not a doctrine, Engels explains, but a working-class movement growing out of the establishment of large-scale capitalist industry and its social consequences. $4.00